HAYMARKET THEATRE
161 WEST MADISON ST.
CHICAGO.

CATHER STUDIES 9

Willa Cather and Modern Cultures

Edited by
Melissa J. Homestead
and Guy J. Reynolds

UNIVERSITY OF NEBRASKA PRESS
LINCOLN AND LONDON

© 2011 by the Board of Regents of the University of Nebraska

All rights reserved

Manufactured in the United States of America

♾

The series Cather Studies is sponsored by the University of
Nebraska–Lincoln in cooperation with the Willa Cather Pioneer
Memorial and Educational Foundation.

Library of Congress Cataloging-in-Publication Data

Willa Cather and modern cultures / edited by

Melissa J. Homestead and Guy J. Reynolds.

 p. cm.—(Cather studies; 9)

Includes bibliographical references and index.

ISBN 978-0-8032-3772-8 (pbk.: alk. paper)

1. Cather, Willa, 1873–1947—Criticism and interpretation.

I. Homestead, Melissa J., 1963– II. Reynolds, Guy.

PS3505.A87Z93527 2011

813'.52—dc22   2011021067

Frontispiece:

Willa Cather in Chicago, 1895.

Philip L. and Helen Cather Southwick Collection, Archives and
Special Collections, University of Nebraska–Lincoln Libraries.

CONTENTS

EDITORIAL POLICY

Cather Studies, a forum for Cather scholarship and criticism, is published biennially by the University of Nebraska Press. Submissions are invited on all aspects of Cather studies: biography, various critical approaches to the art of Cather, her literary relationships and reputation, the artistic, historical, intellectual, religious, economic, political, and social backgrounds to her work. Criteria for selection will be excellence and originality.

Manuscripts may vary in length from 4,000 to 10,000 words and should conform to the MLA *Style Manual*, 3rd edition. Please submit manuscripts in duplicate, accompanied by return postage; overseas contributors should enclose international reply coupons. Because *Cather Studies* adheres to a policy of anonymous submission, please include a title page providing author's name and address and delete identifying information from the manuscript. Manuscripts and editorial correspondence should be addressed to Guy Reynolds, Editor, *Cather Studies*, Department of English, University of Nebraska–Lincoln, Lincoln NE 68588-0333.

Introduction

MELISSA J. HOMESTEAD AND GUY J. REYNOLDS

To some, linking Willa Cather to "the modern" or more narrowly to literary modernism still seems an eccentric proposition. As Richard Millington has pointed out, "one will look in vain for Cather's name in the index of most accounts, whether new or old, of the nature and history of Anglo-American modernism" (52). Perhaps she fails to feature in these accounts because in her public pronouncements and certain recurring motifs in her fiction, she appeared to turn her back on modernity. Cather was skeptical about many aspects of the culture that took shape around her in the early decades of the twentieth century, in that most modern place, the United States of America. Born in rural Virginia during the decade following the Civil War, Cather felt herself to be part of a vanished world. She was already in her twenties when the generation of canonical American modernist novelists (F. Scott Fitzgerald, William Faulkner, and Ernest Hemingway) was born, and late-Victorian culture formed her childhood world. By the time the modernist moment had decisively crystallized in the 1920s and 1930s, Cather was issuing jeremiads condemning aspects of modern life she felt to be cheap or "gaudy." In her essay "Nebraska: The End of the First Cycle" (1923) she attacked movies, consumerism, and education policy (including the changes at her alma mater, the University of Nebraska, that, in her eyes, made it a "trade" school). Cather's title for her notorious collection of literary-cultural essays, *Not Under Forty* (1936), conveyed her sense that those younger than that age would not understand her cultural positions, prejudices, and beliefs.

As Millington observes, one strain of Cather scholarship has argued for her status as a modernist artist by focusing on her "affinities with the aesthetic ideals of particular modern artists" (52), and particularly her experiments with form and narrative technique. For example, is *The Professor's House* (1925), with its embedded narrative in the voice of Tom Outland, "modernist"? However, Cather, even at her most formally experimental, is still far removed from the main currents of modernist fiction. Unlike Gertrude Stein or James Joyce, she never wrote prose that radically challenged received ideas of conventional syntax; her sentences remained clean and classical, lapidary in their simple effectiveness. Her narrative structures, though more complex and experimental than many critics have acknowledged, never equaled the avant-garde complexity we associate with Faulkner. Furthermore, the themes and subject matter that define modernist storytelling are either absent or only marginally present in Cather's work. The urban cultures of Chicago and New York certainly feature in some of her fiction, but the city is not the cynosure of her literary imagination, as it is in John Dos Passos's *Manhattan Transfer*. His novel points to another thematic dimension where Cather is idiosyncratic: she does not share modernism's fascination with new technologies of the early twentieth century. *The Great Gatsby*, with its cars and movies and phones, best exemplifies the way American fiction of the 1920s registered the massive shift in the sheer "stuff" of everyday life. In contrast, Cather's fiction—much of it set in the late nineteenth century or earlier—can seem fetishistically wedded to imagined worlds where such technology was either absent or remained the object of suspicion.

Millington advocates a different approach to Cather's engagements with modernity—a historicist, cultural studies one in which scholars are "interested less in the formal qualities of Cather's fiction than in the relation between the content of that fiction and the context of her society and culture" and "work to specify the nature of her engagement with the definitive experiences and ideological movements of twentieth-century life—migration and immigration, nostalgia, Progressivism, the emergence of a fully fledged culture of consumption, and so on" (52). The essays in this collection extend this contextual approach, adding more "experiences and ideological movements" for understanding Cather's engagements with what this volume terms "modern cultures." Our contributors write about the role of railways in Cather's work, her understanding of art history, music, and performance, her response to the opening up of the American Southwest to archaeology and anthropology, and her recurring engagements in her life and her fiction with the city of Chicago. Chicago was the first large modern city Cather encountered, and it was the site of the twelfth International Cather Seminar in 2009, at which earlier versions of many of the essays in this volume were presented. Throughout, the essays explore how Cather used fictional narrative to engage salient aspects of the complex, modern world emerging around her. While she sometimes feared or resented this world, it also prompted her to create her own distinctive narrative mappings of modern cultures.

The essays in this collection fall into two distinct clusters. As we approach the centenary of the inauguration of Cather's career as a novelist with the publication of *Alexander's Bridge* (1912), each group demonstrates how far Cather criticism has come. Essays in the first group focus on Cather's representations of place in the modern world, whether those places are the places traditionally associated with regionalism (farms, small towns, or the frontier) or are cities (particularly Chicago, but also New York). Although Cather is often identified as a Nebraska writer, in these essays she emerges as a writer able to move through and to imagine a whole range of different cultures. Deploying so-

MELISSA J. HOMESTEAD AND GUY J. REYNOLDS

phisticated conceptualizations of place and writing, these essays redefine Cather as a multifaceted regionalist with roots in strikingly heterogeneous places.

A second group of essays explores Cather's relationship with the visual arts and music, "culture" in its most obvious form. Commentators have only recently begun to recognize the full extent of Cather's achievements as a cultural critic and as a writer with a profound and idiosyncratic enthusiasm not only for literature but also for music, theater, and the visual arts. Because of the major anthologies of Cather's late-nineteenth-century journalistic writings and reviews—*The World and the Parish* and *The Kingdom of Art*—literary historians have long had access to and have acknowledged the quality of her early writings on the visual and performing arts (and the Cather Journalism Project, produced by the *Willa Cather Archive*, will soon provide digital access to these writings in the form in which they originally appeared in newspaper and magazines). Essays in this group broaden and deepen this critical tradition by considering how turn-of-the-century visual arts shaped her fiction. Other essays suggest that the representation of music and musicians remains a fertile area for inquiry: Richard Giannone's *Music in Willa Cather's Fiction* (1968) inaugurated but did not conclude scholarly inquiry on this topic. From direct quotations from arias or popular songs to plots centered on performance or artistic apprenticeship, Cather's fiction teems with knowledge of the arts.

The cluster of essays on Cather and place begins with essays on Cather's West, a region that was both real and an imagined subject of an expanding range of stories and images in the early twentieth century. John Swift charts Cather's engagement with the West and the Western in an essay that links her to one of the major figures in the growth of Western genre fiction. In "Willa Cather in and out of Zane Grey's West," Swift emphasizes the importance of this commodified form of the West to the American national project in the region. Swift, like many other critics, identifies the Southwest as a major site for Cather's imaginative rendering of the modern and reactions against the modern, and in particular, what cultural historian T. Jackson Lears calls antimodernism. Swift also brings a distinctively psychoanalytic slant to his meditation, arguing that figures such as Grey and Cather brought a therapeutic passion to their writing about this region of pueblos and mesas, a passion both individual and symptomatic of a broader cultural anxiety.

The Song of the Lark is the subject of many essays in this collection. A novel of place and places, saturated with Cather's knowledge of music and the visual arts, the book is at the center of arguments about her sense of modern cultures. Our contributors explore the text's mapping of apparent opposites: the rural and the urban, Chicago and the Southwest, the modern and the ancient. In "Thea's 'Indian Play' in *The Song of the Lark*," Sarah Clere considers the dynamic interplay between the modern and the antimodern in Cather's representation of Native cultures. Tracing the "discovery" of the Southwest by anthropologists and explorers at the end of the nineteenth century as a context for Thea's encounter with Indian artifacts in Panther Canyon, Clere shows how this particular place fed into American culture's ambiguous sense of progress and empire: in the Southwest, a once-powerful culture had seemingly vanished. Clere argues that a reconsideration of ideas of the modern provides new ways to approach old questions about how Cather represents female characters. In the 1970s Ellen Moers praised this novel for its feminized landscapes and its exploration of womanly creativity, but Clere argues that Cather's representation of landscape and female creativity is conflicted and troubled. Avoiding the critical dichotomy of praise or blame, Clere demonstrates the maturity of Cather criticism: we can now appreciate that Cather's work sometimes articulates a new vision of culture while simultaneously being bounded by her era's dominant cultural assumptions.

In her essay on Cather's layered, dense sense of place. "'Jazz Age' Places: Modern Regionalism in Willa Cather's *The Professor's House*," Kelsey Squire extends work of the last decade that has enriched our understanding of how Cather created a textured fictional topography. Focusing on the disparate places of *The Professor's House*, Squire's sophisticated reading revisits America's cultural understanding of region, unpacking the ways in which the rural has often been read as antimodern or backward. The novel grew out of a concerted phase of writing and thinking in 1924 and 1925, when Cather reconsidered her relationship to "the soil" and suggestively meditated on how writing and place interact. During this period, Cather gave an interview in which she discussed the setting of *My Ántonia*, published *The Professor's House*, and wrote an introduction to a collection of stories by Sarah Orne Jewett. Using the term "regional consciousness" to think about attachment to place, Squire analyzes how consumerism and cosmopolitanism complicated traditional linkages between a writer and her place. Professor St. Peter is a cosmopolitan figure, apparently at home in both Europe and the United States, but he is also deeply attached to his house and garden. His final near-death crisis testifies to a morbid, unsustainable form of place consciousness. In Squire's compelling reading of this most haunting of Cather novels, modern place consciousness fostered a profoundly ambivalent mixture of attachment and exile.

Mark A. R. Facknitz's essay "Changing Trains: Metaphors of Transfer in Willa Cather" demonstrates the ways in which a critical focus on a specific historical detail can yield a rich analysis of the writer and her milieu. For Facknitz, the train and its networks help us see how a language of movement, exchange, and transfer operates throughout Cather's fiction. His essay brings together two themes in the collection: the importance of technological change to an understanding of modern culture, and the centrality of place to Cather's conceptions of modernity. This is an essay about Chicago, about the sweeping changes that the development of the railroad and the expansion of that city brought to the Midwest as a whole. Cather, Facknitz shows, developed train travel—and particularly the experience of changing trains at the rail hub of Chicago—into an aesthetic, a way to think about borders, boundaries, and thresholds. The literal "line" of the railroad is crucial, becoming a link to other "lines" in Cather's work, such as the Divide on the prairie in *O Pioneers!* The centrality of movement in train travel, the sense of a visual apprehension that is so fleeting as one looks through the train car window, also becomes, according to Facknitz, a way for Cather to explore a technology to arrive at a modern aesthetic.

As Facknitz's essay demonstrates, Cather's fiction not only focuses on a single place but holds together disparate topographies through complex narrative shapes. Her fictional world, as Joseph Urgo demonstrated in *Willa Cather and the Myth of American Migration* (1995), is founded on displacement, movement, and migration. Cather's own journey from Virginia to Nebraska as a child became her primal scene, a real-life prefiguring of the journeys, epic and unsettling, that provided the basis of her stories. Movement and migration are the deep background for her characters, who, even as they forge new attachments to place, remain shaped by journeys they have made.

For Cather, culture was a conversation, and Michelle E. Moore uncovers just such a conversation in Cather's representation of Chicago in "Chicago's Cliff Dwellers and *The Song of the Lark.*" According to Moore, 1890s Chicago was a cauldron of conflicting ideas about culture. A commercial and highly materialistic city, Chicago was also home to boosters who wanted to "raise" the place culturally and aesthetically. Moore moves between literal and metaphorical notions of "raising" or of being "up high," and focuses in particular on the ways Henry Blake Fuller's Chicago novel *The Cliff-Dwellers* (1893) created a suggestive language in which skyscrapers and ideals of cultural aspiration mixed and cross-fertilized. Furthermore, the Anasazi people of the Southwest, culturally advanced but ultimately doomed, were also cliff dwellers. Cather appropriated this provocative mixture of motifs drawn from both modern urbanism and the late-nineteenth-century's fascination with primitivism in

MELISSA J. HOMESTEAD AND GUY J. REYNOLDS

her work from *The Song of the Lark* through to *The Professor's House*. Cultural uplift becomes an ideal in her fiction, but it is threatened both by contemporary commercialism and the realization that the utopian world (of the ancient cliff dwellers or the modern artist) is ultimately doomed.

Fuller's work is also central to Richard C. Harris's essay, "Willa Cather and Henry Blake Fuller: More Building Blocks for *The Professor's House*." Harris recovers the Chicago novelist as a central inspiration for a Cather novel that Harris tellingly describes as a "collage." For Harris, Cather's sense of place is profoundly intertextual, shaped by other narratives as much as by place itself. He reads Cather as a creative borrower, able to see how she might reenergize and redeploy themes and motifs in an earlier writer's work. Intriguingly, Harris concentrates on two Fuller novels published in the 1890s (*The Cliff-Dwellers* and *With the Procession* [1895]), again suggesting that to understand Cather's sense of the modern we must look back to her intellectual roots in late-Victorian, fin de siècle culture.

As Amber Harris Leichner shows in "Cather's 'Office Wives' Stories and Modern Women's Work," the city as place was important to Cather on a professional level. As an editor and journalist in Pittsburgh and New York, Cather became part of a new modern workplace, the office, increasingly populated by women workers in the early twentieth century. The modern office culture in American cities was open not only to professional women like Cather but also to working-class immigrant women, and Leichner explores Cather's fictionalization of that milieu in her small body of office stories published in magazines in the 1910s. Her essay demonstrates that to read Cather in terms of modern culture allows us to revisit important questions and shed new light on them. Leichner shows that Cather's sense of the office as a place is deeply and complexly bound up with gender—indeed, Leichner reads these stories (including "Her Boss" [1919]) as contributions to a feminist examination of office culture.

Matthew Lavin's essay, "It's Mr. Reynolds Who Wishes It:

Profit and Prestige Shared by Cather and Her Literary Agent," moves from the topographies of the regional and the urban to a more abstract and national topography, the literary marketplace. Lavin shows that as a national literary marketplace developed, writing's "place" as defined by its origin and dissemination became more complex. New hierarchies of value developed, and writers balanced the desire for profit with concern for the symbolic capital of artistic reputation. Publishers, editors, and literary agents increasingly entered the terrain of writing. Focusing on Cather's relationship with her literary agent, Paul Revere Reynolds, Lavin pushes the received understanding of the literary modernism as a stylistic or formalistic movement to the background. Instead, he attends to the fine detail of how Cather and Reynolds together situated her as an author in a stratified and very modern marketplace, negotiating complex hierarchies of elite and mass culture in the process.

For three contributors to this volume, Cather engages modern culture through the visual arts. In "Thea at the Art Institute," Julie Olin-Ammentorp weds an investigation into Cather's representations of art and artists to a site-specific analysis of the cultural impact of the Art Institute of Chicago on Thea in *The Song of the Lark*. Olin-Ammentorp rereads Cather's novel of music and female maturation as a text in which encounters with the visual arts play a central role in the protagonist's self-development. Serendipitously wandering around the Art Institute, a curious and engaged Thea makes herself. A provincial girl with little experience of the city or high culture, Thea encounters art on her own terms. Olin-Ammentorp shows that Cather is interested in the *how* of cultural encounter as process, as well as the *what*. Across her fiction, Cather references specific paintings and works of music, but what most concerns her are the particularities of how a character engages with a work, meets it, understands it and then remembers it.

Diane Prenatt, in "Art and the Commercial Object as Ekphrastic Subjects in *The Song of the Lark* and *The Professor's*

House," focuses on Cather's use of the classical rhetorical device as means to critique modern cultures. Ekphrasis—instances in which a verbal work of art references a visual one (as in Keats's "Ode on a Grecian Urn")—structures *The Song of the Lark,* a novel that takes its very title from Jules Breton's 1884 painting. Cather, Prenatt claims, uses this ancient literary device to open up a discussion about culture and commodification. Defining ekphrasis broadly enough to include Cather's representations of Thea's encounter with the cliff-dweller artifacts in Panther Canyon, Prenatt moves on to *The Professor's House,* charting Cather's extended meditation on the function of art in supposedly primitive cultures and its denigration through commodification. Ekphrasis thus acts as a key for understanding the earlier novel's valorization of non-classical art and the later novel's critique of the apparent triumph of modern consumer culture.

Janis Stout's essay reads Cather's relationship with modern visual art through the prism of Katherine Anne Porter's complex rivalry with Cather. Seeing Porter's "Reflections on Willa Cather" as "an essentially duplicitous essay," Stout considers how Porter sought to strengthen her own reputation as an author by undermining the status of the senior writer. Analyzing (and sometimes inventing or misrepresenting) Cather's reactions to various modern artworks, Porter creates a portrait of Cather as resistant to modernism. Stout sees modern art as a mirror in which the writer imagines herself and sees other writers. Writing and painting enter into a complex dance, with authors using the visual arts as a means to define their own work and the work of their peers (in a deeply conflicted relationship based around admiration and rivalry). Stout's essay richly revisits debates about the "sisterhood" of female writers and shows how modernity became a vital term in the conversation between authors.

In "'The Cruelty of Physical Things': Picture Writing and Violence in Willa Cather's 'The Profile,'" Joyce Kessler analyzes a 1907 Cather story, reading it through a conceptual framework drawn from art history. Cather's "visual semiotics" are central

to Kessler's analysis of what she calls Cather's "picture writing." Cather's story focuses on Virginia Gilbert's facial scar, and
Kessler unpacks the significance of the scar through a contextual discussion of representations of female beauty in late-nineteenth-century visual culture. Linking Cather's story to Manet's
revolutionary 1863 painting *Olympia*, Kessler's interdisciplinary
analysis draws on art history, feminist studies, and knowledge of
the transatlantic cultural world that shaped the young Cather's
imagination.

Cather was a friend to many singers, a devotee of opera, and
an author of stories about the growth of musical creativity. In
"'Before the Romanzas Have Become Street Music': Cather and
Verdi's *Falstaff*, Chicago, 1895," John H. Flannigan describes
the eclectic range of music that animated Cather's imagination.
Through a forensic reconstruction of a single musical encounter
in Chicago early in Cather's career, Flannigan develops a reading
of Cather and the changing nature of "taste" at the turn of the
century. Tracing evidence of Cather's interest in both elite and
popular (or folk) forms of music, Flannigan reads her eclecticism
as emblematic of her fondness for both "high" and "low" forms
of culture.

The writers in this volume create a layered, multivalent sense
of what "modern cultures" might mean. What unifies many of
the essays is an understanding of Cather as a writer of transition: she straddled the late-Victorian and modernist eras and
saw many aspects of the contemporary world emerge over time.
As a result, her fiction set in the late nineteenth and early twentieth centuries meditates on the transition into the modern. Her
sensibility forged by this shift, Cather captures the massive and
irrevocable cultural change that had taken place. This cultural
dynamic structures many of her novels, which foreground the
processes of looking back, memorializing, and remembering, as
if to acknowledge how much had altered in the period between
the 1880s, when the young Cather moved to Nebraska, and the
1920s, when she entered her major creative phase.

The profoundly elegiac cast of Cather's works relates complexly to the passing of time and to the realization that—for good and ill—her protagonists were living in modern times. Cather's characters, like Cather herself, often exhibit profound disquiet about this passage to the modern. However, we can see in the distinctive shapes of her novels, with their recursions into memory and their attempts to synchronize and bridge very different cultural eras, the modern emerging with full force. Protagonists such as Jim Burden and Professor St. Peter try to recall and capture the past in order to understand the present and, perhaps, create a bridge to the future. In this desire, they are fully modern.

WORKS CITED

Cather, Willa. *The Kingdom of Art: Willa Cather's First Principles and Critical Statements, 1893–1896.* Ed. Bernice Slote. Lincoln: U of Nebraska P, 1966.

———. *The World and the Parish: Willa Cather's Articles and Reviews, 1893–1902.* Ed. William M. Curtin. Lincoln: U of Nebraska P, 1970.

Giannone, Richard. *Music in Willa Cather's Fiction.* Lincoln: U of Nebraska P, 1968.

Lears, T. J. Jackson. *No Place of Grace: Antimodernism and the Transformation of American Culture, 1880–1920.* New York: Pantheon, 1981.

Millington, Richard H. "Willa Cather's American Modernism." *The Cambridge Companion to Willa Cather.* Ed. Marilee Lindemann. Cambridge: Cambridge UP, 2005. 51–65.

Moers, Ellen. *Literary Women.* Garden City NJ: Doubleday, 1976.

Urgo, Joseph. *Willa Cather and the Myth of American Migration.* Urbana: U of Illinois P, 1995.

Willa Cather Archive. Ed. Andrew Jewell. Oct. 2007. U of Nebraska–Lincoln. 20 Jan. 2011. http://cather.unl.edu.

1 Willa Cather in and out of Zane Grey's West

JOHN N. SWIFT

In her fictions and elsewhere in her life Cather frequently invoked the landscapes and themes of the American "Western": the Protean, multimedia genre, rooted in the fantastic inscription of European desires on the American continent and people, which achieved its most self-conscious and finished form in almost exactly the period of Cather's writing career, from Wister's *The Virginian* in 1902 to the midcentury films of John Ford and others.[1] The popular Western of the early twentieth century was a quintessentially modern project, made possible by emergent transportation technologies and large-scale commodity tourism, and by the advent of film, radio, and eventually television. All of these dramatically expanded the reach of and audiences for a new kind of exotic regionalism, one suited to a new age. Moreover, the Western's pastoral individualism (and its mysterious, ambivalent relation to American indigenes, or "ancient people," as Cather called them in *The Song of the Lark*) made it a broadly available site for the expression of vague antimodern anxieties. As an avid tourist, a self-conscious regionalist, a hard-headed commercial writer, and (eventually) a cultural conservative, Cather explored the Western in all these functions.

The Western doesn't begin with Wister; its antecedents stretch back past Twain and Cooper, perhaps as far as Cabeza de Vaca.

But its modern form seems to many of its fans almost the personal invention of Zane Grey, the prolific New York dentist-turned-author who wrote about sixty cowboy romances between 1910 and his death in 1939. It is the mirroring of Cather's and Grey's careers that concerns me here. At first glance and in their best-known personae, they are almost polar opposites: she an aesthetic minimalist and a representative of beleaguered high culture and good taste, he a popular (and spectacularly successful) purveyor of florid sentimentality. Cather, in her rare public comments on the Zane Grey phenomenon, was scornful. In a May 1925 talk at Bowdoin College, for instance, she observed testily that Grey's work had displaced Longfellow's *Golden Legend* on booksellers' shelves, and went on to link him to all that was wrong with a modern mass-produced literature responding to debased public demand. Grey's art, she suggested to her audience, was the chief manifestation of a three-pronged menace to culture itself: the modern popular novel, modern cinema, and the nascent radio show (Bohlke 155). (Grey was by 1925 not only a hugely best-selling novelist but also a major player in Hollywood. Radio and comic strip adaptations of his work were still in the future.) And that autumn she told Fanny Butcher of the *Chicago Tribune*, speaking of the newly published *The Professor's House*, that "I could have written ["Tom Outland's Story"] like a Zane Grey novel, but I would have died of boredom doing it" (O'Connor 238).

Her highbrow disdain is only part of the story, however. Cather appears to have enjoyed the West in its showier popular representations, from the dime novel *Life of Jesse James* that Jim Burden brings to Nebraska, and from whose pages appears to step the picturesque cowboy Otto Fuchs, scars, high-heeled boots, and all (*My Ántonia* 4), to her interest in the Rin Tin Tin movie phenomenon of the late 1920s, the high point of which was her meeting the canine celebrity himself on a train crossing New Mexico (Jewell and Stout 0832, 0875). She apparently even had a soft spot for the cultural menace Grey himself, and probably read at least some of his work: only a month after her interview with Butcher, she admitted privately to her friend Harriet Whicher that she had spent a delightful summer roaming in the Southwest and "living like a Zane Grey character" (Jewell and Stout 0797). Most interestingly, while Cather certainly found Grey's style deplorable and his popularity evidence of the public's bad taste, she understood, as her comment to Butcher makes clear, that she herself might also be a sort of cowboy writer: no Zane Grey, but a co-habitant of his chosen landscapes and motifs, telling similar stories of idealistic cowpunchers, mysterious mesas, and lost cultures, but telling them differently. In fact, she had at a critical moment in her early career seriously intended a full-length novel of the Southwest ("The Blue Mesa," abandoned in 1916 in favor of *My Ántonia*, as I describe below). Through the late 1920s the romanticized far West made frequent appearances in her work, twice as entire "Western" stories within stories, "The Ancient People" in *The Song of the Lark* and "Tom Outland's Story" in *The Professor's House*. In the remainder of this essay I explore Grey's and Cather's apparently improbable meeting in the literary West, arguing first that both appropriated that landscape's emerging mythologies to historical and personal purposes that they shared with a host of early-twentieth-century Americans.[2] More specifically, I suggest that through the conventions of the Western they identified and explored a problem with love and sexuality, to which they responded very differently.

Despite their obvious differences, Willa Cather and Zane Grey had much in common. Almost the same age, they were midwesterners who came to New York with big literary dreams shortly after the turn of the century. They were passionate, ambitious self-fashioners: in constructing their public faces, both altered names and ages. Each broke from obscurity to fame following holidays in the Grand Canyon/Four Corners region (Grey between 1907 and 1913, Cather in 1912 and 1914–16), during the national surge of southwestern tourism set in motion by the expansion of the rail lines across New Mexico and Arizona, a

4

west-flowing tide that popularized a set of readily reproducible landscapes and emblems: trackless deserts, hidden canyons, sturdy cowboys, hot-blooded Mexicans, taciturn Indians, and so on. Both were struggling to become self-supporting writers, and they reported in letters and journals that these vacations were personally transforming; the subsequent energizing of their careers bears this judgment out. In the 1910s they wrote the emerging iconic West into their novels, while they themselves inhabited the different world of literary New York, where their work was reviewed, kindly or unkindly, by the same reviewers (in Grey's case, mostly unkindly). Finally, and most important for my purposes here, Grey and Cather shared a profound nostalgia for *authentic* or *uncorrupted* experience and feeling, which for each hardened after World War I into social conservatism, a mistrust of the modern world's practices. Cather regretfully contemplated, in her well-known words, a "world broke[n] in two" (*Not Under Forty* v), while Grey distrusted a "new order of things . . . a vastly different America" (*Code of the West* 81). Their discomfort with the present was nothing very unusual, but expressed a broader cultural movement that historian T. J. Jackson Lears identified a generation ago as "antimodernism," a countercurrent of protest against the rational but soul-starving efficiencies of late-nineteenth- and early-twentieth-century progressive bourgeois American culture.[3] Antimodernism significantly shaped Cather's and Grey's encounters with the West: for both of them, as for middle-class Americans generally, the West's newly minted emblems, popularized in the service of rail-based domestic tourism, came to have therapeutic antimodern value, suggesting as they did strong, accessible (but exotic) alternatives to the debilitations of modernity.

I will approach both authors' antimodern uses of the West through one of these emblems, the abandoned Anasazi cliff dwellings of the Four Corners region, which both visited and wrote into their centrally important fictions of the mid-1910s. Grey encountered ancient pictographs and burial sites near the

Grand Canyon on his first dude ranch expedition of 1907, and he traveled to the more remote cliff cities across the Painted Desert at Betatakin and Keet Seel four years later; these became the setting for the escape and romance of Bern Venters and the "Masked Rider" Bess in his first best-seller, *Riders of the Purple Sage* (1912). Cather first saw cliff dwellings at Walnut Canyon outside Flagstaff in 1912, and made them the site of Thea Kronborg's creative revitalization and romance with Fred Ottenburg in *The Song of the Lark* (1915); she returned with Edith Lewis in 1915 to the well-known excavations at Mesa Verde, which became the subject matter and setting of "Tom Outland's Story" of *The Professor's House* (published in 1925, but probably begun in 1916). Cather and Grey were not unusual in their interest in these distinctively western sites: the cliff dwellings were ubiquitous in popular American consciousness from the 1890s through the 1920s, vigorously marketed by boosters and advertisers as picturesque destinations competitive with the ruins of old Europe and the Near East. "We have a Sphinx of our own in the West," effused the travel writer Agnes Laut in 1913, "and stone lions older than the columns of Phrygia, and kings' palaces of 700 and 1000 rooms" (x). Cather well understood the commercial and iconic values of the cliff dwellings by the early summer of 1915, when she proposed to Ferris Greenslet, her editor at Houghton Mifflin, that he use them in his marketing campaign for *The Song of the Lark*, noting that all the people who usually vacationed in Europe—even her friend the singer Geraldine Farrar—were heading to the Southwest to visit the cliff dwellers (Cather to Greenslet, [July 1915]). She was right: not only she and Grey, but many thousands of others undertook the cliff-dwelling pilgrimage before and after the turn of the century. They included scores of literary-minded visitors (including writers of tour guides) from Charles Fletcher Lummis to Teddy Roosevelt, who like Grey and Cather created in their writings about such encounters a pervasive, stylized narrative of modern America's experience of its mythic past, a narrative that served a particular antimodern purpose.

The story that modern America read into the empty cliff dwellings, formulated repeatedly as a meditation on their vanished inhabitants, most often involved peacefulness, domesticity, and love. As early as 1892 Frederic Chapin identified the lost Mesa Verdeans as "a great population, a people well advanced in many arts . . . a race who loved peace rather than war" (182). Teddy Roosevelt echoed this language after a 1913 trip to Betatakin, where he envisioned an "industrious race of advanced culture and peaceful ideals" (44), as did Cather herself in "Tom Outland's Story," in Father Duchêne's speculative descriptive of the Blue Mesa's vanished Indians, "a superior people" who "in an orderly and secure life . . . developed considerably the arts of peace" (*Professor's House* 219). In their perceived orderly tranquillity, the cliff dwellers offered an appealing image of "natural" sociopolitical man and a healing counterpart to the well-known chaos of modern American urban life. Moreover, their domesticity—the homely artifacts and implements of private life exposed for tourist eyes (as if, as many commented, their users had just departed)—reminded viewers of the fundamental constructive energies of desire that hold culture together. Contemplation of domestic detail led Charles Francis Saunders to muse sentimentally in a 1918 guidebook to the ruins of the Southwest that "men never lose a supreme interest in men; stronger than all is the yearning of the human heart for other human hearts" (169). In *The Song of the Lark*, Thea Kronborg's extended meditation on potsherds in Panther Canyon discovers an originary desire for beauty: "they had not only expressed their desire, but they had expressed it as beautifully as they could. Food, fire, water, and something else—even here, in this crack in the world, so far back in the night of the past!" (305). For Grey in *Riders of the Purple Sage*, the cliff dwellers' pottery becomes the literal agent of social repair, as his runaway lovers-to-be Bern and Bess set up housekeeping in Surprise Valley with crockery borrowed from a nearby cliff city (129), in a first step toward mending the novel's various broken families and communities.

In fact, we may read the lure of the cliff dwelling and the West, for modern American culture generally and in the works of Grey and Cather, as a special case of what Lears calls the antimodern "turn toward a premodern unconscious" (166), a therapeutic regression from a state of enervated "neurasthenia" (47) toward elemental yearnings and desires, the primal erotic bedrock of human society and the human condition. The cliff dwelling (and the entire mythologized western landscape) was not only a corrective alternative to an alienating, dysfunctional society, but it was also the potential site of *individual* erotic rehabilitation, a place of "natural" or "authentic" love. Thus Grey in his first western fiction, *The Heritage of the Desert* (1910), wrote of a city-weary, sickly easterner, John Hare, who undergoes a kind of libidinal correction in the Southwest, recovering health and vital identity in an erotic liaison with the alluring Spanish-Navajo maiden Mescal. Cather told a similar, though less picturesque, story five years later in *The Song of the Lark*, in which Thea trades her Chicago depression (a classically described "neurasthenia") for the bright vitality of Panther Canyon and Fred's love. Cather had, in fact, already rehearsed a version of this plot with *herself* as heroine (a version whose exoticism brings it closer to Grey's story of Mescal than to Thea's affair with Fred) in her private 1912 letters from Arizona to Elizabeth Shepley Sergeant, in which she presented the overwhelming and romantic figure of her admirer Julio, the beautiful Mexican-Indian singer, as an implicit agent of *her own* personal revitalization (Jewell and Stout 0228, 0229, 0236; Sergeant 80–82). Grey, who in his journals even more overtly fantasized his own western travels as sexual encounters (Pauly 96–98), would repeat this formula (whereby an effete easterner is restored to erotic health by a western encounter) more subtly in the wildly successful *Riders of the Purple Sage*: hero Bern is also an obscurely depressed drifter from Illinois, "a lonely outcast . . . sick in mind" (123), until he finds redemption with Bess. Grey would employ the same plot with minor variations in a half-dozen or more of his nov-

els of the 1910s and 1920s: *Desert Gold, Light of the Western
Stars, The Rainbow Trail, The Call of the Canyon, Code of the
West, The Vanishing American,* and others. In short, for both
Grey and Cather, the West was a place of unfettered "natural"
passion, of a "real" love that, like the harmonious communities of the cliff dwellers, might provide a corrective to modern
relationships' corrosive confusion. Surely it is no accident that
both Cather's Thea and Fred *and* Grey's Bern and Bess discover
their love in a cave during a thunderstorm (*Song* 322–27; *Riders* 184–89). In these Virgilian moments, a natural tumult out of
doors mirrors a human passion only barely contained within ("a
storm of real love," Bern muses, discovering his passion for Bess
[189]): Eros is represented in the very moment of its domestication, literally beneath the authenticating signs of the "ancient
people."[4]

But in exploring the fundamental nature of desire, both authors also uncovered its dark side, a core of pain and violence
that repelled even as it drew them. "Down here at the beginning," Thea concludes her meditation on potsherds and original
desire in Panther Canyon, "that painful thing was already stir-
ring; the seed of sorrow, and of so much delight" (*Song* 305).
For Grey, the pastoral domesticities of familial and sexual love—
like Bern and Bess's housekeeping in Surprise Valley—were often inseparable from extraordinary pain (significantly, Bern must
shoot Bess, nearly killing her, in order to bring her into the para-
disal valley and erotic health). Grey repeatedly caricatures authentic love in terrifying images of masculine brutality, rape,
and incest. In *Riders of the Purple Sage* he gathers these images around the Mormon elders, polygamy, and violated child
brides, culminating in Bern's fantasy of Bess's past, held as a sexual prisoner in her outlaw father's remote cabin. This cabin—the
demonic counterpart of the couple's cave of love—reappears in
various guises throughout Grey's work as a place of unspeakable
sexual violence done to young women: in the Mormon town of
Stonebridge (a harem colony of "sealed wives") in *Purple Sage*'s

sequel, *The Rainbow Trail*; at the Death Valley camp in *Wanderer of the Wasteland*, where the effete maniac Virey methodically stones his wife, Magdalena, to death; as the storied cave of the giant outlaw Gulden in *The Border Legion*, where he may or may not have eaten a young girl. A different version of the demonic cabin appears in the apparently good-natured romance *Code of the West*: Cal Thurman holds his kidnapped and forcibly married bride, Georgiana, captive in a cabin until she unlearns her modern eastern notions of women's freedoms. Perhaps the strangest of these related images is the "Strong-Arm Club" of 1922's *The Day of the Beast*, Grey's overwrought nonwestern novel of social criticism, in which men maintain a clubhouse for illegal drinking, heavy petting, and the occasional rape of teenage girls.

Cather is less repetitively extravagant but equally anxious in exploring desire's bleaker faces. Unless desire can be held at arm's length—as Thea and Fred do with each other—or mastered through framing ironies, love—and particularly heterosexual, marital, and reproductive love—also abuses and kills. To contextualize Thea's skittishness about marriage one need only consider the long parade of spectacularly bad marriages across Cather's novels, many ending fatally: the Alexanders of *Alexander's Bridge*, the Shabatas of *O Pioneers!*, the dancing Swedes whose story Thea tells, the Russian bridal party and the Cutters of *My Ántonia*. Other marital relations are haunted by infidelity, madness, or merely the stifling ennui experienced by Godfrey St. Peter, who dreams idly of "Medea's way" out of the trap of Eros. And although Cather makes the Southwest the site of Thea's erotic redemption, the cave of love in Panther Canyon reflects darkly in her other southwestern fiction: in "Tom Outland's Story" in the tomb of the putatively unfaithful and murdered Mother Eve; in Buck Scales's murderous family cabin on the lonely road to Mora in *Death Come for the Archbishop* (where, as for Grey in *Wanderer of the Wasteland*, another curiously named Magdalena suffers horrendous masculine violence); or in the weirdly sexualized, unspeakable horror of that novel's "Stone Lips" episode. Whatever threatens Latour in the ancient cave—hints of the fetid womb, rumors of phallic snakes, the specter of infanticide—is also authentically primal, as primal as anything in Panther Canyon, and "the oldest voices of the earth" speak there (*Death* 130), sexual and fearful. Cather developed these unsettling places' meanings most explicitly in 1920's "Coming, Aphrodite!," in Don Hedger's unlikely prelude to the seduction of Eden Bower, his telling of the story of the "Queen's House," a grotesque but apparently sexually energizing tale of rape, castration, serial infidelity, and murder. Not coincidentally, Cather claimed to have learned this story of the passionate Southwest, which so brutally intrudes into the careful civilities of Washington Square, from the exotic Julio, her partner in exotic southwestern romance in 1912 (Sergeant 81).

The sources of desire's inextricably intertwined strands of love and aggression, delight and pain, are not my focus here. Psychoanalysis, which focuses on crossed or self-canceling desire, suggests a number of speculative approaches to desire's sources—personal, political, even biological. Acknowledgment of love's core ambivalence is hardly unusual in literary history or in popular culture, however, and antimodernism, in its typical movement backward toward stronger, more authentic times, sensations, and emotions, encountered some fearful demons as well. Lears suggests that those antimodernists who saw only desire's happy face in the healing journey toward premodern eroticism "trivialized unconscious mental and emotional life by denying its darker dimensions of aggression, rage, and conflict" (166–67). Neither Cather nor Grey could ignore the "darker dimensions," and perhaps for Grey his novels' concerns spilled over into his personal life (or vice versa), in his string of teenage mistresses and his private career as a pornographic photographer (Pauly 10). More important for my argument here are Grey's and Cather's different *literary* responses to the West and to the simultaneously therapeutic and threatening passions that they first located there in the 1910s. Simply put, despite their common attraction to the West, Cather did not become a writer of popular western romances, and Grey did. This distinction may not be as self-evident as it sounds. In the summer of 1916—the fourth summer of her first round of trips to the Southwest— Cather wrote to Greenslet about her literal compulsion to write a southwestern novel: she felt forced to write it, she told him; it would eventually write itself, and until then she begged him to publish no one else's (Cather to Greenslet, 30 June 1916). She tentatively called it "The Blue Mesa" and described the unwritten work as filled with passionate desires and hatreds (Cather to Greenslet, 22 August 1916). Most scholars understand "The Blue Mesa" as the prototype of "Tom Outland's Story," begun but set aside in late 1916 in favor of *My Ántonia*, but Cather's extravagant description suggests that she at first envisioned a narrative very different from Tom Outland's disciplined, poised "story of youthful defeat" (*Professor's House* 176): in fact, "The Blue Mesa" sounds something like a romance, even a Zane Grey romance. The work she envisioned in the summer of 1916, despite her conviction of its compulsive inevitability, remains (as she intimated to Fanny Butcher) the Zane Grey romance that she never wrote, and her letters to Greenslet point along a literary path—Zane Grey's path—that she was even then already abandoning.

How may we understand their divergence and its significance? I have argued that for both writers the Southwest—the cowboy West—held out a promise of picturesque and restorative romance, behind which adult heterosexuality disclosed itself as a lethal trap. This intolerable dilemma informed their non-western fictions as well, but a West newly mythologized and eroticized by antimodern longing made the paradoxes of desire particularly vivid. Grey's response to this discovery (of love's ambivalence) was to send himself and his protagonists compulsively into that trap again and again, for the remainder of his career. One result was a torrent of superheated, often inexplicably intense language. In Jane Tompkins's description of Grey's prose, "reading him was like being caught in a waterfall or a flood . . . at the mercy of a natural force" (157). Another result was structural repetition of plots, characters, and landscapes: Grey told and retold a few simple stories of desire, authenticity, and danger. Like Cather's unwritten "Blue Mesa" story, they were filled with passionate desire and hatred, usually driven by dimly understood forces of doom, such as Wansfell's senseless crisscrossing of the Mojave in *Wanderer of the Wasteland*, although almost any Grey novel provides good examples. All of his books unselfconsciously represent a quest for "truth" in love, and all are haunted by the monsters that love awakens, the cruelties that it inflicts. Such a driven repetitiveness of subject and form is "compulsive" in exactly the psychoanalytic sense: in Freud's words, "a thing which has not been understood inevitably reappears; like an unlaid ghost, it cannot rest" (122). Moreover, Grey's compulsion made possible his success as a novelist: having gropingly found a formula for a good story, even a great story, by 1912, he never let it go.[5] I am tempted to say that the unresolved, unresolvable riddle of the desire that brutalizes its objects never let him go either.

Not so with Cather. Like Grey, she experienced an overwhelming, anti-rational power in the Southwest, and like him she associated it consistently with Eros and sexual desire. Moreover, her June 1916 letter to Greenslet about her plan to write "The Blue Mesa" suggests that she, too, sensed something irresistible, compulsive, in her relation to the Southwest and its stories. Her career's arc, however, was anything but repetitive. Despite Carl Linstrum's famous remark in *O Pioneers!* that "there are only two or three human stories, and they go on repeating themselves as fiercely as if they had never happened before" (119), Cather found in art precisely a way out of biological experience's repetitions. She made the refusal of repetition central to her formal practice, and commented on it frequently herself in private and public assessments of her work. She insisted on each work's intentional uniqueness, chiding those who would see *A Lost Lady* as another *My Ántonia* (Jewell and Stout 0824) or *Shadows on the Rock* as another *Death Comes for the Archbishop* (Jewell and Stout 1089), who would ask that Claude Wheeler visualize his world like Jim Burden (Jewell and Stout 0859), or who would judge any of her novels by the conventions of its predecessors. As she wrote a little ruefully to E. K. Brown in the last year of her life, she had probably disappointed some readers by her changefulness, but she had always "kept working and trying to learn" (Jewell and Stout 1741).

In short, while Grey's work was sustained by the intensity of his blind, repeated struggle with a love that was always wrong, Cather's work drew power from the perpetual newness of writing, its ability to encounter directly and explore the unresolvables of human experience and then leave them behind. Again in classical psychoanalytic terms, this is exactly the difference between "repeating" and "remembering," or between submitting to compulsion and consciously mastering it, the difference between, finally, the symptom and its cure. Cather's specific techniques for mastery were the complex and playful framing devices, the paradoxes, doublings, and structural ironies ("the magic of contradictions," in Niel Herbert's phrase in *A Lost Lady*), that marked her work and allowed her to examine passion intimately while holding it at a safe distance. The dominant trope for such mastery was departure and new beginning, both in her novels, whose characters with few exceptions are always moving on despite nostalgia's backwards lure, and perhaps in her own life's similar form, as a succession of unrepeatable experiences and places.[6] She could not go back to places once she had written about them, she told an admirer in a letter of 1943 (Jewell and Stout 1622), as if the act of writing itself made compulsive return unnecessary.[7]

The impassioned, vital Southwest exemplified in Grey's writings seems to have been one of the places that Cather found hardest to write out of her system—I suspect because this version of the Southwest was so closely tied to dreams of love and sexuality both cultural and personal, dreams harder than most to confront and master. After writing "The Ancient People" she returned to the Southwest in 1915 and 1916. Over the following decade, "The Blue Mesa" transformed itself slowly in her imagination into the coolly framed "Tom Outland's Story" of 1925 (we may recall again Cather's comment that, had "Tom Outland's Story" been a simple repetition of Grey's cowboy plots, she would have "died of boredom"). As I have suggested, the Southwest resurfaced also as a troubling set of allusions in 1920 in "Coming, Aphrodite!," another "story of youthful defeat." Like *The Professor's House*, the short story self-consciously bids farewell to youth, to sexual passion, and to the picturesque, romantic West itself, represented as a passing moment in a young artist's career (Don Hedger's New Mexico phase, a style approved by Frederic Remington but "something [Hedger] didn't wish to carry further,—simply the old thing over again and got nowhere" [18]).[8] Even after *The Professor's House* (which is, among other things, a perfectly clear and conscious good-bye to cowboys), Cather still was not done with the Southwest. She visited again in 1925 and 1926 to prepare for *Death Comes for the Archbishop*, a novel that reframes and sanctifies the land, transforming her cowboys into missionary priests and the "happy family" of misfits into the Holy Family. If such a transformation did not entirely lay to rest the ghosts that inhabited the cave of love, it pacified them enough to allow her to move forward, unencumbered and open-eyed.

In placing Grey and Cather side by side and holding up for comparison their responses to the riddle of the passionate desire that wounds even as it vitalizes in the forms of Grey's repetitions and Cather's innovations, I do not mean to suggest Cather enjoyed a "sanity" or psychic health that Grey failed to achieve. Instead, I have invoked some broad concepts of psychoanalysis, particularly as they involve repetition, as a useful exploratory metaphor rather than as an instrument of individual diagnosis.

In fact, although I find the personal life stories of both authors compelling, I am most interested in how they and their work participated in the largest cultural dreams of the early twentieth century: ponderous, nostalgic dreams of authenticity, vitality, and significance (dreams which, as Lears argues, often served the interests of the very modern condition that they sought to escape). In this respect Cather's and Grey's engagement with the West as a setting for the exploration of salvific love reflected, not a personal experience, but a cultural one, and the continuing popularity of "the Western" and its familiar pleasures through the rest of the twentieth century suggests something of that experience's energy.

Nor do I want to claim for Cather's work superiority to Grey's based on an aesthetic standard that values experiment and invention over formulaic repetition. Grey and Cather were simply different kinds of authors and thinkers, able to achieve effects of great power through very different means. The intensity or very "compulsive" quality of Grey's work, its over-the-top failure to deal with the monsters it summons, sets it apart from the pragmatically formulaic work of most of his imitative successors in the history of the Western. Nevertheless, Cather's work, particularly after 1915, is lighter in its touch than Grey's, more playfully willing to assume emotional positions temporarily, explore them, and then move on. This is not to say that Cather lacked depth or powerful emotional commitments—what we know of her life points entirely in the opposite direction. Rather, her famous reserve was perhaps the mark, not of repression or denial of the imagined realm of love's passionate excess that snared Grey so thoroughly, but rather of her deep familiarity with that place, and of her respect for its finally unfathomable mysteries. To put it differently: perhaps Cather, unlike more naive antimodern modernists (such as Grey, and perhaps some other, more highbrow modernist masters of repetition and the return), recognized at the core of experience a wound, erotic or otherwise, that simply could not be healed, in a mythic western landscape or elsewhere. This recognition, far from binding her to compulsive returns, freed her to imagine the *other* world of clear-eyed adulthood where love is still a possible, if temporary and imperfect, performance, and where there are new variants of old stories to be told. In this other world, for instance, Godfrey St. Peter, in Chicago at the opera, looks with wonderment at his wife, Lillian, recalling Turgenev and observing simply, with "a smile not altogether sad," that "the heart of another is a dark forest, always" (*Professor's House* 95).

NOTES

1. Several scholars have placed Cather in or against the cowboy Western tradition, most notably Janis Stout, who suggests in *Picturing a Different West* that Cather, Mary Austin, and other women artists imagined and depicted a "different West" from the masculine, individualist, violent West of Frederic Remington and other late-nineteenth-century male mythographers. Susan Rosowski devotes several chapters to Cather's West (although mainly to her relations to the western plains) in *Birthing a Nation*, and Audrey Goodman's *Translating Southwestern Landscapes* usefully places both Cather and Grey in the historical context of the development and exploitation of a tourism-driven southwestern iconography.

2. I am not concerned with the question of direct influence or of an intentional "conversation" between the two writers in their works, although Cather clearly knew of Grey and it seems unlikely that he would not have been aware of her work. There may be an allusion to *O Pioneers!* or *My Ántonia* in *Code of the West* (1923), whose heroine Georgiana recalls having read "some book about a pioneer girl . . . [who] sure had it coming to her" (118). Some points of similarity are genuinely remarkable: the love-in-the-cave scenes from *Riders of the Purple Sage* (1912) and *The Song of the Lark* (1915) that are important to my argument in this essay, for example, suggest powerfully that Cather might have picked up and remembered Grey's best-seller during the time of *The Song of the Lark*'s composition. But it seems best to consider the two as writing in a particular historical moment, with particular shared cultural and artistic needs: thus it is hardly surprising that each wrote a World War I novel about a young farmer who enlists (*The*

Desert of Wheat and *One of Ours*), or that various of their characters hold similar negative opinions of modern jazz and dancing, or even (to take a very specific scene) that Wansfell's apostrophe to the condor in *Wanderer of the Wasteland* (1923) echoes Thea's earlier famous exultation to the eagle in Panther Canyon. These seem to be useful implements, like the cliff dwelling itself, from a literary-historical toolkit that the two authors shared.

3. See Lears 4–7 for a summary of his sweeping account of the antimodernist critique of the modern, an apparently regressive cultural tendency that often paradoxically supported the development of modern liberal culture and consumer capitalism. Leona Sevick has perceptively traced the politically repressive uses of two of Lears's categories of antimodernist thought, therapeutic nostalgia and religious aestheticism, in "Catholic Expansion and the Politics of Depression in *Death Comes for the Archbishop.*"

4. The passion that Grey and Cather associated with the Southwest had two faces, one picturesque and sentimental, the other primal and overwhelming. Cather tended to keep these separate; thus her "Julio," or the bantering courtship of Fred and Thea, seem stock figures of romance, only distantly related to the powerful unconscious forces of desire released in Thea and perhaps Cather by the desert landscape. Grey, on the other hand, mixed the two faces, sometimes to comical effect, as characters declare their elemental maleness or femaleness in the stilted language of the proto–Harlequin Romance. I agree with Jane Tompkins, who sees in Grey's super-eroticized landscapes forces of desire that appear to transcend sexuality and that threaten the very autonomy of the rational, civilized self (169–70); such anti-rational forces—what Lears calls "primal irrationality" (166)—are an important characteristic of the "unfettered" aspect of the Southwest in the literary imagination of the 1910s and 1920s (apparent, for instance, in Mary Austin, Mabel Dodge Luhan, D. H. Lawrence, and others as well as in Grey and Cather). Both the picturesque and the primal freedoms associated with the West represent urgent desires, and both are clearly opposed to the confining rules of the conventional urban world that the traveler into the West leaves behind.

5. Grey's repetitions were frequently noted by his critics; in 1923, his biographer notes, even he himself became disturbed by the serialized *Code of the West*'s undeniable similarity to its immediate predecessor, *The Call of the Canyon* (both were stories of eastern flappers con-

verted to true womanliness by western experiences and men), and held off publishing *Code* in novel form for more than ten years (Pauly 203).

6. In this connection I am particularly struck by another part of the August 1916 letter to Greenslet, written from Wyoming after a holiday in New Mexico. Looking back over the difficult year that had seen Judge McClung's death, Isabelle's marriage, and increasing tensions for her own family in Red Cloud, she wrote characteristically that although the previous winter had been positively infernal, she had put it and its memories behind her, left them in the Rockies (Cather to Greenslet, 22 August 1916). It would be nine years before she would return to the Southwest.

7. This statement, written about her final visit to Virginia during the writing of *Sapphira and the Slave Girl*, is no doubt extreme, since Cather returned frequently to many places she had written about—not only the Southwest up through the 1920s, but also and obviously her family home in Red Cloud—as well as Europe, Grand Manan, and Northeast Harbor. Nonetheless, she clearly returned to those places, including Red Cloud, as a visitor, not a native coming home, and this is an important distinction: like the returns of Jim Burden or Niel Herbert, hers were defined by her alienation. Her burial in Jaffrey—a favorite vacation spot, and one about which she had never written (although she had written there) is telling in this regard.

8. "Coming, Aphrodite!" brings together three significant scenes of Cather's early career: the small midwestern town (the Huntington of Eden Bower's past), lower Manhattan, and the exotic landscape of the West, figured not only in "The Forty Lovers of the Queen" and this allusion to Remington, but also in Hedger's blankets from Arizona, Eden's identification of him as an "old friend from the West," and the unexpected strains of Puccini (whose romantic opera *La Fanciulla del West* [*The Girl of the Golden West*] opened in Manhattan in 1910) that he hears Eden singing.

WORKS CITED

Bohlke, L. Brent, ed. *Willa Cather in Person: Interviews, Speeches, and Letters*. Lincoln: U of Nebraska P, 1986.

Cather, Willa. "Coming, Aphrodite!" *Youth and the Bright Medusa*. New York: Knopf, 1920. 11–78.

———. *Death Comes for the Archbishop*. New York: Knopf, 1927.

———. Letters to Ferris Greenslet. Houghton Library, Harvard U, Cambridge MA.

———. *My Ántonia*. Boston: Houghton Mifflin, 1918.

———. *Not Under Forty*. New York: Knopf, 1936.

———. *O Pioneers!* Boston: Houghton Mifflin, 1913.

———. *The Professor's House*. New York: Knopf, 1925.

———. *The Song of the Lark*. Boston: Houghton Mifflin, 1915.

Chapin, Frederic. *The Land of the Cliff Dwellers*. Boston: Clarke, 1892.

Freud, Sigmund. "Analysis of a Phobia in a Five-Year-Old Boy." 1909. *The Standard Edition of the Complete Psychological Works of Sigmund Freud*. London: Hogarth P, 1955. 10:1–149.

Goodman, Audrey. *Translating Southwestern Landscapes: The Making of an Anglo Literary Region*. Tucson: U of Arizona P, 2002.

Grey, Zane. *Code of the West*. New York: Grosset and Dunlap, 1934.

———. *Riders of the Purple Sage*. New York: Grosset and Dunlap, 1912.

Jewell, Andrew, and Janis P. Stout, eds. *A Calendar of the Letters of Willa Cather: An Expanded, Digital Edition*. *Willa Cather Archive*. Ed. Andrew Jewell. U of Nebraska–Lincoln. 8 March 2011. http://cather.unl.edu.

Laut, Agnes. *Through Our Unknown Southwest*. New York: McBride, 1913.

Lears, T. J. Jackson. *No Place of Grace: Antimodernism and the Transformation of American Culture, 1880–1920*. Chicago: U of Chicago P, 1983.

O'Connor, Margaret, ed. *Willa Cather: The Contemporary Reviews*. Cambridge: Cambridge UP, 2001.

Pauly, Thomas. *Zane Grey: His Life, His Adventures, His Women*. Urbana: U of Illinois P, 2005.

Roosevelt, Theodore. *A Book-Lover's Holidays in the Open*. New York: Scribner, 1916.

Rosowski, Susan. *Birthing a Nation: Gender, Creativity, and the West in American Literature*. Lincoln: U of Nebraska P, 1999.

Saunders, Charles Francis. *Finding the Worth While in the Southwest*. New York: McBride, 1918.

Sergeant, Elizabeth Shepley. *Willa Cather: A Memoir*. Philadelphia: Lippincott, 1953.

Sevick, Leona. "Catholic Expansionism and the Politics of Depression in *Death Comes for the Archbishop*." *The Cambridge Companion* to *Willa Cather*. Ed. Marilee Lindemann. Cambridge: Cambridge UP, 2005. 191–204.

Stout, Janis. *Picturing a Different West: Vision, Illustration, and the Tradition of Cather and Austin*. Lubbock: Texas Tech UP, 2007.

Tompkins, Jane. *West of Everything: The Inner Life of Westerns*. New York: Oxford UP, 1992.

2 Thea's "Indian Play" in *The Song of the Lark*

SARAH CLERE

Much critical attention has been paid to the role of southwestern Indian ruins in *The Professor's House*; however, far less space has been devoted to the use Cather makes of indigenous culture in *The Song of the Lark*. In *The Professor's House*, Tom Outland's experiences with cliff-dweller culture include concrete historical and anthropological qualities that appear to be largely absent from Thea Kronborg's encounters with Native ruins. Tom excavates and catalogs relics; Thea has transcendent moments of identification with long-dead Native women. On the surface, Thea's response to Panther Canyon appears to be entirely emotional and almost intentionally ahistoric. Yet her sojourn in Panther Canyon is, in reality, heavily grounded in contemporary antimodern anxiety surrounding gender roles and the appropriation of American Indian culture. By allowing Thea to identify herself so closely with these non-white women, Cather is indulging in a variation of the practice Philip Deloria terms "playing Indian." Thea's identification with the long-dead Native women of Panther Canyon allows her to identify herself as an artist without completely abandoning the qualities of domesticity that Cather's successful female characters invariably possess.

Both ethnographers and tourists found Native peoples of the

21

Southwest more historically and aesthetically compelling than the tribes who occupied the Great Plains. Plains Indians' role as nomadic hunters seemed less appealing and less "civilized" to white Americans than the agrarian lifestyle practiced by the Native occupants of the Southwest.[1] In terms of the evolutionary continuum upon which late-nineteenth-century anthropologists placed non-white peoples, southwestern Indians seemed closer to European culture (and thus more advanced) than their counterparts in the central United States.[2] By the time Cather wrote *The Song of the Lark*, stereotypical images of Plains Indians dominated popular perceptions of Native peoples. Their aggressive attacks on wagon trains formed the plots of dime Westerns, and their feathered war bonnets were staples of the period's numerous Wild West shows. As non-Indian Americans imbibed these images, individual Plains tribes were being systematically removed and exterminated.[3] The omnipresence of these stereotyped depictions meant that to middle-class culture seekers, Plains Indians lacked authenticity. In contrast, southwestern Indians appealed to literate tourists, who felt they had a legitimate intellectual and aesthetic interest in Native peoples.

In the early years of the twentieth century, preoccupation with the southwestern corner of the United States was not unique to Cather. She joined a range of intellectuals, including Mary Austin and Mabel Dodge Luhan, in traveling to and writing about the area. With its ethnically diverse population and flexible borders, the Southwest in the later nineteenth century was not quite "American." This vision of the Southwest as space set aside from the main course of westward expansion is particularly relevant to *The Song of the Lark*, where it becomes for Thea a refuge from modernizing America. Unlike the rest of the western United States, southwestern territory could still function as a regenerative, imaginative space, allowing individual Americans who visited to recuperate and escape from the complexity of the modern United States. The central feature of the southwestern United States that enthralled everyone from archaeologists, to tourists, to Willa Cather herself, was the presence of sites of Anasazi ruins, known simply as "cliff-dweller" ruins.[4] These structures, actually built into the rock face, were abandoned hundreds of years before the first white settlers arrived in the Southwest. Archaeological evidence shows an agrarian culture that had evolved a settled, domestic lifestyle. The exact fate of the former occupants of these dwellings has never been determined, adding a compelling layer of historical mystery to the region. On a national level, this interest in the cliff-dweller ruins reflected not only a need for another trajectory of exploration but a very real sense of ambiguity regarding the whole project of empire, both within the borders of the United States and abroad. Michael Tavel Clarke asserts, "The failure of the Cliff Dwellers contradicted American faith in the foreordained victory of civilization over savagery and thus also challenged American faith in its new program of overseas imperialism" (400). The notion that a people as "culturally superior" as the Anasazi could simply disappear made Americans uneasy, as it seemed obliquely threatening to the continuance of their own civilization. Americans, eager to lengthen their own national history and produce historic monuments and ancient artifacts that could vie with Europe's, showcased these ruins as national treasures. Paradoxically, though, the very ruins they proudly exhibited not only had no direct connection with their own national history but also emphasized the tenuous positioning and potential for extinction of all civilizations, regardless of how advanced.

That the Southwest and its prehistoric buildings became a fin de siècle antidote to antimodern anxiety is unsurprising. Richard Slotkin maintains, "The moral landscape of the Frontier Myth is divided by significant borders, of which the wilderness/civilization Indian/White border is the most basic. The American must cross the border into 'Indian country' and experience a 'regression' to a more primitive and natural condition of life so that the false values of 'the metropolis' can be purged and a new, purified social contract be enacted" (15). The escape the region offered was not only geographic but temporal: imaginative visitors could go back in time to a land that had not yet felt the imprint of European colonization and experience the mythic freedom of frontier America. Journeying to the southwestern United States and viewing the cliff-dweller ruins allowed Americans (including Willa Cather) to make this theoretical border crossing and escape modernity. Culture-seeking white Americans were even able to imagine themselves connected with these ancient civilizations. Such identification, Caroline Woidat explains, was enabled by the ruins' lack of living Indian inhabitants: "While the modern Native American was in many ways 'other' to the tourist, visitors thought they could identify with the ancient people whose homes they wandered. Like Cather, they were inspired to claim Native America as part of their own historical past" (33).

Thea's own retreat into Panther Canyon represents a flight from the hectic pace and "false values" of the modern metropolis of Chicago. Her seemingly fruitless winter of musical study in Chicago has exhausted her physically and mentally. Sitting in a restaurant with her friend Fred Ottenburg, she is a dismal sight indeed: "Thea was as gray as the weather. Her skin looked sick. Her hair, too, though on a damp day it curled charmingly about her face, looked pale" (288). Thea's lackluster appearance and overall despondency inspire Ottenburg to suggest a summer in the Southwest: "I don't think I told you, but my father owns a whole canyon full of Cliff-Dweller ruins. He has a big worthless ranch down in Arizona, near a Navajo reservation, and there's a canyon on the place they call Panther Canyon, chock full of that sort of thing" (289). Tellingly, Cather is careful to avoid any hint that Biltmer's ranch might be one of the West's touristy "dude ranches," established in the 1890s and ubiquitous by 1915. The text emphasizes the ranch's identity as a private residence run by an accommodating caretaker. A vacation at a for-profit dude ranch with other tourists would interfere with the authenticity of Thea's private, regenerative experience with Indian culture. Ottenburg suggests that a summer in the open air will make a "new woman" of Thea. His use of the phrase is unintentionally ironic, since a "New Woman" is exactly what Thea, with her frantic routine of study and work in an urban center, has become. Thea's ill-health may be partially explained by a bout of tonsillitis; however, her listlessness and general sense of malaise also resemble neurasthenia. An oft-diagnosed ailment at the turn of the twentieth century, neurasthenia was thought to be the consequence of a too-active involvement in the competitive arena of modern life. Women, who were considered constitutionally weaker and less fitted for the aggressive nature of the public sphere, were diagnosed with the malady more often than men. The treatment for both genders involved what Tom Lutz calls "a reconstitution of the subject in terms of gender roles" (32). Women were forced to go on bed rest and were prohibited from any physical exertion, while men, who were thought to be feminized by the disease, were prescribed rigorous physical activity, often in a wilderness setting. Notably, both male and female neurasthenics were encouraged to forgo intellectual activity. Fred's plan for Thea's regeneration combines the female rest cure with the male exercise cure. Thea is sent to an unfamiliar place and cared for by people she has no connection with; however, that locale is in the rugged American West near a "canyon full of Cliff-Dweller ruins." The presence of Panther Canyon and the Indian ruins it contains also help Thea reconstitute and reinvigorate herself. Early-twentieth-century Americans understood Indian life as simple and authentic and viewed it as a healthful antidote to the enervating confusion of modernity.

Neurasthenia and an interest in Indian cultures, particularly those of southwestern tribes, were both important characteristics of the impulse historian T. J. Jackson Lears refers to as antimodernism. In *The Song of the Lark*, Thea's retreat to Panther Canyon is a definite antimodern escape, a movement outside the boundaries of mainstream America. For Thea, who has failed to find contentment in the small town of Moonstone and found the urban center of Chicago similarly uncongenial, the Southwest functions as a refuge from both the provincial town and the anonymous city.

The long-dead Native people whose homes and relics Thea appropriates are the Sinaguas, a tribe that disappeared before Europeans entered the Southwest. An interest in "primitive" and "exotic" cultures was characteristic of fin de siècle reactions to the increasing urbanization and mechanization of America that Lears terms antimodernism. According to Deloria, modernity was a "paradigmatic moment" for playing Indian that "used Indian play to encounter the authentic amidst the anxiety of urban industrial and post-industrial life" (7). Turn-of-the-twentieth-century America, fully invested in the myth of the vanishing American, increasingly reached back to its own prehistory and viewed American Indian peoples with retrospective nostalgia. In *Playing Indian*, Deloria establishes two contradictory ways Americans have historically viewed and appropriated Indian peoples. Native Americans could be viewed as either interior figures "situated within American societal boundaries," or exterior figures "outside the temporal (and societal) boundaries of modernity" (103). The view of Indians as interior, authentically American figures populated the imaginations of Revolutionary and nineteenth-century Americans, while the view of Indians as exterior figures removed from normative American life dominated the early-twentieth-century United States. As outsiders who had been both literally and figuratively pushed beyond the periphery of American society, these exterior Indians, in Deloria's words, "represented positive qualities—authenticity and natural purity—that might be expropriated, not for critique (as in the case of the traditional noble savage), but as the underpinning for a new, specifically modern American identity" (103).

The Song of the Lark views Native peoples as exterior figures removed from America's national consciousness. Leah Dilworth lists several ways of appropriating Indian culture; the first example she gives is collecting: "Once collected (or represented) southwestern Indian life circulated as a spectacle for middle-class consumption in museum displays, books, magazines, and galleries, and as tourist attractions" (7). Tom Outland engages in the process of collecting in *The Professor's House* with his carefully excavated and cataloged finds and his trip to the Smithsonian. *The Song of the Lark*'s Henry Biltmer, the elderly German caretaker of the Ottenburg ranch, is another collector who "had gathered up a whole chestful of Cliff-Dweller relics which he meant to take back to Germany with him some day" (303). In Biltmer we perhaps see an earlier prototype of the German collector in *The Professor's House* who buys the artifacts Tom and Roddy have collected and returns with them to Germany. Thea, although surrounded by artifacts in Panther Canyon, does not collect these objects: "Thea had a superstitious feeling about the potsherds, and liked better to leave them in the dwellings where she found them. If she took a few bits back to her own lodge and hid them under the blankets, she did it guiltily, as if she were being watched" (305). Sarah Wilson notes that, in contrast to Tom, who paternalistically possesses and mediates the relics on behalf of a country that is ignorant of their true value, Thea considers the cliff-dweller artifacts outside of a specifically American worldview: "Unlike Tom, Thea sees the ancient Native American dwellings as neither a national right nor a national possession. Rather, she feels herself 'a guest' and finds in the ruins an individual inspiration to resist the worst side of American nationality, its assimilative hometown conventionality" (580). That Thea views the Southwest as a personal rather than a national possession does not make her identification with Native peoples wholly positive and uncomplicated. Although she does not gather artifacts the way Tom does, she makes other intangible appropriations. Her self-proclaimed status as a "guest" assumes a welcome that has never been proffered and becomes a disingenuous means of legitimizing her presence in the Sinaguas' long-abandoned homes.

Although Tom's anthropological and nationalistic appropriation of the culture of Indian people is easy to condemn, the uses to which Thea puts Native culture present problems that are more difficult to articulate. In the vein of Wilson's article, most analyses of *The Song of the Lark* have cited Thea's experience with Native culture as wholly positive, devoid as it is of the anthropological scrutiny and possessiveness that characterize Outland's time on the Blue Mesa.[5] This attitude crystallizes in Deborah Lindsay Williams's statement that "When the two novels are juxtaposed, what emerges is Cather's subtle condemnation of the desire to possess something as intangible as landscape: a critique of the colonizing impulse" (163). In an early feminist reading of the novel, however, Ellen Moers remarks, "The whole Panther Canyon section of the novel is concerned with female self-assertion in terms of landscape; and the dedication to landscape carries with it here the fullest possible tally of spiritual, historical, national, and artistic associations" (258). Williams is correct that Thea's occupation of Panther Canyon does not involve physical possession and control, but as Moers indicates, Thea's "self-assertion in terms of landscape" is not without a range of cultural and nationalistic ramifications. Both Williams and Moers are alive to the female dimensions of both the canyon itself—what Moers famously calls "the most thoroughly elaborated female landscape in literature"—and the artifacts that Thea finds there. What these critiques do not address is Thea's whiteness and the distance it imposes between her and American Indian cultures.

When Moers claims that Thea's "own artistic commitment makes her one with the Indian women, who with their pottery began the creation of beauty" (258), then several lines later remarks that "Thea relishes her aloneness" (258), she unwittingly reveals one of the great contradictions at the heart of Cather's use of Pueblo culture. The cliff-dweller ruins Thea explores are a model of communal endeavor, yet Thea repurposes them as a tribute to individual autonomy. Her treatment of Panther Canyon as a source of, in Wilson's words, "individual inspiration" bears a startling resemblance to the uses New Age Americans would make of Native peoples.[6] Writing about appropriation of American Indian culture in the New Age, Shari Huhndorf remarks that "'Native' traditions generally reflect a heavily European ethos" and that "the fixation on self-discovery and self-healing articulate the very Western ideology of bourgeois individualism" (163). Thea's use of the Native ruins for both "self-discovery and "self-healing" allows her to take her place as an individual in modern America. This anxiety about American individualism runs through the novel and is intimately connected to the fraught role of the female artist. *The Song of the Lark* frequently and somewhat stridently emphasizes the importance of individual achievement; however, according to Joseph Urgo, "Thea's belief in her self-sufficiency is sharply qualified in the novel, for Cather makes it clear that one does not climb without stepping on something or someone" (137). This is certainly true, but there seems to be a kind of inevitability determining the roles of both the favored individuals who climb and those less fortunate ones on whose shoulders they stand. Ray Kennedy tells Thea fatalistically that the world is composed of winners and losers and "halfway people" who are "foreordained" to "help the winners win and the failers fail" (123). Sixteen pages later, Dr. Archie informs Thea, "The people who forge ahead and do something, they really count. . . . We all like people who do things even if we only see their faces on a cigar-box lid" (139). The "halfway people" who are fated to be mere instruments in others' success or failure are not ultimately as important, or even worthwhile, as those who "do things."

The Song of the Lark's consistent linear focus on Thea's upward climb echoes Frederick Jackson Turner's conception of American settlement and progress. In his 1893 address, "The Significance of the Frontier in American History," Turner recounts how "the Indian trade pioneered the way for civilization. The buffalo trail became the Indian trail, and this became the trader's 'trace'; the trails widened into roads, and the roads into turnpikes, and these in turn were transformed into railroads"

(14). Turner's spatial paradigm of the Indian's relation to the European allows him to naturalize European incursions into the North American continent. He continues: "The trading posts reached by these trails were on the sites of Indian villages which had been placed in positions suggested by nature, and these trading posts, situated so as to command the water systems of the country, have grown into such cities as Albany, Pittsburgh, Detroit, Chicago, St. Louis, Council Bluffs, and Kansas City" (14). Turner imagines Indian villages fluidly transforming into large cities; these cities, by virtue of their location on Native sites "suggested by nature," are themselves a part of nature rather than a corruption and a violation of the natural world. Turner depicts the transformation of the American landscape and the disappearance of Native peoples as a process both natural and inevitable. The Sinaguas disappear before European contact, so Cather is able to sidestep the issues of European conquest, land partition, and removal, topics that were particularly acute in the temporal context of *The Song of the Lark*'s action. Turner performs a similar evasion, hypothesizing, "Long before the pioneer farmer appeared on the scene, primitive Indian life had passed away" (13).

Turner's designation of the Indian as the forerunner of the modern American dismantles the binary relation of savage and civilized that many white Americans used to understand their relation to indigenous people, creating a new paradigm with the Indian as the white American's evolutionary ancestor. Huhndorf comments: "For Turner, it was the actions of individuals (in this case individual pioneers) engaged in historical processes, rather than the development of the race as a whole, that enabled civilization to advance. Turner's thesis thus develops social evolutionary theory by emphasizing competitive individualism and also articulates the ideology of industrial capitalism" (57). This aspect of Turner's thesis is what allows Ray Kennedy earlier in the novel to link his own individual achievements as a nineteenth-century American with those of the pre-Columbian tribes who occupied the Southwest (118). Thea endorses such "competitive individualism" with regard to the cliff dwellers when she places the labor of the tribe's women on a hierarchical scale of value: "The stupid women carried water for most of their lives; the cleverer ones made vessels to hold it" (303). This value-laden division of labor comes very close to an articulation of a modern, capitalist ethos. Even as Thea revolts from not only the village of Moonstone but the modern city of Chicago, she brings some of the values of those communities with her to Panther Canyon.

Thea's regeneration is not only an individual project but also a completely bodily one. The manner in which Thea engages in Indian play differs from more mainstream examples of the phenomenon. In contrast to many of her male contemporaries, who donned ersatz Indian dress and participated in Indian-influenced ceremonies as part of fraternal organizations, Thea's behavior is devoid of the props, pageantry, and communal activities that characterized more typical Indian play. Thea experiences purportedly Indian culture through acts of bodily mimicry that are not dependent on costumes or ceremony. The lack of material culture trappings enables Cather to convert a fairly typical American activity into something portentous and mythic. Williams notes Thea's "physical, even visceral appreciation of the past" (157), and Marilee Lindemann describes *The Song of the Lark*'s "fierce and exuberant reclaiming of the body as a site of power, pleasure, and utopian possibility," claiming "the text stands not simply as a resistance to coercive heteronormativity but as a positive alternative to it" (56). In the Southwest, Thea resists the "coercive heteronormativity" that would have her stay in Moonstone and participate in one of the novel's disastrous marriages by enacting a kind of perfect domesticity, free of the often messy and tedious circumstances of childbearing and homemaking. Climbing the trail to Panther Canyon, Thea thinks about the Native women before her who wore the path into the earth, carrying water to the houses above: "She found herself trying to walk as they must have walked, with a feeling in her feet and knees and loins which she had never known be-fore,—which must have come up to her out of the unaccustomed dust of that rocky trail. She could feel the weight of an Indian baby hanging to her back as she climbed" (302). Cather illus-trates Thea vicariously experiencing that most female of activi-ties, motherhood. Until now, maternity and the heterosexual re-lations that precede it have been things to be avoided at all costs. In fact, the domestic sphere in *The Song of the Lark* is consider-ably less idyllic than in Cather's other fiction. Although Thea's mother is an admirable housekeeper and a wholly sympathetic character, her homekeeping appears to be more of a herculean effort against chaos than the rhythmic and creative process it is in many other Cather texts.

The novel's problems with domesticity, as Lindemann indi-cates, reach back to heteronormativity itself. Marriage is almost invariably a problematic institution in this novel. Although in many of her other works Cather exhibits a similar unease re-garding marital ties, she reaches new and striking levels of vitriol in *The Song of the Lark*. Dr. Archie has a disastrously unhappy marriage, and his stingy wife eventually dies gruesomely in an explosion caused by her use of gasoline to clean the household's upholstery. Fred Ottenburg and his disagreeable wife live entire-ly separate lives, and we learn later in the novel from Dr. Archie that she has "general paresis," a complication of advanced syph-ilis. Both the doctor and Fred are essentially tricked by their conniving wives into their respective marriages. Even more troubling is the chilling Norwegian folktale Thea tells at the Nathanmeyers' house that depicts an adulterous wife being danced off a cliff by her husband and smashing with him on the rocks below. Themes of marital infidelity followed by graphic violence also occur in *The Kreutzer Sonata* by Leo Tolstoy, lent to Thea by a designing medical student. In this novella, after de-ciding that romantic love is a fiction, a man catches his wife in adultery and brutally murders her. Moving from her characters' experiences to folk culture to Russian literature, Cather takes every opportunity to produce examples of marriages that have terrifying consequences, particularly for women. The paradigm in both the real and fictitious bad marriages is the same: the men are ensnared and betrayed by women, who are then doomed to die grotesquely.[7] Most disturbing is the subtext that somehow these women deserve their violent ends, echoed a decade later in *The Professor's House*, where Father Duchêne cheerfully designates the preserved prehistoric woman named Mother Eve as an unfaithful wife who has been murdered by her husband.

Urgo interprets Thea's story about the wife being danced off a cliff as a kind of warning to Fred through which Thea "communicates the necessity of avoiding volitional dependence on others" (138). Indeed, when Fred, sitting with Thea in Panther Canyon, asks, "suppose I were to offer you what most of the other young men I know would offer a girl they'd been sitting up nights about: a comfortable flat in Chicago, a summer camp in the woods, musical evenings and a family to bring up. Would it look attractive to you?" Thea replies to his proposition with the exclamation, "Perfectly hideous!" (317). Both the middle-class home life of the small town and the upper class, urban domesticity that Fred offers are equally unpalatable to Thea. Through mimicking the movements of Native women carrying both water and babies, Thea is able to experience female domestic labor and motherhood at their most ideal and organic, divorced from the cluttered and increasingly programmatic twentieth-century domestic realm.

Deloria suggests that for women at the turn of the twentieth century, "Indian role models demonstrated the difference between natural, domestic labor and unnatural work outside the home. They claimed a transcendent existence as expressions of the universal female activities of childraising and homemaking" (113–14). This elision of indigenous and European-American women's roles found its most concrete cultural expression in the organization known as the Camp Fire Girls, founded in 1910. Camp Fire Girls began as the companion movement to the Boy Scouts and illustrated the fear of the modern New Woman and her separation from the traditionally feminine roles of housekeeping and motherhood. According to Deloria, "If camping and boy scouting were about restoring masculinity to post-frontier city boys, Camp Fire was about reaffirming female difference in terms of domesticity and service" (113). The Camp Fire movement viewed Native American women, traditionally seen as outside modernity, as domestic role models for American girls. Young women gave themselves what they thought of as Indian names, dressed in fringed and embroidered "ceremonial gowns," and did supposedly Indian dances, all the while earning "honor beads" for largely domestic activities.[8] These correlations between traditional domesticity and Indian play tap into what Deloria terms "the importance of preexisting symbolic links between Indians and women" (111).

Such "symbolic links" undergird contemporary descriptions of the origins and purpose of the Camp Fire movement. A 1912 article by Hartley Davis on Camp Fire Girls in the Protestant newspaper *The Outlook* rhapsodizes about the prehistoric roots of the firmly gendered division of labor on which the group was based: "It was also in primitive days that the first grand division of labor was made. The man, the provider and defender of the family, went out into the wilderness to hunt, and the woman stayed at home and kept the fire burning and the pot boiling. And that division, with all the consequences that it entailed, has remained to a very large extent, in spite of all the changes in social life, until this day" (182). Davis views women's domestic labor as a kind of eternal verity enduring, "in spite of all the changes in social life," right into the early twentieth century, but he tolls an ominous note with the phrase "until this day," implying that without a hasty intervention traditional femininity faces extinction. Writing in 1919, James Franklin Page connects Camp Fire Girls' formation more explicitly to the perceived difficulties of modern America: "The general aim of the Campfire Girls is to help girls prepare for a new social order, and to en-able them to overcome the grinding tendency of modern machine work; to show that common life contains the materials for romance and adventure—that even the most commonplace tasks may prove adventuress; to show the significance of the modest attainments of life; to put women's work into measurable bundles; to develop in girls the power of cooperation, the capacity to keep step" (81). Page acknowledges an altering "social order" and emphasizes the need to "keep step"; however, he believes, somewhat contradictorily, that young women can best acclimate themselves to such changes by embracing the pleasures of "common life" and "commonplace tasks"—that is to say, domestic labor. Regarding this strange paradox, Mary Jane McCallum explains, "Modern messages were imbued with anti-modernist appeal as Camp Fire organizers devised new ways for girls to participate in an increasingly industrial society without renouncing domesticity" (56).

In the Camp Fire movement, striving and ambition, while encouraged, were carefully placed inside a narrowly conceived regulatory framework. According to the Camp Fire Girls' manual, *The Book of the Camp Fire Girls*, young women could earn honor beads in seven areas: "Home Craft, Health Craft, Camp Craft, Hand Craft, Nature Lore, Business, and Patriotism" (11). Notably, the categories in which girls could achieve recognition were limited to activities deemed socially acceptable for middle- and upper-class women. Honors in "Patriotism," for example, did not involve agitating for the right to vote. Regarding women's suffrage, the organization maintained a determinedly impartial official position.[9] *The Book of the Camp Fire Girls* briefly addresses the issue with regard to the wearing of the ceremonial gown: "In the matter of partisan parades such as woman's suffrage, the Camp Fire organization cannot take sides either for or against, although individual members among the girls and Guardians are entirely free to identify themselves as they choose. In such cases the ceremonial gown should not appear" (17). Despite Camp Fire's stated neutrality regarding suffrage, the organization's emphasis on female domesticity aligned them philosophically with anti-suffrage reformers, who argued that woman's primary civic duties were enacted within the home. In Elizabeth Duffield's *Lucile the Torch Bearer*, one of the many novels that capitalized on Camp Fire's popularity, when Lucile tells her father that she hopes to be a Camp Fire girl, he responds, "Camp-fire girls you say? What's that? Anything like a suffragette?" Lucile "contemptuously" replies, "Well, Hardly," and enjoins her father to let her explain the goals of the Camp Fire movement in order that he "can never make such a mistake again" (8). Thea's own experiences in Panther Canyon resemble those enshrined by the Camp Fire movement: She hikes up ancient rock paths, ponders the soot from the cooking fires of the site's prehistoric inhabitants, marvels at the fragments of woman-crafted pottery she finds, regains her physical and mental health, and contemplates her own place in the long line of historical endeavor.

Although Thea's own Indian play initially revolves around the domestic roles of the tribe's women, Cather soon enacts a subtle shift from the traditional female role of the homemaker to the less traditional one of artist. The more Thea discovers regarding the tribe's women and their roles, the more she identifies with them, until even her daily bath, in Cather's words, "came to have a ceremonial gravity. The atmosphere of the canyon was ritualistic" (304). Thea learns from Henry Biltmer that the women of the tribe were responsible for procuring and storing water, a vital task in that arid region (303). Despite her earlier bodily identification with the water carriers on the path, Thea is not destined to remain one of the stupid women who carry the water (or by extension the stupid women who carry infants strapped to their backs). In a highly modernist epiphany, Thea suddenly integrates the domestic and the artistic, the contemporary and the eternal. This realization occurs during one of her baths in the canyon stream:

The stream and the broken pottery: what was any art but an effort to make a sheath, a mould in which to imprison for a moment the shining, elusive element which is life itself,—life hurrying past us and running away, too strong to stop, too sweet to lose? The Indian women had held it in their jars. In the sculpture she had seen in the Art Institute, it had been caught in a flash of arrested motion. In singing, one made a vessel of one's throat and nostrils and held it on one's breath, caught the stream in a scale of natural intervals. (304)

Thea unites the functional art of the Indians, high art enshrined in a museum, and her own ability to create music, recognizing all of these things as valid means of capturing what she sees as the indefinable essence of life.

Thea's experiences in the Southwest seal her exile from her family and her community of origin. While there she completes the process of maturation and separation begun during the previous summer, when her open-air concert with her Mexican neighbors embarrassed her racist siblings and she made the painful realization that her brothers and sister "were among the people she had always recognized as her natural enemies" (240). In Panther Canyon, Thea recalls her experience of the summer before and determines to jettison "whatever was left of Moonstone in her mind," citing the "older and higher obligations" (308) the cliff dwellers have taught her, which replace the more typical bonds to relatives, friends, and neighbors. Again, there is the transformation of a complex and nuanced community into a monolithic expression of individual desire. In *The Song of the Lark*, playing Indian allows Thea to formulate an alternative female identity in which the role of the woman artist absorbs and contains the more traditionally feminine roles of mother and homemaker. In this all-encompassing feminine role, Thea, as Sharon O'Brien asserts, becomes "reborn as an artist—daughter to the earth and the women potters, mother to herself" (417).

This creative rebirth echoes Harsanyi's dictate early in the novel that "Every artist makes himself born" (175) and Wunsch's even earlier remark, "The world is little, people are little, human life is little. There is only one big thing—desire" (76). The advice of her male teachers, both talented artists in their own right, does not resonate with Thea, who must see those ideas expressed in female form.

The end of *The Song of the Lark* shows Thea as a great opera singer. At the height of her success, she tells Fred, "I don't know if I would have gotten anywhere without Panther Canyon" (463), indicating how significant this contact with prehistoric people has been to her career. Native cultures inspired Cather in much the same way. What is not clear is the effect of narratives like Cather's on actual American Indians. Dilworth claims that "as American writers brought the Indian into literature . . . as the Indian was 'written,' Native Americans vanished. And furthermore this was a necessary transformation. The Indian was usable only as past" (187). Although in 1915, when *The Song of the Lark* was published, a number of Indian tribes occupied Arizona, Cather makes few references to living Native Americans. The glimpse she gives the reader of the Navajos, or Diné, is telling, "The great pines stand at a considerable distance from one another. Each tree grows alone, murmurs alone, thinks alone. They do not intrude upon each other. The Navajos are not much in the habit of giving of or asking help. Their language is not a communicative one, and they never attempt an exchange of personality in speech. Over their forests there is the same inexorable reserve. Each tree has its exalted power to bear" (295).[10] Here, Cather effectively elides the Navajos into the landscape, equating individual Indian people with trees and relegating them to the status of natural resources. She also describes the Navajos as isolated from each other and from other tribal groups and dismisses their language as a means of effective communication. The Navajos surface again later in "The Ancient People" when Thea and Fred take "long rides into the Navajo pine forests" to purchase "turquoises and silver bracelets from the wandering Indian herdsmen" (322). The "wooly red and gray blankets" Thea uses to cushion the floor of her rock house are made by the Navajos as well. The contemporary Navajos were noted silversmiths and weavers, yet Cather does not elaborate on the artistry of either the blankets or the jewelry Thea encounters. The role of the artist in *The Song of the Lark* is exclusively reserved for the long-dead occupants of the cliff city, and, now, for Thea herself.

A peripheral and stereotyped presence in *The Song of the Lark*, the Navajos gain more attention and more nuance twelve years later in *Death Comes for the Archbishop*; their artistic accomplishments are recognized and admired, and Bishop Latour's friend Eusabio emerges as an expressive and sympathetic character.[11] Cather's detailed description of Eusabio's clothing illustrates her newfound appreciation for Navajo artistry: "He always dressed very elegantly in velvet and buckskin rich with bead and quill embroidery, belted with silver, and wore a blanket of the finest wool and design. His arms, under the loose sleeves of his shirt, were covered with silver bracelets, and on his breast hung very old necklaces of wampum and turquoise and coral" (220). *The Song of the Lark*'s "turquoise and silver bracelets" and "wooly red and gray blankets" transform from cheap trinkets and ignored domestic objects into expressions of Navajo aesthetics and craftsmanship. When Latour journeys to meet his friend after Eusabio's only son has died, Eusabio greets him with the single remark, "My friend has come" (232). Of this greeting the text states, "That was all, but it was everything; welcome, confidence, appreciation" (232). Here we see *The Song of the Lark*'s clumsy description of the Navajos as profoundly mute recast as one man's individual reserve. As Latour settles into the hogan Eusabio has provided, he notices the "grove of tall, naked cottonwoods—trees of great antiquity and enormous size—so large they seemed to belong to a bygone era. They grew far apart and their strange, twisted shapes must have come about from the ceaseless winds that bent them to the east and scoured them with sand, and from the fact that they lived with very little water—the river was nearly dry here for most of the year" (231). As with Eusabio's verbal economy, there are echoes here of the somewhat silly description of the "great pines" in *The Song of the Lark* that "grow alone" (295). Instead of being personified, however, the trees in *Death Comes for the Archbishop* are beautifully described and integrated into the natural world. Furthermore, the offensive equation of the trees with the Navajos that Cather makes in *The Song of the Lark* is nowhere to be found.

By the time of the publication of *Death Comes for the Archbishop* in 1927, Cather had obviously begun considering indigenous Americans as individuals rather than cultural exemplars. Both Eusabio and Jacinto, Latour's Pueblo guide, emerge as distinct characters in the novel. Most interestingly, in contrast to Thea's and Tom's blithe assumptions of a shared consciousness with Indian people, Latour realizes that there are aspects of indigenous culture that as a non-Indian he cannot experience. Regarding Latour's relationship with Jacinto, Cather writes, "There was no way he could transfer his own memories of European life into the Indian mind, and he was quite willing to believe that behind Jacinto, there was a long tradition, a story of experience, which no language could translate to him" (97). Latour's acknowledgment that Jacinto's culture is uniquely his own and not available for export or appropriation illustrates Cather's own evolving cultural awareness and her abandonment of Indian play. Unlike both *The Song of the Lark* and *The Professor's House*, each of which features Native culture as experienced and mediated through the consciousness of a central non-Indian character, *Death Comes for the Archbishop* depicts individual indigenous people as possessing their own desires and agendas independent of the preoccupations of the novel's white characters. In their introduction to *Willa Cather and the American Southwest*, John Swift and Joseph Urgo affirm the continuing relevance of the ideas articulated in *Death Comes for the Arch-*

bishop, citing the text as "providing grounds for analysis and debate of issues that remain central to contemporary visions of the nation's future as a multi-racial, multi-ethnic society" (10). Published in 1927, Cather's final southwestern novel depicts the region as something other than a vacation spot for disillusioned white Americans. Although *Death Comes for the Archbishop* is by no means free of imperialism and Eurocentric ideas, it reflects Cather's willingness to grapple with the extraordinary and exhilarating idea that the Southwest, and by extension the United States, might be more than a place of imaginative and economic possibility for Americans of European descent.

NOTES

1. According to the 1911 *Encyclopaedia Britannica*, Pueblo Indians possessed "sedentary agricultural characteristics" and lacked "the warlike disposition of the Plains Indians" (633).
2. Itinerant southwestern tribes like the Apaches and the Navajos were often ignored by ethnographers who found them overly "primitive."
3. Mike Fischer provides a discussion the absence of Plains Indians in Cather's Nebraska novels.
4. Ann Moseley notes that the ruins Cather viewed in Walnut Canyon (the real-life counterpart of the fictional Panther Canyon) belonged to a pre-Columbian tribe retroactively named the Sinaguas (219).
5. One notable exception is Lisbeth S. Fuisz, who not only recognizes the imperial dimensions of Thea's use of the Southwest but argues provocatively that critics are often guilty of unintentionally "reinscribing" such imperialism by wholeheartedly endorsing Cather's own autobiographical designation of the Southwest as a place of potential and renewal (40).
6. Cather is truly ahead of her time. The mystical, kinesthetic appropriation of Native "essence" she shows Thea experiencing in 1915 greatly resembles the countercultural interest in indigenous spiritual practices during the 1960s and 1970s.
7. There is a somewhat ironic contrast here between the numerous examples of deceitful women and Fred's duping of Thea during their trip to Mexico.
8. The use of beads as markers of achievement added another quasi-

Indian touch to the Camp Fire Girls, while avoiding the masculine and militaristic connotations surrounding the giving of badges.

9. The 1914 edition of *The Book of the Camp Fire Girls* lists both Jane Addams, who by the twentieth century was noted for her support of women's suffrage as well as her settlement work (Knight 380), and Kate Douglas Wiggin, author of the beloved children's book *Rebecca of Sunnybrook Farm* and an opponent of suffrage (United States Congress 5), as members of the "Board of Electors" (Camp Fire Girls 6). Such disagreement on the specific nature of reformist principles reflects the miscellany of attitudes that could and did exist under the rubric of Progressive Era American thought.

10. This passage, one of Cather's rare lapses of precise description, illustrates the ludicrous metaphoric conceits otherwise excellent writers can be moved to use when they attempt to describe Indians. Janis Stout pointedly remarks, "What, one wonders, would a noncommunicative language be? And how would a tree 'bear'—in the sense of having to bear a burden, not in the sense of producing or conveying an implication—an 'exalted power'" (147).

11. According to Edith Lewis, the character of Eusabio is based on Mabel Dodge Luhan's husband, Tony Luhan, who was himself Navajo (143). Lois Palken Rudnick concurs, noting that "many of the characteristics that Mabel and other associated with Tony" may be found in Cather's description of Eusabio (188).

WORKS CITED

Camp Fire Girls. *The Book of the Camp Fire Girls.* New York: Camp Fire Girls, 1914.

Cather, Willa. *Death Comes for the Archbishop.* 1927. Willa Cather Scholarly Edition. Ed. John J. Murphy and Charles W. Mignon. Lincoln: U of Nebraska P, 1999.

———. *The Song of the Lark.* 1915. Lincoln: U of Nebraska P, 1978.

Clarke, Michael Tavel. "Lessons from the Past: The Cliff Dwellers and New Historicism." *Western American Literature* 42.4 (2008): 395–425.

Davis, Hartley. "The Camp Fire Girls." *The Outlook* [New York NY] 25 May 1912.

Deloria, Philip. *Playing Indian.* New Haven: Yale UP, 1998.

Dilworth, Leah. *Imagining Indians in the Southwest: Persistent Visions of a Primitive Past.* Washington DC: Smithsonian Institute Press, 1996.

Duffield, Elizabeth M. *Lucile the Torch Bearer*. New York: George Sully, 1915.

Fischer, Mike. "Pastoralism and Its Discontents: Willa Cather and the Burden of Imperialism." *Mosaic* 23.1 (1990): 31–44.

Fuisz, Lisbeth S. "Rediscovering the Southwest: Imperialism in Willa Cather's *The Song of the Lark* and Sharon O'Brien's *Willa Cather: The Emerging Voice*." *Willa Cather Pioneer Memorial Newsletter* 46.2 (2002): 39–42.

Huhndorf, Shari. *Going Native: American Indians in the Cultural Imagination*. Ithaca: Cornell UP, 2001.

Knight, Louisa W. *Citizen: Jane Addams and the Struggle for Democracy*. Chicago: U of Chicago P, 2005.

Lears, T. J. Jackson. *No Place of Grace: Antimodernism and the Transformation of American Culture, 1880–1920*. Chicago: U of Chicago P, 1981.

Lewis, Edith. *Willa Cather Living*. 1953. Lincoln: U of Nebraska P, 2000.

Lindemann, Marilee. *Willa Cather: Queering America*. New York: Columbia UP, 1999.

Lutz, Tom. *American Nervousness, 1903: An Anecdotal History*. Ithaca: Cornell UP, 1991.

McCallum, Mary Jane. "'The Fundamental Things': Camp Fire Girls and Authenticity, 1910–1920." *Canadian Journal of History* 40.1 (2005): 45–66.

Moers, Ellen. *Literary Women*. Garden City NJ: Doubleday, 1976.

Moseley, Ann. "The Creative Ecology of Walnut Canyon: From the Sinagua to Thea Kronborg." *Cather Studies 5: Willa Cather's Ecological Imagination*. Ed. Susan J. Rosowski. Lincoln: U of Nebraska P, 2003. 216–36.

O'Brien, Sharon. *Willa Cather: The Emerging Voice*. New York: Oxford UP, 1987.

Page, James F. *Socializing for the New Order or Educational Values of the Juvenile Organization*. Rock Island IL: James F. Page, 1919.

"Pueblo." *Encyclopaedia Britannica*. 11th ed. 1911.

Rudnick, Lois Palkin. *Mabel Dodge Luhan: New Woman, New Worlds*. Albuquerque: U of New Mexico P, 1984.

Slotkin, Richard. *Gunfighter Nation: The Myth of the Frontier in Twentieth Century America*. New York: Athenaeum, 1992.

Stout, Janis P. *Picturing a Different West: Vision, Illustration, and the Tradition of Cather and Austin*. Lubbock: Texas Tech UP, 2007.

Swift, John N., and Joseph R. Urgo. "Introduction: Literate Tourism and Cather's Southwest." *Willa Cather and the American Southwest*. Ed. Swift and Urgo. Lincoln: U of Nebraska P, 2002. 1–12.

Turner, Frederick Jackson. "The Significance of the Frontier in American History." *The Frontier in American History*. 1920. Tucson: U of Arizona P, 1997. 1–38.

United States Congress, Senate Committee on Woman Suffrage. *Hearings on S.J. Res. 1: Joint Resolution Proposing an Amendment to the Constitution of the United States Extending the Right to Vote to Women*. 63rd Cong., 1st sess. Washington DC: GPO, 1913.

Urgo, Joseph. *Willa Cather and the Myth of American Migration*. Urbana: U of Illinois P, 1995.

Williams, Deborah Lindsay. "'Fragments of Their Desire': Willa Cather and the Alternative Aesthetic Tradition of Native American Women." *Willa Cather and Material Culture*. Ed. Janis P. Stout. Tuscaloosa: U of Alabama P, 2005. 156–71.

Wilson, Sarah. "'Fragmentary and Inconclusive' Violence: National History and Literary Form in *The Professor's House*." *American Literature* 76.1 (2003): 571–99.

Woidat, Caroline M. "The Indian-Detour in Willa Cather's Southwestern Novels." *Twentieth-Century Literature* 48.1 (2002): 22–49.

3 "Jazz Age" Places
Modern Regionalism in Willa Cather's
The Professor's House

KELSEY SQUIRE

To appreciate Cather as a modern writer, we must come to terms with her complex relationship to regionalism; her vivid depictions of the Midwest, although celebrated, can also relegate her to the margins of American modernism. As Guy Reynolds suggests, "this, finally, is the lesson that Cather teaches us about regional thinking: that we need ever more supple, inflected, nuanced definitions in order to understand the complexities of the inter-connections between writing and place" (18). In this essay I suggest that Cather is a modern regionalist; that is, her complex regional consciousness encompasses both rural and urban places. *The Professor's House* (1925), with its cosmopolitan protagonist, Professor Godfrey St. Peter, proves to be the ideal text for exploring Cather's position as a modern regionalist because the novel gains momentum from the meaningful juxtaposition of disparate places.

I propose three texts published in or just before 1925, the same year as *The Professor's House*, as a contextual field for understanding Cather's position as a modern regionalist: Cather's introduction to *The Best Stories of Sarah Orne Jewett* (1925), her interview with *New York Times* reporter Rose Feld (21 December 1924), and F. Scott Fitzgerald's *The Great Gatsby* (1925). Cather's introduction and interview provide insights into regionalism as an affective relationship between artists and the world around them. This relationship between artists and the *modern* world can be explored through correspondences between *The Great Gatsby* as an exemplary modern text and *The Professor's House*. Both novels complicate traditional literary regionalism as they examine how urbanization, consumption, and exile impede the acquisition of place attachment.

Traditional definitions of literary regionalism can be traced back to Hamlin Garland's assertion in *Crumbling Idols* (1894) that "*local color in the novel means that it has such quality of texture and back-ground that it could not have been written in any other place or by any one else than a native*" (54, emphasis in original). More than century later, literary critics still return to his definition as a means of identifying "regional" texts; however, Garland's insistence on the contemporary nature of the "local color" novel often remains forgotten. He writes, "conventional criticism does not hamper or confine [local color writers]. They are rooted in the soil. They stand among the cornfields and they dig in the peat-bogs. They concern themselves with modern and very present words and themes" (50). While Garland helped through his criticism and his fiction to establish the association between regionalism and rural places filled with soil and cornfields, it is important to note his use of the word "modern" and his insistence that regional literature confronts present-day social concerns. His story "Under the Lion's Paw" from *Main-Travelled Roads* (1891) perfectly captures a regional text addressing modern social themes through the attempts of his protagonist, the tenant farmer Tim Haskins, to buy the farm he has improved from a corrupt land speculator.

Contradictions abound as twentieth-century critics look back on and attempt to define traditional expressions of literary regionalism; although the feature of rural places remained central, this location was imagined to be situated in the past. Consider Richard Brodhead's description of regionalism in *Cultures of Letters*: "[Regionalism] requires a setting outside the world of modern development, a zone of backwardness where locally varied folkways still prevail. Its characters are ethnologically colorful, personifications of the different humanity produced in such non-modern cultural settings. Above all, this fiction features an extensive written simulation of regional vernacular, a copious effort to catch the nuances of local speech" (115–6). This definition demonstrates a clear shift in the American cultural understanding of place as terms like "backward," "antimodern," "rural," and "past" become entangled (and in some cases, synonymous). The additional link between these terms and regionalism leads critics to misconstrue the term, for to invoke a region (especially one that features rural places) evokes assumptions of backwardness and antimodernism. It is surely no coincidence that literary regionalism has flourished at moments when the tensions between modern and antimodern America were most apparent.

In *Writing Out of Place*, Judith Fetterley and Marjorie Pryse attempt to circumvent the "antimodern" classification of regionalism by redefining regional texts as those "where region becomes mobilized as a tool for critique of hierarchies based on gender as well as race, class, age, and economic resources" (14). In a sense, their understanding captures Garland's vision of regionalism as a social and political commentary on present and pressing issues facing common Americans. Yet Fetterley and Pryse's assertion that regional writing is *women's* writing becomes more narrow and problematic than Brodhead's list of criteria. An equally troubling feature of Fetterley and Pryse's definition concerns the very nature of regions themselves; echoing critic Frank Davey, Fetterley and Pryse situate regionalism as "a discourse . . . rather than a place" (7).

Places, regions, and the land form the anchor of Cather's regionalism, and while Cather clearly appreciated the representation of regions in works by other writers, she resists classifying herself within the "limited" scope of regional writing. Cather's complex engagement with the history of regionalism threads through several projects that emerged in 1925. In her introduction to the writing of Sarah Orne Jewett (an exemplar of traditional literary regionalism), Cather praises Jewett's ability to write "of the people who grew out of the soil and the life of the country near her heart" ("Best Stories" 55). Yet Cather also downplayed the importance of the "soil" in her own work around this time. In a 21 December 1924 *New York Times Book Review* interview with Rose C. Feld, Cather was asked, "Is *My Ántonia* a good book because it is a story of the soil?" Cather responded, "No, no, decidedly no. . . . I expressed a mood, the core of which was like a folksong, a thing that Grieg could have written. That it was powerfully tied to the soil has nothing to do with it" ("Restlessness" 72). Cather qualifies that while "Ántonia was tied to the soil," the story itself was not; "Chicago could have told the same story." Cather demonstrates the flexibility of her regional consciousness as she continues, imagining the mood of this urban story: "It would have been smearier, joltier, noisier, less sugar and more sand, but still a story that had as its purpose the desire to express the quality of these people. No, the country has nothing to do with it; the city has nothing to do with it; nothing contributes consciously" (72). Cather's statement demonstrates her resistance to regionalism as she refuses to celebrate a stereotypical reading of *My Ántonia* as "a good book" simply because it takes place in the country. While Cather scholars continue to embrace her modern complexity, her remarks invite an investigation of how places contribute to the "core" or "mood" of her stories, especially the "smearier, joltier, noisier" places.

In this essay I argue that we can further appreciate Cather's complexities of place by understanding regionalism not as fiction about rural places or with vernacular speech, but as a "way of seeing" places—what I would like to call it a "regional consciousness." This regional way of seeing emphasizes the interconnections between places and communities as a larger spatial network.[1] In this view of regionalism, to borrow Cather's phrasing, "the country has nothing to do with it, the city has nothing to do with it," not because place itself is irrelevant but because both country and city can be represented within a region. Cather effectively embodies this definition of modern regionalism[2] in *The Professor's House*: "regional" because her characters form intense attachments to particular places and use their awareness of place distinctiveness to construct regional and communal borders; "modern" because the organic, spiritual meanings of places are complicated by twentieth-century economics, consumerism, and cosmopolitanism.

One of Cather's concerns that surfaces both in her introduction to Jewett and in her interview with Feld is the influence of place on artists as inspiration for artistic creation. In her introduction to a select collection of Jewett's works, Cather defines two aesthetic approaches in Jewett's sketches, one that is "fluid and formless" but full of "perception and feeling," and one that is "tightly built and significant in design" ("Best Stories" 48–49). It is through the unity of these two approaches that Jewett achieves the height of aesthetic quality, Cather argues, as Jewett's "sketches are living things, in the open, with light and freedom and air-spaces about them. They melt into the land and the life of the land until they are not stories at all, but life itself" (49). Although Cather does not use the word "regionalism" in her description of Jewett's work here, these stories that "melt into the land" are in fact regional in nature because her impressions of the landscape allow Jewett to capture a community situated within a wider spatial network. In the Feld interview Cather is much more critical of American literature and art; however, she returns to the natural, organic relationship between the artist and his or her life by inventing a fictional French artist and examining his artistic philosophy and activities: "The Frenchman doesn't talk nonsense about art, about self-expression; he is too greatly occupied with building the things that make his home. His house, his garden, his vineyards, these are the things that fill his mind. He creates something beautiful, something lasting. And what happens? When a French painter wants to paint a picture he makes a copy of a garden, a home, a village. The art in them inspires his brush" ("Restlessness" 71). This philosophy can also describe Jewett, whose "brush" was inspired by the villages, gardens, and landscapes around her.

In *The Country of the Pointed Firs*, Jewett exemplifies how an artist sees through a regional consciousness as her characters form place attachments by appreciating the aesthetic, communal, and spiritual dimensions of places. Through this "topophilia,"[3] or love of place, Jewett's characters recognize regions not only by distinctive geography but by the stories and emotional sensations that connect places to each other. Jewett's unnamed narrator, an outsider to the Dunnet Landing community, facilitates her place attachment through an aesthetic appreciation of physical geography. As she sails to Green Island with her hostess, Almira Todd, the narrator delights in the island landscape; she admires small farms and fish houses, and the sharp shapes of the firs against the sky. She concludes that "one could not help wishing to be a citizen of such a complete and tiny continent" (407). The narrator's love of place facilitates her desire to become a citizen and belong to this community.

In *The Professor's House*, Cather too incorporates aesthetic appreciation of geography as a way to express place attachment to areas where the characters feel most "at home." Tom Outland expresses his attachment to the Blue Mesa through his sensory observations: the "bluish rock in the sun-tanned grass, under the unusual purple-grey of the sky, gave the whole valley a very soft colour" (198). St. Peter holds a similarly multi-textured memory of Lake Michigan. As he recalls his childhood, he sees the geography of the "shaggy pines" of the shore and brilliant chunks of lake ice, "crumbly and white, throwing off gold and rose-coloured reflections from a copper-coloured sun behind grey clouds" (31). Like Jewett and Cather's imaginary French painter, Tom and St. Peter appreciate the inherent "art" in the physical geography of regional landscapes. Unlike the French artist and Jewett, however, St. Peter is unable to express the physical geography of the landscape and the spiritual feelings it evokes in him. He tries to explain the nature of "le Michigan" to the two boys he tutors in France as a young man, but he finds that his descriptions are inadequate: "it is altogether different. It is the sea, and yet it is not salt. It is blue, but quite another blue. Yes, there are clouds and mists and sea-gulls, but—I don't know" (32). St. Peter's inability to adequately articulate and convey the impressionistic sense of the lake is only one instance of communicative failure concerning the affective dimensions of place throughout *The Professor's House*. In fact, there are several such occurrences: St. Peter struggles to express the value of his old house, and Tom fails twice to explain the value of the mesa, first to Rodney, then to the Washington officials. It is important to note that both men have successful communicative experiences as well: St. Peter's books and articles capture the Southwest to the satisfaction of Father Duchêne, and Tom fascinates St. Peter and his daughters with his vivid tales of the mesa. Both men, however, see their inability to communicate their love of place as a deep crisis. Cather illustrates that this crisis has its roots in the incompatibility between traditional patterns of place attachment as established in literary regionalism and the current modern experience.

While Tom and St. Peter clearly identify with and become attached to particular regional places, their attachment is complicated by their genealogical backgrounds. One of the primary modes of forming a lasting attachment to place, according to environmental psychologist Setha Low, is a family history of occupying the same area for generations. For ancient cultures, a history of occupation promoted an intimate understanding of physical geography that was necessary for survival and facilitated a place-based, communal identity in children through the telling of regional stories and family history. Many regional texts employ genealogical references in order to establish a similar occupational history. In *The Country of the Pointed Firs*, for example, the citizens of Dunnet Landing repeatedly tell stories that emphasize their residency through familiarity with the community's past. The narrator becomes aware of her role as an empathetic insider[4] in this community when Mrs. Todd brings her to a "sainted" place where pennyroyal grows; Mrs. Todd had "never [shown] nobody else but mother where to find this place" (416). Such access to the intimate places of a region allows the narrator to participate actively in community life. Her sense of place attachment and her participation in storytelling together allow the narrator to surmount her status as a genealogical outsider, to the extent that she even takes part in the Bowden family reunion.

In *The Professor's House*, however, Cather demonstrates that the lack of genealogical belonging cannot be overcome so easily. Tom's childhood migration to the West and the subsequent death of his parents emphasize his lack of genealogical connection. Through Tom's experiences, Cather explores genealogical revision as a means of place attachment, as Tom claims the ancient Pueblos as his "grandmothers." This move is clearly, in his eyes, a testament to the attachment that he feels toward the mesa. Within the context of the novel, however—especially in the unacknowledged actions of the conquistadores that St. Peter devotes his life to studying—Tom's attempts to adopt himself into the Native community are on the borderline between deep appreciation and acquisitiveness. As Deborah Lindsay Williams argues, Tom "links understanding with uncovering and ownership" (164). When Tom returns to the mesa after his falling out with Rodney over the artifact sale, he examines the landscape and realizes that it was "the first time [he] ever saw it as a whole" (249). Tom does not state what this vision consists of, but it seems to be a synthesis of all of the mesa's individual parts—the landscape, its colors, its ancient inhabitants, its architecture, its history, stories, and myths—into a collective whole. Tom describes this feeling, saying, "it was possession" (250). While Tom's holistic understanding of the intimate connections between place and community do promote his appreciation of the mesa's intrinsic value, his assertion of his genealogical "rights" to the landscape move him from a position of citizen to owner, and from a feeling of belonging to one of possessing.

The other path of genealogy—the one most frequently adopted by American regionalists—is to trace one's roots back to pre-colonial geographies of origin. This move strangely undercuts one of the presumed aims of regional literature: to be truly "American." For Cather, the tension in negotiating this type of genealogical attachment is embodied in St. Peter's garden. The garden is described as "French": "there was not a blade of grass," but instead gravel, carefully planned hedges and walls, and symmetrical trees (15). These features emphasize the "unnatural" qualities of the garden and suggest that it is an "imported" place. Mark Facknitz interprets the garden as a sign of St. Peter's repression, arguing that the garden seems determined "to make something work where it does not belong" (297–98). The Professor himself seems to acknowledge the "out of place" character of the garden, as he sits in the garden and attends to it especially when he feels homesick for "other lands" (15). Ultimately, the garden represents St. Peter's genealogy of mixed French Canadian and American farmer stock; even those American farmers are "imported" from somewhere else, and St. Peter relishes this imported quality in both the garden and himself, particularly through remembering his experiences in France.[5]

When seen in the light of Cather's praise for Jewett and the art of the imagined Frenchman, the positive qualities of St. Peter's garden emerge. The garden is a place where land melts into life itself. It was built through a sometime-shared effort between St. Peter and the landlord; although the landlord refuses to pay for any repairs to the house, he pays for part of the garden wall, participates in the gardening, and dispenses advice (14–15). The garden also figures into the family's relationship with Tom Outland. St. Peter is working in the garden when Tom first arrives at the house; it is the site of their first conversation. In the garden are grown not only ornamental plants but also salad greens. The family holds meals in the garden, and it is the place where Tom enacts imaginary adventures with the girls. Perhaps most importantly, the garden is a place of mentoring and friendship where the Professor and Tom "used to sit and talk half through the warm, soft nights" (16). Overall, the garden commingles natural and cultural aspects of gathering, hospitality, and belonging.

In these two places—Tom's mesa and St. Peter's garden—Cather raises serious questions concerning how individuals participate in place. She celebrates place attachment through the experiences of Tom and St. Peter, but she recognizes the challenges to forming such attachments. How is Tom, as a non-indigenous American, to form a meaningful place attachment without "possessing" the landscape? How can St. Peter's garden, with its rigid structure and foreign elements, inspire organic relationships and inclusiveness? Tom and St. Peter experience genuine attachments to place, but because they are unable to articulate an appropriate expression of the place's meaning, these relationships to place are unstable. As a result, several of Cather's characters embrace market or economic value as a way to overcome their inability to express place attachment. This tension between "love of place," attachment, and market value defines the modern experience of place and represents Cather's more modern approach to regionalism.

Identifying Cather's works as modern can be challenging, as elements of her own life seem at odds with the "modern" era. Novelist Fanny Hearst notes that the traditional furnishings of Cather's domestic space and her circle of friends were "no more a part of Fitzgerald's twenties than of Mars" (qtd. in Acocella 24). As Hearst demonstrates, Cather's and Fitzgerald's lifestyles were radically dissimilar. In "Echoes of the Jazz Age" (1931), Fitzgerald describes the 1920s as "the most expensive orgy in history," a time marked by gaiety and cynicism, sexual exploration, and drunkenness, and he attributes such wild behaviors and intense feelings to "all the nervous energy stored up and un-expended in the War" (21, 13). Cather was two decades older than Fitzgerald, and Joan Acocella notes that Cather retained more nineteenth-century qualities in her lifestyle and her writing than other modernists did (23). Yet Fitzgerald himself was a vo-cal enthusiast of Cather's work. He called *My Ántonia* "a great book!" in his letters, and he ranked Cather—along with Whar-ton, Dreiser, and Norris—among those "literary people of any pretensions . . . [who] have been more or less bonded together in the fight against intolerance and stupidity" (*Correspondence* 78–79).[6] He deeply admired *A Lost Lady* (1923), and anxiously apologized to Cather because he believed his portrait of Daisy Buchanan too closely resembled Marian Forrester; Cather ad-mitted that she did not notice any correspondence between the two women in her own reading.

Walter Benn Michaels's examination of modernism in *Our America* remains foundational for understanding how both *The Professor's House* and *The Great Gatsby* participate in the con-struction of national identities. Michaels primarily investigates who counts as a native, that is, who "belongs" as an insider in a particular place; my interest lies in *how* people belong, which can be seen through the regional consciousness that permeates Fitzgerald's and Cather's novels. Earlier regional novels, such as Jewett's *The Country of the Pointed Firs*, suggest that outsiders can become insiders through an appreciation for regional geog-raphy, which forms the foundation for place attachment. In their novels of 1925, both Cather and Fitzgerald question the ability of individuals to form attachment to place as our understanding of regions shifts in the modern era to encompass urban centers and to accommodate greater mobility. Although her characters are able to form some attachments to place, Cather also exam-ines how materialism and feelings of exile or rootlessness im-pede such attachments. Through an understanding of Fitzger-ald's and Cather's common ground concerning the anxiety of forming place attachment, we can not only better understand

Cather's engagement with modernism but also add complexity to our conceptions of literary modernism.

Tom Lutz initiates a modernization of regionalism in *Cosmopolitan Vistas*; as his title suggests, he advocates increased attention to the cosmopolitan features that appear in regional literature when insiders meet outsiders, the local meets the global, and the rural meets the urban. Commenting on one of the "hallmarks" of regional literature—a city visitor who narrates his or her trip to the country or provincial enclave—Lutz notes that while "in these texts the urban visitor's perspective is represented as in some ways clearly superior to the rural ones," this perspective "is far from reliable" (30). He continues, arguing that "the visitor does not, in the end, determine our reading, but helps give these texts their cosmopolitan flavor, since the competing cultural views voiced by visitors and visitees mirror and contend with one another." Just as the city forms an integral part of regional writing, "the provinces" inform notable modern texts.[7] Susan Hegeman questions the assumption that "the city" is the primary inspirational source for modernism: "why would Faulkner write about life in the rural South; or why would Georgia O'Keefe abandon her fascination with New York skylines to paint the rural environs of Taos, New Mexico?" she asks (21). Through her examination of anthropology's professionalization in the early twentieth century, Hegeman convincingly argues that the "spatial reconstruction of one's relationship to the past," particularly through objects, is central to modern thought (37). I would argue further that modern writers reconstruct their spatial relationships to the present through a negotiation of regions, and particularly through the relationship between one region and another, or between an urban center and the surrounding region.

Fitzgerald illustrates the urbanization of landscapes in the Midwest through the eyes of narrator Nick Carraway in *The Great Gatsby*. He writes: "That's my middle-west—not the wheat or the prairies or the lost Swede towns but the thrilling, returning trains of my youth and the street lamps and sleigh bells in the frosty dark and the shadows of holly wreaths thrown by lighted windows in the snow" (184). Nick effectively captures several elements that traditionally define regional places, such as pastoral landscapes (wheat, prairies) and provincial towns that have a shared genealogical background (lost Swede towns). At the same time, Nick provides an alternative definition that reflects a dynamic, urban landscape. Specifically, his focus on trains suggests mobility, industrialization, and a movement away from genealogical definitions of belonging. Nick's alternative regional definition does more than simply shift the cultural regional consciousness from rural to urban areas. His attachment to place highlights things—street lamps, sleigh bells, wreaths, and windows—and this emphasis asserts the role of an increasingly commodified culture as part of the modern regional experience.

In the Feld interview, Cather teases out the modern conflation of the market value of objects and their aesthetic beauty. She says that while "so many more of us are buying chiffoniers and bureaus and mirrors and toilet seats," this new purchasing power should not be confused with culture; homes have increased in "comfort and luxury," she continues, but "every home has not increased in beauty" ("Restlessness" 69). In contrast to the aesthetic appreciation of geography, which facilitates place attachment and communal belonging, the cosmopolitan lifestyle of St. Peter requires an erasure of regional boundaries. His picnic lunches—"chicken sandwiches with lettuce leaves, red California grapes, and two shapely, long-necked russet pears," served with linen napkins (100); his alcohol—taken through "the City of Mexico . . . without duty" (97); his furs and furniture; and his trips abroad all reflect his epicurean tastes and his efforts to surround himself with the beauty, craftsmanship, and quality.[8]

The true effects of this cosmopolitan lifestyle and the practice of conspicuous consumption, however, become clear during St. Peter's two trips to Chicago; although these trips have very different purposes and opposite emotional outcomes, both emphasize his acquiescence to luxury. After arriving by train in the middle of a snowstorm, St. Peter and his wife join the Marselluses at their hotel, Chicago's famous Blackstone: "tea was served in Louie's suite on the lake front, with a fine view of the falling snow from the windows. The Professor was in a genial mood; he was glad to be in a big city again, in a luxurious hotel, and especially pleased to be able to sit in comfort and watch the storm over the water" (89). In contrast to other place experiences, such as Tom Outland's awestruck depictions of the mesa and St. Peter's vivid childhood memories of Lake Michigan, the Blackstone experience lacks vivacity. The simplicity of the diction (the "fine view," the "big city") reinforces St. Peter's complacent mood; the place is smooth and mesmerizing, and any details that could disturb his comfort have dissolved into generalities. Underneath St. Peter's ease, however, is a sense of disconnection; in this Chicago scene, Cather demonstrates the difficulty of forming an attachment to place within a cocoon of luxury that walls off the individual and dulls the senses.

The ramifications of disconnection and a lack of attachment to place are apparent in St. Peter's second trip to Chicago, as he accompanies Rosamond and Louie to select furniture for their new estate. Chicago is not valued as a place of spiritual renewal; it does not facilitate a sense of belonging, and it does not foster relationships between individuals. Instead, St. Peter and his family have created a marketplace identity for Chicago; its function is to provide access to luxury items, such as Spanish bedroom furniture and fur coats. As William Cronon points out in *Nature's Metropolis*, in the nineteenth century Chicago developed into a gateway marketplace that extended the distance between the point of production and the point of consumption. As a result, goods "were valued according to the demands and desires of people who for the most part had never even seen the landscapes from which they came" (266). While an increased distance between production and consumption points can significantly increase an item's luxury (through desirability, financial worth, or cultural value), it simultaneously diminishes the affective relationship between people and places. The consequences of this disconnect to place can be seen in St. Peter's condition after the trip: fatigued and detached.

St. Peter himself does not attribute the commodified turn of mind in his family to a particular place, however, but rather to a person: Louie, who is Jewish. The stereotypical link between Jews and materialism in *The Professor's House* has led to charges of anti-Semitism, most notably in Michaels's *Our America*. Cather's anti-Semitic stereotypes are regretful; however, Louie's cultural heritage becomes a vehicle for the exploration of a torn, modern relationship to place through themes of diaspora and exile.

Howard Wettstein explains that, especially from a Jewish standpoint, diaspora and exile can be seen as opposing terms.[9] He defines *diaspora* as a "geopolitical dispersion," which may be involuntary, but the term also encompasses a voluntary dispersion for people who "simply [decide] to leave, say for want of economic improvement or cultural enrichment" (47). *Exile*, in contrast, is a more religious concept that involves "involuntary removal from homeland" and "being somehow in the wrong place," often as punishment. Louie embodies the more positive concept of diaspora, rather than exile, as he voluntarily moves between and within regions. This mobility allows him to pursue economic improvement and cultural enrichment, and his characterization suggests a link between diasporic behavior and cosmopolitanism. Although Louie's pursuit of money and cultural opportunity is explicitly critiqued by his brother-in-law Scott McGregor and St. Peter, the latter, in particular, exhibits similar diasporic tendencies. Any critiques of Louie could be applied to St. Peter; any acceptance of St. Peter's pursuit of improvement—likewise, it seems—could also be applied to Louie. Through St. Peter's criticism of Louie and the novel's underlying critique of St. Peter, Cather exemplifies her fears concerning cosmopolitanism, as both men fail to investigate the relationship between their consumer lifestyles, the "cultural enrichment" these lifestyles propose, and the effects of consumption and cosmopolitanism on their own sense of place. Fitzgerald echoes these failures at self-investigation when Nick considers the Buchanans' decision to live in New York: "Why they came east I don't know. They had spent a year in France, for no particular reason, and then they drifted here and there unrestfully wherever people play polo and were rich together" (10). The cosmopolitan Buchanans "drift" toward opportunities of cultural enrichment (playing polo) and economic improvement (being surrounded by other rich people), but as a consequence they fail to develop any type of meaningful attachments to, or even distinctions between, the places they inhabit.

In both Fitzgerald's and Cather's novels, conspicuous consumption provides one means of pursuing these missing place attachments; through the acquisition of more goods, especially goods that are aesthetically pleasing or luxurious, the characters increase their potential avenues of attachment. The Marsellus mansion, Outland, provides an excellent example. While the mansion was ostensibly created to honor its namesake (particularly through museum spaces for Tom Outland's laboratory materials and library), many of its features are incongruent with this purpose. Instead, the mansion functions as a showcase to display opulence and wealth. Louie and Rosamond select a pristine location on Lake Michigan, where their Paris-trained architect plans to build "a Norwegian manor house, very harmonious with its setting, just the right thing for rugged pine woods and high headlands" (40). Clearly, the Marselluses consider the aesthetics of place as they build their home; however, Outland becomes a cosmopolitan marketplace—like Chicago—where products are to be consumed and displayed, such as the perfect wrought-iron hinges and latches that are more distinctive (and expensive) than Colonial glass knobs. In addition to the Outland mansion, St. Peter's (new) house and Gatsby's mansion constitute Cather's and Fitzgerald's critical portraits of erratic consumerism, one driven by preoccupations with display and excessiveness. Each of these places embodies the critique against modernization that Cather expressed in her Feld interview, for these houses have indeed increased in "comfort and luxury," but not necessarily beauty, through the accumulation of goods (see "Restlessness" 69).

Cather's characters are not blind to consequences of consumption and their ramifications for attachment and belonging. St. Peter recognizes that his attachment to his garden was cultivated through an intimacy with the place, his own work to create the garden, and its role in facilitating community. As St. Peter prepares to move, he anticipates that the new occupants will not value the garden, since they were not involved in its production and history. After one gardening session he asks his wife, "what am I to do about the garden in the end, Lillian? Destroy it? Or leave it up to the mercy of the next tenants?" (76–77). In contrast to Louie's embrace of diasporic mobility, in this instance St. Peter leans toward exile and regret in anticipation of his move because he is painfully aware of the difficulty of forming an attachment to a new place.

As the novel closes the garden remains intact, and it seems safe to say that St. Peter does not follow through with his destructive suggestion. But the full impact of his thoughts can be seen in light of the story of the cliff dwellers that haunts the text. These ancient people, by choice or by force,[10] did what St. Peter is afraid to do: they left everything behind. St. Peter's anxiety concerning the appreciation of place is realized through the experience of the cliff dwellers, for while Tom becomes attached to the mesa through his aesthetic appreciation of physical geography, and even attempts to form a genealogical attachment to this place and people, the belongings of the cliff dwellers have been left "to the mercy of the next tenants." Tom's endeavors to preserve this historic place cannot be sustained through modern regional consciousness: he and Rodney fight over the economic value of the artifacts, Tom's requests for government aid go ignored, and dozens of objects—including human remains—are disturbed in the process. Ultimately, Cather's novel suggests that an individual sense of place attachment, one that cannot be successfully communicated or shared with others, will be unsustainable due to the competing definitions of value that face a modern industrial world.

The Professor's House represents a modern approach to place as Cather examines and questions the formation of place attachment in a changing modern landscape. The concluding section of the novel considers a concept that remains unexplored in earlier forms of regional writing: the attempt to learn to live in exile, or in "the wrong place." In *The Great Gatsby*, Nick Carraway recognizes his own exile when the East becomes "haunted" for him, like a grotesque El Greco painting, after Gatsby's death (185). When Nick confidently states that he "decided to come back home," he suggests that mobility is the key to defeating exile. A similar act of returning to a place is celebrated in Jewett's *The Country of the Pointed Firs*; the opening chapter is appropriately named "The Return" as the narrator comes back to Dunnet Landing for a second visit. In *Country* there is no doubt that the narrator will be able to resume her life and attachment to the community. In *The Professor's House*, in contrast, Cather emphasizes the impossibility of return due to changes in time. The Professor can renew his attachment to place through his childhood memories and his memories of Tom Outland and their time on the mesa, but it is impossible for him to return to the past; St. Peter's attempt to literally live in the past of the old house nearly kills him. His resulting acquiescence to life in the new house, in a place where he does not feel at home, suggests that exile is a permanent condition. Cather, who seems unwilling to leave "the old house" of regionalism, ultimately suggests that returning to a place does not circumvent exile, but that through knowing one's place, exile can be endured: "at least," the Professor notes, "he felt the ground under his feet. He thought he knew where he was" (283).

NOTES

1. I appreciate Wendy Katz and Timothy Mahoney's effective definition of a regional identity as "a sense of belonging, and awareness of similar traits among people living under similar conditions, or not coincidentally, of how their cultural patterns are distinctive in comparison to other regions or places" (xi). A regional *identity*, however, seems problematically tied to a single region; as Cather demonstrates in her life and in her fiction, individuals may identify with and belong to several regions. As a result, I prefer the term "regional consciousness" to convey how individuals use concepts related to regional affiliation in order to make meaning.

2. Reynolds, Michaels, and Herring place "regional" before "modern" (as in "regional modernist" or "regional modernism") to describe Cather and her work. By identifying Cather as a "modern regionalist" I seek to position her as a regional writer who experiments with modern forms and engages in topics associated with literary modernism.

3. "Topophilia," broadly defined by Yi-Fu Tuan, includes "all of the human being's affective ties with the material environment" (93).

4. Edward Relph uses the term "empathetic insider" to distinguish between several levels of insider and outsider as part of place-based identities. He explains that "to be inside a place empathetically is to understand that place as rich in meaning, and hence to identify with it, for these meetings are not only linked to the experiences and symbols of those whose place it is, but also stem from one's own experiences" (54–55).

5. James Woodress and Kari Ronning's detailed explanatory notes to the Scholarly Edition reveal the degree of importation that St. Peter's garden contains. While the plants are notable for their popularity in European gardens, several have transcontinental origins, including the geraniums (native to Africa), the French marigolds (native to Brazil), and the dahlias (native to Mexico and Central America).

6. This quote is from a letter to Thomas Boyd, the literary editor of the *St. Paul Daily News*, which Boyd subsequently printed as a feature item in the newspaper. Fitzgerald discusses the current state of literary art in America by beginning with the argument that the "history of a young man" formula has been overworked. He turns to an examination of the upper-class reading public who simply "read what they're told" and believe that they are cultured.

7. Lutz's arguments continue an avenue of inquiry established by Stephanie Foote, who suggests that "although regional texts focused

almost exclusively on rural concerns, their nostalgic tone shows then to have been profoundly shaped by an awareness of the globalizing and standardizing tendencies of urbanization and industrialization" (3). Foote's reading of regionalism addresses globalization and urbanization more directly than Brodhead or Fetterley and Pryse; however, as this quote indicates, Foote still situates regional literature as nostalgic and rural. Lutz's argument, and my own, investigates a less dichotomous approach to the relationship between regional and urban places.

8. Christopher Nealon argues that St. Peter's "nostalgia for French and Spanish culture" and his distaste for the "feminine" shopping spree of his daughter form the foundation for his domestic alienation (84). Further treatment of the significance of objects in Cather's fiction can be found in Janis Stout's edited collection *Willa Cather and Material Culture*.

9. Wettstein opens his essay by explaining that "diaspora is a relatively new English word and has no traditional Hebrew equivalent" (47). According to his notes, the first OED reference occurs in 1876, and by 1881 the term was used by *Encyclopaedia Britannica* to refer specifically to Jewish relocation (58 n. 1).

10. In the novel, Father Duchêne hypothesizes that the able-bodied members of the tribe were ambushed by a hostile tribe while farming away from the cliff dwellings, and that the elderly population remaining in Cliff City abandoned the site when the farmers did not return. Anthropologists continue to examine evidence from several different types of ancient structures, including the cliff dwellings, to understand their migration. David Stuart analyzes Chacoan settlements and argues that an increasingly class-stratified society, in combination with drought, put communities under tremendous stress that ultimately led to increased ritualistic behavior, possible violence, and abandonment. Mark Varien and Richard Wilshusen's collection of anthropological essays on the Mesa Verde region are more technical in nature but offer intriguing investigations of environmental and community stress that could cause depopulation or migration.

WORKS CITED

Acocella, Joan. *Willa Cather and the Politics of Criticism*. Lincoln: U of Nebraska P, 2000.
Brodhead, Richard H. *Cultures of Letters: Scenes of Reading and*

Writing in Nineteenth-Century America. Chicago: U of Chicago P, 1993.

Cather, Willa. "The Best Stories of Sarah Orne Jewett." 1925. *Willa Cather on Writing: Critical Studies on Writing as an Art*. New York: Knopf, 1949. 47–59.

———. *The Professor's House*. 1925. Willa Cather Scholarly Edition. Ed. James Woodress and Frederick M. Link. Lincoln: U of Nebraska P, 2002.

———. "Restlessness Such as Ours Does Not Make for Beauty." Interview by Rose C. Feld. *New York Times Book Review*. 21 Dec. 1924. Reprinted in *Willa Cather in Person: Interviews, Speeches, and Letters*. Ed. L. Brent Bohlke. Lincoln: U of Nebraska P, 1986. 67–72.

Facknitz, Mark A. R. "Character, Compromise, and Idealism in Willa Cather's Gardens." *Cather Studies 5: Willa Cather's Ecological Imagination*. Ed. Susan J. Rosowski. Lincoln: U of Nebraska P, 2003. 291–307.

Cronon, William. *Nature's Metropolis: Chicago and the Great West*. New York: Norton, 1991.

Fetterley, Judith, and Marjorie Pryse. *Writing Out of Place: Regionalism, Women, and American Literary Culture*. Urbana: U of Illinois P, 2003.

Fitzgerald, F. Scott. *Correspondence of F. Scott Fitzgerald*. Ed. Matthew J. Bruccoli and Margaret Duggan. New York: Random House, 1980.

———. "Echoes of the Jazz Age." November 1931. *The Crack-Up*. Ed. Edmund Wilson. New York: New Directions, 1945. 23–33.

———. *The Great Gatsby*. 1925. Ed. Matthew J. Bruccoli. New York: Scribner, 1992.

Foote, Stephanie. *Regional Fictions: Culture and Identity in Nineteenth-Century American Literature*. Madison: U of Wisconsin P, 2001.

Garland, Hamlin. "Local Color in Art." *Crumbling Idols*. 1894. Ed. Jane Johnson. Cambridge: Harvard UP, 1960. 49–58.

———. *Main-Travelled Roads*. 1881. Lincoln: U of Nebraska P, 1995. 130–44.

Herring, Scott. "Regional Modernism: A Reintroduction." *Modern Fiction Studies* 55.1 (2009): 1–10.

Hegeman, Susan. *Patterns for America: Modernism and the Concept of Culture*. Princeton: Princeton UP, 1999.

Jewett, Sarah Orne. *Novels and Stories*. Ed. Michael Davitt Bell. Library of America Series. New York: Penguin, 1996.

Katz, Wendy J., and Timothy R. Mahoney. "Regionalism and the Humanities: Decline or Revival?" *Regionalism and the Humanities*. Ed. Wendy Katz and Timothy Mahoney. Lincoln: U of Nebraska P, 2008. ix–xviii.

Low, Setha M. "Symbolic Ties That Bind: Place Attachment in the Plaza." *Place Attachment*. Ed. Irwin Altman and Setha M. Low. New York: Plenum P, 1992. 165–85.

Lutz, Tom. *Cosmopolitan Vistas: American Regionalism and Literary Value*. Ithaca: Cornell UP, 2004.

Michaels, Walter Benn. *Our America: Nativism, Modernism, and Pluralism*. Durham NC: Duke UP, 1995.

Nealon, Christopher. *Foundlings: Lesbian and Gay Historical Emotion before Stonewall*. Durham NC: Duke UP, 2001.

Relph, Edward. *Place and Placelessness*. London: Pion Limited, 1976.

Reynolds, Guy. "The Politics of Cather's Regionalism: Margins, Centers, and the Nebraskan Commonwealth." U of Nebraska–Lincoln, Digital Commons, 2003. http://digital commons.unl.edu/.

Stout, Janis P., ed. *Willa Cather and Material Culture*. Tuscaloosa: U of Alabama P, 2005.

Tuan, Yi-Fu. *Topophilia: A Study of Environmental Perception, Attitudes, and Values*. Englewood Cliffs NJ: Prentice Hall, 1974.

Varien, Mark D., and Richard H. Wilshusen, eds. *Seeking the Center Place: Archaeology and Ancient Communities in the Mesa Verde Region*. Salt Lake City: U of Utah P, 2002.

Wettstein, Howard. "Coming to Terms with Exile." *Diasporas and Exiles: Varieties of Jewish Identity*. Ed. Howard Wettstein. Berkeley: U of California P, 2002. 47–59.

Williams, Deborah Lindsay. "'Fragments of Their Desire': Willa Cather and the Alternative Aesthetic Tradition of Native American Women." *Willa Cather and Material Culture*. Ed. Janis P. Stout. Tuscaloosa: U of Alabama P, 2005. 156–70.

4 Changing Trains
Metaphors of Transfer in Willa Cather

MARK A. R. FACKNITZ

From the beginning truths of the unconscious
belie circumstantial surfaces of things.
—*Susan Rosowski,* The Voyage Perilous

It seems almost silly to write that during all of Willa Cather's life, trains were the primary mode of transport between cities. Even towns of modest size—for example, wayside Red Cloud—might have at least one eastbound and one westbound trunk-line stop each day. Yet the fact that trains are casually omnipresent, as routine as windows, walls, and doors are to rooms, does not make them non-essential. Rather, they are key elements of what Guy Reynolds characterizes as the "shifting historical matrix" of Cather's rural Nebraska childhood, and "it would be a patronizing mistake" to assume that the elements of this matrix are "inevitably quiet or conservative or . . . insignificant" (19). Indeed, Cather's trains "narratively" move much like Melville's *Pequod,* the Rouen diligence in Flaubert's *Madame Bovary,* or Kerouac's motorcars in *On the Road.* They travel the edge between the naturalist's environmental machinery and the romantic idealist's impulse to essentialize, however subtly, our second nature. Famously, in "The Novel Démeublé" Cather looked to retire Balzac's aged "property man" because for too long the novel had been "over-furnished" (5) and, as realism exhausted its momentum in romantic novels or naturalism, "the city . . . on paper [was] already crumbling" (6). For a model she instead chose Tolstoy, in whose writing "the clothes, the dishes, the haunting interiors of those old Moscow Houses, are always so much a part of the emotions of the people that they are perfectly synthesized; they seem to exist, not so much in the author's mind" (or in physical reality) "as *in the emotional penumbra of the characters themselves*" (emphasis added, 6). Cather reminds her reader that "the higher processes of art are all processes of simplification" and, referring to *The Scarlet Letter*, she comments, "the material of the story is presented as if unconsciously" (6).

As if. The author's challenge is not to invest the fictional world with a clutter of verisimilar accoutrements, as if there can be no reference to the world without "red meat thrown into the scale to make the beam dip" (6), nor is she obliged to brashly allegorize. Her poor "drudge, the theme-writing high school student," cannot go to *The Scarlet Letter* for "information regarding the manners and dress and interiors of Puritan society" (6), and the meanings of the rattlesnake and the plow in *My Ántonia*, unmistakably metaphoric though they are, depend on circumstances and landscape inhabited by Jim and Ántonia. They are not there for the herpetologist and the ironmonger. They are bursts of literary light on the ordinary topography of the narrative, wholly teachable moments most of us theme-writing drudges can grasp. However, if asked to choose, Cather prefers a more discreet luster, "whatever is felt upon the page without being specifically named . . . the inexplicable presence of the thing not name, of the overtone divined by the ear but not heard by it, the verbal mood, the emotional aura of the fact or the thing or the deed" (6).

Cather's railroads are eloquent examples of what she means by this superbly enigmatic comment. At once they reveal her subtle attention to the emergence of Chicago as "second city" and the broader historical transformation of the upper Midwest; they reiterate her own experience of moving out of a hostile landscape into the civilized comforts of New York and France; and, most suggestively, they consistently lay down lines of nuance and metaphoric transfer across her midwestern and southwestern landscapes. Trains, not barbed wire or property deeds, redefine Cather's Midwest and West. The new American second nature, according to Cather, is less about the use and ownership of the land than it is about movement across the landscape.

In 1893, during the Columbian Exposition, the American Historical Association heard from Frederick Jackson Turner that the essence of the American story was in the union of the ideas of wilderness and westward settlement. Chicago was the city through which the mineral, agricultural, and human wealth of the West moved in direction of the industrial, financial, and cultural centers of the East. Thus Chicago became "nature's metropolis," as William Cronon aptly dubbed it, in effect the hub city of a new American mythos because "Turner's frontier, far from being an isolated urban society, was in fact the expanding edge of the boosters' urban empire" as "frontier and metropolis turned out to be two sides of the same coin" (51). In material terms, Chicago was originally dependent on its geographical relationship to waterways—lakes and rivers, later the canal—and it continued to thrive when as a major rail center it became a twentieth-century metropolis. Nineteenth-century Chicago, in other words, was a city of profound adaptations to environment and events. For example, at midcentury it was a dank and sprawling shantytown of wooden structures, but after the fire in 1871 Chicago rebuilt as a city of stone and steel; architects vied to endow the ambitious capital of the heartland with unique and ever more imposing buildings.

Cronon argues that the rise of the rail network of which Chicago was a hub is more than a merely economic narrative. "Wherever the rails went," he writes, "they brought sudden sweeping change to the landscapes and communities through which they passed"; their "power to transform landscapes partook of the supernatural, drawing upon a mysterious creative energy that was beyond human influence or knowledge" (72). Indeed, the railroads, and the telegraphs the wires of which ran along the tracks, "shrank the perceptual universe of North America" (76). In fact, trains made the Midwest inhabitable for the new settler population; they were means of moving safely in the cold of winter and the heat of summer, and of moving at all in the muds of spring. Within a generation of the Civil War, settlement and social patterns in the upper Midwest depended entirely on the railroads. For Cronon, "the railroad left almost nothing unchanged," and "to those whose lives it touched, it seemed a at once so ordinary and so extraordinary—so second nature—that the landscape became unimaginable without it" (73). Railroads quickly became second nature, fundamental structures in the midwestern conception of time and space, or "the unnatural instrument of a supposedly 'natural' destiny," one that defines Chicago as if it were "an artificial spider suspended at the center of a great steel web," for to grasp the city and its relation to the West "one must first understand the railroad" (74).

Cather, I believe, had an entire and intuitive grasp of this transformation, as the railroad became a ubiquitous and unobtrusive trope for narrative effects as varied as transfer, estrangement, correspondence, serendipity, and fate in her works, up to and including *Death Comes for the Archbishop* (1927) and, arguably, *Lucy Gayheart* (1935). My thesis is consistent with Joseph Urgo's premise that "migration is the keystone of American existence," for our "picture of life in the United States is a moving picture; our sense of community is in transit; the consciousness we share is migratory" (13). The integument of Cather's fiction is largely made of iron rails, for by train we make the journey by which, as Urgo argues, "the past is no burden on the present; the burden comes from the future, where migrants must utilize what they have that is portable to make the journey in the world" (37). I would add that with trains Cather implies a network of journeys and transferences, such that "her novels provide a way of seeing American society and history as spatialized phenomena, countering many of the dominant myths that have sustained the culture in this century" (Urgo 39). Or, to embellish my analogy, as tracks are laid and trains move over them, so moves the mythos. Enclosing us in darkness as we cross great spaces in search of new "temporary permanence," trains are uniquely capable of shifting us into new forms of being, and as Urgo demonstrates, Cather's "emphasis on transit—including the great fact of migration—reinforces the idea that the past must often be forgotten if one is to succeed in transferring self and value to a new environment" (39).

Moreover, the historical context for trains is as complex as the already rich narratives of migration. In *Memorial Fictions*, Steven Trout comments that Cather's "seventy-four years extend from the final volleys of the age of black powder to the detonation of the atomic bomb—from the last of Indian wars to the beginning of the Cold War" (1). The limits of her life also correspond to the age of rail. Cather was born four years after the completion of the Transcontinental Railroad, and by the time she died the railroads were already beginning to wane, giving way to highways, and even air travel was becoming commonplace in the late 1940s. In arguing that the Great War is pervasive and a surreptitious presence in *The Professor's House*, Trout reminds readers that "Cather herself encourages in 'The Novel Démeublé' . . . a definition of literary achievement that holds subtlety and suggestion over 'mere verisimilitude'" (151). As an example of such he mentions the Professor's houses as "point[s] of interchange between Europe and America" (159). What comparable freight or passengers might not a train carry? Trains, not wagons, bring Cather's migrants westward to the prairie; eastward, trains take them to education, careers, money, war, and European culture.

A peripatetic midwesterner with cosmopolitan ambitions, Cather traveled much and her letters often refer to train travel, which almost invariably includes a change of trains—with its challenges to comfort and tranquillity—in Chicago. As early as 1896, only a few hours after arriving in sooty Pittsburgh, she writes to Mariel Gere about how she began to feel happy once her train was east of Chicago and she saw hills, streams, and trees (Jewell and Stout 0025). Later in life, when established as editor and novelist, Cather traveled more. Letters ran ahead of her travels, as when, for example, in summer of 1916 she wrote to Charles Cather from the Brown Hotel in Denver to ask that a deposit check be sent ahead to the La Salle Hotel in Chicago, adding that her night on the train was pleasantly cool (Jewell and Stout 1907). In October 1918 she wrote from Red Cloud to Irene Miner Weisz with the information that she would arrive in Chicago midmorning on Thursday and leave that afternoon at four for Toronto, presumably on the Grand Trunk Railway (Jewell and Stout 0436). These are details of a sort that any-one traveling in that day might have reported. Judging from nu-merous references to train travel in her letters, Cather's pattern is the same as anyone's who traveled beyond Chicago. Indeed, when Cather traveled to Red Cloud or points further west, in-variably she would have traveled by the Pennsylvania Railroad or New York Central to Chicago and there changed to the Bur-lington (through Nebraska) or the Santa Fe (to the southwest). For example, on 9 June 1927 she wrote to brother Roscoe to say she soon was leaving Chicago on the Burlington no. 1, would pick up Helen Louise in Hastings, and arrive in Denver that day, spend the night, and go on to Casper the following morning (Jewell and Stout 2088). After the change in Chicago, travel was slower, grimier, noisier, smellier, and—for the storyteller—more portentous.

From the moment of her earliest stories, Cather was able to exploit the metaphoric resonances of the railroads. The early story "A Death in the Desert" (1903) opens with Windermere Hilgarde "conscious that the man in the seat across the aisle was looking at him intently" on board the "High Line Flyer, as this train was derisively called among railroad men, . . . jerking along through the hot afternoon over the monotonous country between Holdredge and Cheyenne" (109). Windermere, with his Wildean name (when the story appears in *The Troll Garden*, he is less-obtrusively named Everett), is the spitting image of his brother, Adriance, a celebrated pianist whose student and paramour, Katharine Gaylord, is dying. She is utterly *dépaysée* outside of Cheyenne, Wyoming; ill with consumption, she has been taken in by her prosperous and kind but mildly rustic brother. When the story opens she can still ride in a phaeton about the high plains, or else she would not have seen Windermere, whose resemblance to his brother readers have already learned. Katharine otherwise lives sequestered in a music room packed with memories of a brief and brilliant European career. Susan Rosowski characterizes "A Death in the Desert" as a story about "the seductive power of illusion over mortals who can never enter the rarified realm of great art" (25).

Taken to Katharine by her brother, compassionate Windermere lengthens his stay while she declines. Unlike his celebrated and narcissistic brother, who "usually did the right thing, the opportune, graceful, exquisite thing—except when he did very cruel things," Windermere, according to Katharine Gaylord, is "the kindest man living" (117). Adriance is a genius, however; Windermere is, by contrast, merely moral. Yet Windermere brings new memories of his brother, and even performs Adriance's newest sonata, music that provokes a rush of confession and feeling in the dying woman. He gives Katharine occasion for a torrent of memory, characterized by its similarity to "that prelude of Chopin's with the ceaseless pelting of rain-drops in the bass," which Chopin wrote "when George Sand carried him off to Majorca and shut him up in a damp grotto in the hill-side, and it rained forever and ever, and he had only goat's milk to drink" (119). Thanks to her chance visitor, in a high dry place and at the threshold of death, Katharine rides back on the strength of Windermere's agency to the stormy defining moment of her life

when "somehow the wind with all its world pain had got into
the room, and the cold rain was in our eyes, and the wave came
up in both of us at once—that awful vague, universal pain, that
cold fear of life and death and God and hope—and we were like
two clinging together on a spar in mid-ocean after the shipwreck
of everything" (119).

For subtlety of construction and pathos, Cather soon exceed-
ed "A Death in the Desert" in three other "train" stories—"A
Wagner Matinée" of 1904 and "Paul's Case" and "A Sculptor's
Funeral" of 1905—yet while "A Death in the Desert" is an overwrought story, more feverish than even the topic of tuberculosis warrants, in many respects it shakes out the impulses of the
Europhile and the aesthete as surely as *Alexander's Bridge* (that
other early Cather fiction which includes a train that lets off passengers at a significant moment). Written the year after Cather's
first European travels, "A Death in the Desert" suggests a struggle to find an aesthetic equilibrium between the landscape and
ethos of her youth (as well as the heady precepts of aestheticism)
and the seductions of classical and romantic music. In this respect, Katharine Gaylord is surely a predecessor to Thea Kronborg, whose talent is comparable and whose self-reliance and
luck are far greater. She is also a predecessor to Lucy Gayheart,
whose last name is remarkably similar and whose inability to get
to New York, much less establish herself in Europe, proves fatal.
Similarly, Windermere, in his capacity for self-effacement and
in his life as an itinerant witness who gets off the train where
the story happens to be, prefigures the more developed Jim Burden. Less obviously, Windermere prefigures the generous Augusta in *The Professor's House*, a *mater dolorosa* who uncannily
appears, narrative alpha and omega, with a measure of comfort during St. Peter's melancholic flirtation with suicide. More
broadly, "A Death in the Desert" announces some of Cather's
durable metaphors; for example, the Gaylord house outside of
Cheyenne is an outpost of gentility, its inhabitants struggling for
dignity, much like the Forrester place outside of Sweet Water in

A Lost Lady. Similarly, the idea that one can hear an air from a cantata based on the spring song of "Proserpine" "on guitars in Old Mexico, on mandolins at college glees, on cottage organs in New England hamlets, and . . . on sleighbells at a variety theater in Denver" (109) turns up again in *O Pioneers!* and *Song of the Lark*, in which European music is played on squeeze-boxes and pianolas, and most pathetically in *My Ántonia*, in which Shimerda's silent violin could play the folk tunes and classical airs of Europe but never does.

For such reasons the train in "A Death in the Desert," as narrative device and as an independent trope, is particularly interesting. At the beginning we learn that Windermere's coach is also occupied by "bedraggled-looking girls who had been to the Exposition at Chicago, and who were earnestly discussing the cost of their first trip out of Colorado" (109). There are another "four uncomfortable passengers . . . covered with a sediment of fine, yellow dust" that "blew up in clouds from the bleak, lifeless country . . . until they were one color with the sage-brush and sand-hills" (109). The train emerges within a natural horizon on which the human hold is fragile, requiring constant grip to prevent the shifting ground from obliterating all effort: "The gray and yellow desert was varied only by occasional ruins of deserted towns, and the little red boxes of station-houses, where the spindling trees and sickly vines in the blue-grass yards were kept alive only by continual hypodermic injections of water from the tank where the engines were watered, little green reserves fenced off in that confusing wilderness of sand" (109). Perhaps this is landscape as disease pathology. One could be tempted to conclude that the moral is that Katharine Gaylord, whose tuberculosis delivers her to the desert, finds that nature first coats, then desiccates, and finally obliterates her talent and her passion. However, the story ends with Windermere "pacing the station siding, waiting for the West-bound train" (121). Katharine's brother waits with him, though neither has anything left to say, and they actually look forward to the "wrench of farewell" (121). When the train at last comes in, it lets off a German opera company, an arrival even more improbable even than Windermere's, and from the troupe emerges a stout woman with a lascivious south German accent, whose "florid face was marked by good living and champagne as by fine tide lines rushed up to him, her blond hair disordered by the wind, and glowing with joyful surprise she caught his coat-sleeve with her tightly gloved hands" (121). This grotesque embodiment of insatiable appetite believes Windermere to be his brother, the second crucial misidentification of the story. Appalled, Windermere tells her that she has confused him with Adriance, "and turning from the crestfallen singer he hurrie[s] into the car" (121). In other words, this chance arrest at rail-side in Wyoming only *seems* to be about nature and chance; more deeply, and pessimistically, it is about human inability to travel beyond the reach of the necessity imposed on us by our character and circumstances.

In the 1904 story "A Wagner Matinée," Cather leaves no doubt of the physical and emotional toll a train from the heartland to the east coast can inflict. The narrator's Aunt Georgiana arrives in Boston looking "not unlike one of those charred, smoked bodies that firemen lift from the *débris* of a burned building," a consequence of her having "come all the way in a day coach" (325). Georgiana's transfer emphasizes the cruel consequence of being stuck in the hinterland. The trains that can carry the body do not, tragically, carry one back to youth or into gentler and more prosperous lives. For most people, the train reiterates the cultural poverty of the wayside stations that are their origin or destination, towns like the little Kansas town where the train will stop in deepest darkness for a brief moment to drop off the body of native son Harvey Merrick in "The Sculptor's Funeral." In that story, the train appears in "the snow [that] had fallen thick over everything; in the pale starlight the line of bluffs across the wide, white meadows south of the town made soft, smoke-colored curves against the clear sky" (329). Into this lyrical landscape the casket of Merrick is tugged from the train by "a number of lanky boys of all ages [who] appeared as suddenly and slimily as eels wakened by the crack of thunder" (329); to these blighted fellows, the palm fronds on the black lid are inscrutable irrelevancies. In other words, when it comes to trains Cather's attitude is at best ambivalent. Indeed, at moments the train is radically destructive. In "Paul's Case" it enables the scandalous escape, and, as Paul discovers in the last instant of being, the train also obliterates the self that anxiously wonders if anyone is watching: "He stood watching the approaching locomotive, his teeth chattering, his lips drawn away from them in a frightened smile; once or twice he glanced nervously sidewise, as though he were being watched" (83). When he jumps he is for an instant aware of "the vastness of what he had left undone" and then he drops "back into the immense design of things" (83).

Could not a train deliver one to a richer story, if not to a more optimistic one? In the prologue to *My Ántonia*, Cather's alter ego chances to meet Burden on a train in Iowa in weather hot enough to wilt oaks. In what appears to be a unique instance, Cather does not allude to the direction the train is moving when they meet. Is the conversation thickened by recently refreshed memories and does the change to a more comfortable express in Chicago await? Or have they already shifted to slower and rougher track, are they trying to contain their dismay at the approach Black Hawk by imagining a story larger and more compelling than the ordinary and cramped existence they may soon need to endure? The reader can only guess. Months later Burden comes east with a manuscript. Remarkably, this narrative travels in two directions; first, west through nostalgia and compromise into the past, from the prairie town that Burden long ago escaped to a place in the here and now, Ántonia's garden. Second, once the story is vivid and coherent, it moves east and penetrates through the geographical, social, and class distances that separated Burden from Ántonia.

Scott Palmer, in his essay on the relation of class and nationality to train travel in *My Ántonia*, treats the novel "as a travel narrative of sorts, one that emerges from the reverie of railway travel to consider the intersecting discourses of nationality, class and gender within the settlement of the American West" (239). Jim, Palmer concludes, is "a product of the retrospective and introspective condition of rail travel"—especially as experienced in the red plush of a Pullman coach—and so "Jim's narrative instinctively embeds itself within the vanishing, nostalgic landscape of Black Hawk because the economic and social forces of class inhibit a shared future for him and Ántonia" (248). Palmer's interpretation begs the question of why Jim writes the narrative, not the author whom he encounters in the observation car somewhere in Iowa. Presumably that anonymous author is a woman (as she was explicitly in early edition), herself a native of Black Hawk, and a rail traveler as well. Yet she writes nothing.

Jim is the "ticket," the narrator and agent of Ántonia's story, and while perhaps Ann Romines is right that the novel is to some extent "the triumph of the written male story, finding its way into print with facilitating female support" (149), it is more importantly true that "Cather makes a housekeeping woman the *center* of a fiction or the first time" (149). This focus of Jim's narrative can only happen because Ántonia trusts him in her home, then at the urging of the children shows him her cellar, and takes him even to the fruitful center of her fertile metaphor, the grape arbor at the heart of her garden. As a result of this openness of spirit, the Ántonia story comes to Jim in a rush. In other words, the railroad is more than a rigid and flat line of masculinity and bourgeois capitalism that a virile manifest destiny lays across the "feminine" divide and undulations of the frontier. Nothing that reductive—nothing that binary—is at work. Jim, in spite of being encumbered by a law degree and a trophy bride, does get back to Ántonia by train, wagon, and force of good will. He grasps who she was and who she has become, comprehends her essential virtuousness, and in spite of differences of gender and class, renders her in a prose adequate to the task of carrying her story intact from Webster County to New York City.

By contrast, in most other Cather narratives, eastbound trains tend to exhaust, corrupt, vitiate, or even annihilate the traveler, making Thea Kronborg in *The Song of the Lark* or Cather herself stark exceptions to the rule. The westbound journey is usually more promising. For Jim Burden, the orphan, the journey is a rich, if anxious, adventure:

> I had been sleeping, curled up in a red plush seat, for a long while when we reached Black Hawk. Jake roused me and took me by the hand. We stumbled down from the train to a wooden siding, where men were running about with lanterns. I couldn't see any town, or even distant lights; we were surrounded by utter darkness. The engine was panting heavily after its long run. In the red glow from the firebox, a group of people stood huddled together on the platform, encumbered by bundles and boxes. I knew this must be the immigrant family the conductor had told us about. The woman wore a fringed shawl tied over her head, and she carried a little tin trunk in her arms, hugging it as if it were a baby. (5–6)

Here is a moment of visual arrest somewhere far west of Chicago. Both Jim and Ántonia stand in the same place and moment, the Black Hawk station in deep night, each in the empty heartland. As soon as Jim and Ántonia move, the place will begin to fill with their life stories. For an instant, the surrounding darkness is complete; the light is red and creates deep shadows. The narrative momentum that drove Ántonia out of Europe and Jim out of Virginia comes to a standstill. Red shapes against a black background, the family presents an image that forever will mark the beginning of Jim's relation to his Ántonia. Later, the image of the black plow against the red horizon will demonstrate the completion of their arrival in the new country.

As they move away from the station in the farm wagon, the boy Jim crawls from beneath the buffalo skin and looks out to see "not a country at all, but the material out of which countries are made," and this under "the complete dome of heaven, all there was of it" (8). Young, an orphan, coming to the still place at the end of a long, jolting journey, he experiences a complete sense of tranquillity that comes from his sense of effacement. Much later, when the memory of Ántonia will swamp his memory with its plenitude, he will recall this moment as one in which "between that earth and sky I felt erased, blotted out," and he neglected his prayers that night for "here . . . what would be would be" (8).

In Jim's case it would seem that the train delivers the boy to a still center, a place at which he conceives of the utter absence of being, as if the train could still bring one to a threshold of wilderness. By contrast, *A Lost Lady* (1923) tends to suggest that Cather understood the closing of the prairie, its domestication and degradation, as one and the same with the growth of the railroads, or a process the traces of which lie adjacent to the rails. The story begins, "Thirty or forty years ago, in one of those grey towns along the Burlington railroad, which are so much greyer to-day than they were then, there was a house well known from Omaha to Denver for its hospitality and for a certain charm of atmosphere" (7). The house is Captain Forrester's, and its chatelaine his wife, who regularly entertains the passing "railroad aristocracy of that time; men who had to do with the railroad itself, or with one of the 'land companies' which were its by-products" (7). From the start, readers know that the railroad divides the population of the prairies into two classes, "the homesteaders and the hand-workers who were there to make a living, and the bankers and gentleman ranchers who came from the Atlantic seaboard to invest money" (7). As a result of the growth of the railroad, the character of rural life begins to change. Rather than a society of families whose lives passed in a relatively narrow range of wealth between subsistence and modest plenty—an agricultural economy for which the tidy farm and amply stocked cellar of Ántonia represents the ideal—rural society begins to divide between haves and have-nots, though to the urbanite the distinction might seem relatively indistinct; the Forrester place in Sweet Water a mile east of town "was not at all remarkable," though "the people who lived there made it seem much larger and finer than it was" (8). To the locals, however, especially the youths for whom Mrs. Forrester is nearly a paragon, the house represents a magnificence and intimacy the interior of which they long to inhabit.

Yet by eastern patrician standards the dwelling might appear squat and pretentious, froufrou carpenter's gothic, much lathing and modest scale, a house best kept covered with vines. A mile outside of a town that for the railroad was nearly a jerkwater town, the Forresters' outpost scarcely appears to represent the suburban colonization of the frontier. To the Captain's credit, he does not drain marsh below the house because he admires the natural and "artless loops" (9) of the creek's meander. Mrs. Forrester is the maven of enchantment, a woman who is most alluring when not fully dressed, which is to say when midway between two states, for "she was attractive in dishabille, and she knew it" (10), even to Cyrus Dalzell, president of the Colorado and Utah Railroad. Here, in a place that might well have been written up as "Prairie Home" in *Good Housekeeping* or *Ladies' Home Journal*, the Captain retires after his fall from the horse prevents him from laying more track, and he grows fat, fiddles with flowering shrubs, and against the background of crop failures the Burlington begins to reduce its service. Ironically, as life becomes more limited in Sweet Water, the Forresters actually spend more time there. The Captain putters and the lady of the house entertains locals; it would appear that the plains were destined to impose their slow regularity of life upon the fancy house and its owners.

For a moment the story is about idle boy stuff—cookies, water snakes, and talk of the poisoning of Judge Pommeroy's spaniel. In comes "Poison Ivy," or Ivy Peters, about eighteen years old, who walks "as if he had a steel rod down his back" (18). He is meanness personified, and he looks like a lizard: "He was

82

MARK A. R. FACKNITZ

an ugly fellow, Ivy Peters, and he liked being ugly" (19). After he drops the female woodpecker with a slingshot he takes out tiny instruments for cutting and sewing—some from a taxidermy kit he purchased by mail order from *Youth's Companion*. He plans for such vileness. The trains bring his tools to him. The bird struggles as the other boys watch, appalled: "There was something wild and desperate about the way the darkened creature beat its wings in the branches, whirling in the sunlight and never seeing it, always thrusting its head up and shaking it, as a bird does when it is drinking. Presently it managed to get its feet on the same limb where it had been struck, and seemed to recognize that perch. As if it had learned something by its bruises, it pecked and crept its way along the branch and disappeared into its own hole" (22). Niel tries to go up to put it out of its misery, but he falls and hurts himself. For the rest of the novel his efforts to intervene in the corruption of Sweet Water are comparably futile. When in the arc of the novel Ivy Peters supplants the Captain, the once virile builder of railroads who went flabby and died, Niel Herbert reckons the end of the transformation of the pioneer prairie. The modern world has settled in. Meanness, once an emotional hazard of hanging on when the prairie was newly settled, becomes—now that the railroad is an ordinary fixture of life—a permanent quality that defines people who get what they want.

In *Willa Cather and Others*, Jonathan Goldberg writes of the "dense transfer points and occlusions around race, gender, and sexuality that link" characters to their narratives, and the narratives of each to the narratives of others (119). The blinded female bird that first links Ivy Peters to Mrs. Forrester is one of many clear examples of his point. As tropes, trains provide similar density but are scarcely occluded; rather, they represent a differently lucid vehicle for Cather, for trains tend to represent the acceleration of the actual. They may redirect or re-pace the story. For example, in *Song of the Lark*, when a train kills Ray Kennedy, Thea sets on her way. In *O Pioneers!* a train brings

Emil back to his fate and carries Alexandra to the interview in the penitentiary. In *One of Ours*, in a Pullman car Enid crushes Claude's foolish expectations. Hence, in their metaphoric quietude, trains are comparable to Cather's skies, prairies, horizons, and dwelling places. There is never a Moonstone, Black Hawk, Hanover, or Sweet Water that does not hinge to the rest of the world by its train station, and in this respect the local and literal actuality of her characters' lives links them, by rail, to broader and distant tropics of meaning. In other words, trains are not just the way her people come and go from their small western towns; banal modern trains also convey her fiction to places as distant as the cultural threshold of New York, the opera houses of Paris and Berlin, and, at the limit, the Virgilian landscapes that adorn *My Ántonia* and *One of Ours*.

Tellingly, most of these trains begin or end in Chicago. Making a transfer in Chicago, an unavoidable hassle one hopes to survive, tests the traveler, who must muster much stoicism, or have a dear and accommodating friend like Irene Miner Weisz. Chicago is the site of crucial symbolic transferences. For example, in *Song of the Lark* (1915), the "lay-over" in Chicago defines the destiny of Thea Kronborg, and after surviving its challenges she can go on to New York and the capitals of Europe. Danielle Russell, in her book on Cather and Toni Morrison, *Between the Angle and the Curve*, conceives of the city—any large city, not merely Chicago—as "masculine space" and a "place of distinct boundaries" (65). Acknowledging the oversimplification, she recalls that in Cather's work, "the city . . . is often treated with ambivalence or outright hostility" (66). Particularly for Thea, Chicago was "simply a wilderness through which one had to find one's way" (*Song* 169; Russell 66), and it represents a set of conundrums that "must be deciphered in order to be navigated" (Russell 68). Nevertheless, Russell concedes, Thea's Chicago experience "is as close as Cather comes to an endorsement of urban life" (68). Thea has talent, voice, and a native shrewdness and pragmatism that keep her unsentimentally focused on her goal. For her, Chicago is hornbook and preparation.

By contrast, in *The Professor's House* (1925) Chicago embodies St. Peter's paralysis, engulfing his cosmopolitan yearnings in a detestable mire of Carson, Pirie, and Scott, whose shabby mid-American novelties beguile his daughters. This is the Chicago of Louis Marcellus—*nouveau riche* and *nouveau gout*; crass, vigorous, and often inanely eclectic, like the big Spanish-Norwegian house named Outland. Cather makes the metaphor of the city darkest for Godfrey St. Peter, her one character who actually settles nearby, though given his attitude toward his increasingly vulgar university it might be appropriate to say he misses his train and gets stuck there. In this respect, the geography of Hamilton is especially interesting. Somewhere on Lake Michigan, well south of Milwaukee and a bit north of Chicago, Hamilton is home to a burgeoning and crass state university; it connects to the rest of the country and world by rail. In "The Family," the opening section of the novel, the first reference to Chicago is as a source of hardware fittings for the new house. Next, Cather mentions Chicago as the city where, after winning his award, the Professor splurges on a luxury hotel and a night at the opera, awakening tender memories of Lillian while listening to "Connais-tu le pays" from Ambroise Thomas's *Mignon* (1866), an aria in which the soprano bemoans her exile from the distant shores and country of youth. Finally, Chicago is the nearby metropolis where in a fictionalized Blackstone Hotel the Professor looks out over Lake Michigan and gloomily recognizes the materialism of one daughter and the bitterness of the other. The city, in other words, is not merely a large industrial, commercial, and cultural center; it is also a metaphor for an exsanguinating new nature that the Professor cannot resist and which worsens his nostalgia and melancholy. Even in Hamilton, at the far margins of the metropolis, he must go to the top of his house and stare toward the distant horizons to get a sense of where he is from or where he would prefer to be.

Hamilton, then, is unlike any other midwestern town in Cather's novels. Moonstone, Hanover, Sweet Water, Haverford, Skyline—all the other remakings of Red Cloud—are remarkable for their quality of clinging to the slender line of rails and the defining and enormous nearness of the prairies. Hamilton, though planted near the place where in earliest childhood Godfrey St. Peter experienced an archetypal vastness of lake and land, is becoming suburban, its relation to its outside horizons newly irrelevant. Rail connects it to Chicago and irresistibly links it to the dehumanization of modern American life. Perversely, towns like Hamilton remind their aging romantics of what they have lost, promoting as they do an unnatural pastoralism and sybaritism as compensation for the ravages of industrial progress. A twelve-minute train ride takes the Professor to his lake where he can sail or immerse himself in the water, staring east across vast openness toward France. Hamilton is also where the Professor once planted a half-acre imitation of the gardens of Versailles. Like the enormous grounds of the palace of Versailles at the limit of the Parisian metropolis—where he lived as a student—the Professor's puny imitation of the Sun King's landscape looked west onto the uninterrupted prairie and was itself entirely free of grass. By contrast, the thousands of acres of royal land at Versailles are a national treasure the horizon of which has long been protected from development. The Professor's garden, once a little folly at the edge of the prairie, will become an absurdity, first isolated and then abolished by the spread of the metropolis. That fate is ironclad, so to speak. It matters only to him, and it will soon disappear.

Tragically, in a place defined by the capacity of the railroads to transport people, goods, and such cultural benefits as opera, paintings, and books, the grim Professor waits. More than his anomie, his alienation from his family, and his disdain for the commercialization of intellectual life at his university, St. Peter suffers from an inability to move. He cannot budge from the old house much less from the pernicious gravitational pull of Chicago. Outland had to take him into the Southwest and lead him about—never mind that the region was central to the Professor's historical studies—and his family's trip to Europe is not enough to induce him to return to the places that were important to him when he was a young student. Finally, with the family returning relentlessly on the *Berengaria*, there comes a point when nothing moves—no schedules are kept, no transfers occur east or west.

For Tom Outland, Chicago is also a transfer point on his way to Europe, but, unlike Thea, or unlike Jim Burden, who travels east of Chicago to mere prosperity and empty marriage, Outland's alacrity in joining the cause of embattled Belgium proves lethal. The fate is similar for idealist Claude Wheeler when he journeys east of Chicago, boarding there the troop train that carries him across the Meadowlands near Hoboken to the ship *Anchises*. For these two rustic Parsifals, rising in the west and looking to the east, Chicago is the cusp of the wasteland of ruined European reason and light, and the Chapel Perilous is somewhere on the other side of the western front. For both Claude and Tom, the abundance of character they draw from the West sustains their enthusiasm but fails to fully protect them. Travel east has become physically easy, but no less deadly than it was for Paul from Pittsburgh decades before. In other words, not everyone who escapes survives, much less thrives.

For the westerner seeking to escape the labor on farms and the tedium of small towns, passage through Chicago, for however many hours or years it took to change trains, involved considerable risk. As William Cronon points out, the countryside "had no wealth to match Potter Palmer's, but it also had no poverty to match the slum neighborhoods that encircled Chicago" (351). For the millions who came to the Columbian Exposition in 1893, the year Cather turned twenty, the trip to the city left them with powerful images of an alabaster city and distressing glimpses of fleshpots, tenderloins, shantytowns, rail yards, and stockyards. It is toward this seductive and dangerous city that Theodore Dreiser sent, by slow train, eighteen-year-old Caroline Meeber with some shoddy luggage and four dollars in 1889. One of two fates, neither very happy, will occur, the narrator of *Sister Carrie* tells us, as "either she falls into saving hands and becomes better, or she rapidly assumes the cosmopolitan standard of virtue and becomes worse" (1). In leaving the small town, young people like Carrie leave behind the possibility of an "intermediate balance" (1), for in the city, "half the undoing of the unsophisticated and natural mind is accomplished by forces wholly superhuman" (1–2). The rest are corrupted by ordinary falsehoods, for "beauty, like music, too often relaxes, then weakens, then perverts the simpler human perceptions" (2).

In fact, Thea Kronborg may be the most successful eastbound transit in Cather's fiction, because few of her characters are as successful in bending the world beyond Chicago to their desire and will. Chicago is the place where Thea sheds her rusticity and gains a degree of education and clarity that eventually allow her to thrive in New York and even Europe. Her trajectory in *The Song of the Lark* (1915) makes the novel Cather's anti–*Sister Carrie*: if Dreiser's Caroline Meeber is absorbed, perverted, and sent east first as a morally crippled woman and finally as a wholly depleted soul, an object lesson about the invincibility of the urban environment, Thea thrives and moves on. By contrast, years later, Cather sends Lucy Gayheart to Chicago with similar intentions but far different results. Lucy does not quite have the talent of Thea, and even if she had, she still lacks the temperament to live as austerely as the divine Kronborg, and she can be victimized by her own sentimental attachments. Lucy's return to Haverford, where she pines for a cad and lets her talent languish, eventually plunges her through the ice. Here is an unambiguous ending, a waste of a dream, and perhaps the cruelest moment in Cather. This is what happens to girls who do not quite have what it takes to change to eastbound trains in Chicago.

After 1902, when the introduction of the Twentieth Century and Broadway Limited made travel between New York and Chicago a luxurious twenty-hour trip, most travelers to or from the West would change only in Chicago. Even so, an astonishing number of Cather's characters change there, explicitly or implicitly, and often before or after the story. Alive, Harvey Merrick went through on his way to Boston and France; his coffin would have transferred at the same junction. Émil in *O Pioneers!*, had he not been murdered, would have changed trains there on his way to law school in Ann Arbor, and we are sure that after the end of "Old Mrs. Harris" young Vickie will make exactly the trip that Émil should have made. In *Death Comes for the Archbishop*, when young Latour first set out on his mission, he needed a year of river travel and horseback to reach his destination; by the time the Archbishop is ready to die, he reflects that "he had come with the buffalo, and he had lived to see railway trains running into Santa Fe. He had accomplished an historic period" (273). In fact, when Latour's friend Jean Vaillant dies, Father Revardy, who in returning from France is waylaid by a terminal illness in a Catholic hospital in Chicago, sees report of the death, and Revardy need only to be driven to a railway station to make his painful way to Vaillant's funeral and die himself a few days later in Denver.

The mythic urbis that depended on tropes of the Phoenix, competition, commerce, and transportation—all archetypal forms of metamorphosis or transit—shuts down in Cather's imagination. When she stopped concerning herself with afflictions of contemporary life—tantamount to saying she stopped writing about trains—for obvious reasons she also stopped sending characters through Chicago. By the mid-1930s, when passenger trains west of Chicago were not noticeably different from those east of the city, and Cather herself had recognized her own sense of being out of step with the postwar world, Chicago no longer "figured" as Cather became interested in the Montreal of *Shadows on the Rock*, the old Virginia of *Sapphira and the Slave Girl*, or the long ago and far away of Avignon in her final and unfinished project. There was no longer need for a significant boundary, not in her art or, for that matter, in American life. The geographical or metaphysical severity of the frontier was passing out of memory. History was shortening the distance between the industrial

East and a prairie of farms, immigrants, and stories of dauntless-
ness in a harsh climate.

Journeying with Isabelle McClung on French trains in 1902
(Woodress 162), Cather would have seen signs in the train stations marked "Correspondances," which at a literal level means
simply the direction one goes to change trains. But, inescapably,
in French the word also refers to the fundamental operation of
metaphor, or the correspondence between vehicle and tenor. In
other words, in France, Cather encounters in the most banal of
situations the double entendre of thing and idea that characterizes metaphor. In going somewhere, you cannot move through
space or language without passing through the point—for example, the iconic moment at the Black Hawk train station—
at which the thing named becomes the unnamable idea. This
is the sense of the word in Charles Baudelaire's poem "Correspondances" in which nature figures as "un temple où de vivants
piliers / Laissent parfois sortir de confuses paroles," a temple
from the pillars of which come confused, and confusing, words.
Through this sacral space, vital and artificial, we pass as if "à
travers des forets de symbols," through a forest of symbols, the
trees of which watch us with friendly insolence. Among distant
echoes, in a "ténébreuse et profonde unité," in a deep and shad-
owy coherence, big as night and all light, we experience things
not named but known by fragrances as fresh as the bodies of
children, as sweet as oboes, and as green as prairies. Baudelaire's
images expand as similes for "des choses infinies," or infinite
things, as if things can be infinite, without particularity, limit,
or horizon. This happens in a song of the transport of "l'esprit
et les sens," a final phrase impossible to tidily translate for the
French word *esprit* can as immediately mean spirit or soul as
it means mind or wit. Moreover, *sens* contains the same indis-
soluble pun as in the English "senses," which can refer either to
our five means of perceiving the physical world or, thereafter, the
senses or meanings that we make of the world.[1] Furthermore,
the French word *sens*, unlike the English, can have a third meaning, specifically, "direction," as in what direction one takes to

change trains for one's next destination. Hence, changing trains, one follows the signs that say *correspondances.*

I do not know how attentively Cather may have read Baudelaire. Yet, her literary use of trains suggests that she would have understood the point of the title and poem, especially the implied parity of correspondence with transfer, or the sense of the metaphor that making meaning means changing trains. Wherever there is a topography cut by rails, there will also be a cusp, a threshold, a horizon, a salience, or a moment in the darkness when a family is momentarily still in the light of a locomotive's fire, or perhaps a transfer as prosaic as a cab ride from LaSalle to Union Station as one changes from the Twentieth Century to the Burlington no. 1. This transfer marks the point at which words stop referring to ordinary matter and become, through the simplification or higher processes of art, the "emotional penumbra" of people made out of words. So Cather's trains, particularly those that arrive or depart from Chicago, make lines across a tropic of meaning that are remarkably like other lines Cather draws across the imagined planes of her novels—for example, the Divide in *O Pioneers!*, Panther Canyon at the edge of the wilderness in *Song of the Lark*, or the tops of mesas against the horizons of *The Professor's House* or *Death Comes for the Archbishop.* In this respect, Cather's technique is true to her understanding, as she puts it in "Light on Adobe Walls," that "at bottom all [an author] can give you is the thrill of his own poor little nerve—the projection . . . of a fleeting pleasure in a certain combination of form and colour, as temporary and almost as physical as a taste on the tongue" (976). Or as fleetingly real as a story glimpsed in the landscape one sees from the moving train.

NOTE

1. "Correspondances" appears in Charles Baudelaire's 1857 *Les fleurs du mal.* Readers can find it conveniently at http://fleursdumal.org/ poem/103, where it is accompanied by half a dozen attempts to translate it.

WORKS CITED

Baudelaire, Charles. *Les fleurs du mal*. Paris: Poulet-Malassis et de Broise, 1857.

Cather, Willa. *Death Comes for the Archbishop*. 1927. New York: Vintage, 1971.

———. "A Death in the Desert." *Scribner's Magazine* 33 (January 1903): 109–21. *Willa Cather Archive*. Ed. Andrew Jewell. U of Nebraska–Lincoln. http://cather.unl.edu.

———. "Light on Adobe Walls." *Stories, Poems, and Other Writings*. Ed. Sharon O'Brien. New York: Library of America, 1992. 976–78.

———. *A Lost Lady*. New York: Knopf, 1923.

———. *My Ántonia*. Boston: Houghton Mifflin, 1918.

———. *One of Ours*. New York: Knopf, 1922.

———. "The Novel Démeublé." 1922. *Stories, Poems, and Other Writings*. Ed. Sharon O'Brien. New York: Library of America, 1992. 834–36.

———. *The Professor's House*. New York: Knopf, 1925.

———. "The Sculptor's Funeral." *McClure's Magazine* Jan. 1905: 329–33. *Willa Cather Archive*. Ed. Andrew Jewell. U of Nebraska–Lincoln. http://cather.unl.edu.

———. *The Song of the Lark*. Boston: Houghton Mifflin, 1915.

———. "A Wagner Matinée." *Everybody's Magazine* Mar. 1904: 325–28. *Willa Cather Archive*. Ed. Andrew Jewell. U of Nebraska–Lincoln. http://cather.unl.edu.

Cronon, William. *Nature's Metropolis: Chicago and the Great West*. New York: Norton, 1991.

Dreiser, Theodore. *Sister Carrie*. New York: Doubleday, 1900.

Goldberg, Jonathan. *Willa Cather and Others*. Durham NC: Duke UP, 2001.

Jewell, Andrew, and Janis P. Stout. *A Calendar of the Letters of Willa Cather: An Expanded, Digital Edition*. *Willa Cather Archive*. Ed. Andrew Jewell. U of Nebraska–Lincoln. http://cather.unl.edu.

Palmer, Scott. "'The Train of Thought': Classed Travel and Nationality in Willa Cather's *My Ántonia*." *Studies in American Fiction* 29.2 (2001): 239–50.

Reynolds, Guy. "Willa Cather a Progressive: Politics and the Writer." *The Cambridge Companion to Willa Cather*. Ed. Marilee Lindemann. Cambridge: Cambridge UP, 2005. 19–34.

Romines, Ann. *The Home Plot: Women, Writing and Domestic Ritual.* Amherst: U of Massachusetts P, 1992.

Rosowski, Susan. *The Voyage Perilous: Willa Cather's Romanticism.* Lincoln: U of Nebraska P, 1986.

Russell, Danielle. *Between the Angle and the Curve: Mapping, Gender, Race, Space and Identity in Willa Cather and Toni Morrison.* New York: Routledge, 2006.

Trout, Steven. *Memorial Fictions: Willa Cather and the First World War.* Lincoln: U Nebraska P, 2002.

Urgo, Joseph. *Willa Cather and the Myth of American Migration.* Urbana: U of Illinois P, 1995.

Woodress, James. *Willa Cather: A Literary Life.* Lincoln: U Nebraska P, 1987.

5 Chicago's Cliff Dwellers and *The Song of the Lark*

MICHELLE E. MOORE

Cather throws Thea, the heroine of *The Song of the Lark*, into the cauldron of social, economic, cultural, and artistic forces bubbling in 1890s Chicago. When Thea needs to recuperate from the exhaustion and illness caused by working in Chicago, she spends time at the Anasazi Indian cliff dwellings in Arizona. Her physical movement from Chicago to the cliff dwellings connects the novel's Chicago chapters and the Panther Canyon chapters and suggests that the two sections inform each other historically and metaphorically.

This essay will show how Chicago embraced the Anasazi Indian cliff dwellers in the years immediately following Richard Wetherill's discovery of the Cliff Palace of Mesa Verde in 1888. By 1893 the phrase "cliff dwellers" had multiple meanings in Chicago: the culturally advanced Anasazi, or "Ancient Ones" of Mesa Verde; Henry Blake Fuller's cliff dwellers, who in his novel of the same name are those members of Chicago society who perch at the tops of the city's skyscrapers; and ideally, the provincial immigrant who has been lifted to a more lofty perch through education, which in turn lifts the higher life of the entire city. The idea of the cliff dwellers also expresses the 1890s concern that the lifted immigrant might knock the cliff-dwelling old European off his perch, and that the entire process of uplift might cause the opposite effect of its stated intents: cultural extinction. I will then examine how reading *The Song of the Lark* through the metaphor of cliff dwelling reveals Thea to be an unknowing participant in Chicago's larger civic project of the "higher life." I will trace her upward trajectory through the novel and then demonstrate how the novel relies on an understanding of Chicago club history to show how fully enmeshed Thea's awakening is with her participation in the business of constructing a higher life for Chicago. This essay argues that the novel develops the Chicago meanings and associations of the cliff dwellers in order to critique the Chicago scene that expects art to be useful (whether as social realism or to raise the city's higher life), treats art as business, and destroys artists by using them up. Cather uses the metaphor of cliff dwelling in the post-fair Chicago sense in order to examine the threat of extinction for the artist contained in the notion of cultural uplift.

In the 1890s, in large cities across America, spiritual, political, and civic leaders began voicing concerns about the "higher life." What they meant was the need to raise the quality of a city through the presence of social projects, social and art clubs, education and intellectual institutions, and moral clubs, institutions, and instruction. Jane Allen Shikoh explains how the idea of the higher life emerged from the fusion of Evangelical Christianity's spiritual project of raising all souls to a higher plane with Darwinian-based ideas about social evolution (3–11). Concern for the "higher life" of the cities was a concern for the spiritual, physical, intellectual, cultural, and artistic evolution of America's cities as almost sentient beings.[1]

Shikoh sets Chicago apart from the other large cities in the United States, writing that "during the 1890s, Chicago was more self-conscious about its 'higher life'" (81). She notes: "Journalists, ministers and others in speaking of Chicago, often mentioned that although in the past the city had been preoccupied with its material growth, it was finally arriving at a 'higher and maturer stage of civic existence'" (81). The Great Fire of 1871 had only recently destroyed Chicago. By the early 1890s, Chicago's boosters announced that the city had successfully rebuilt itself from the ashes with the newest technology available. Before a great deal of the reconstruction had been completed, civic engagement meant bringing wealth to the city, through building and promoting the city as the site for the World's Columbian Exhibition of 1893. Now that the boosters had rebuilt the city, at least according to the promotional rhetoric, Chicagoans could shift their sights from physical construction to promoting and raising the cultural wealth of the city. Chicago's elite, who provided the economic wealth of the city, were most interested in promoting the kind of art that would raise Chicago's higher life.

Henry Blake Fuller was fascinated by Chicago's focus on the higher life and its treatment of artists and art. In "The Upward Movement in Chicago," published in the October 1897 *Atlantic Monthly*, he critiqued the optimism of Chicago politicians and boosters: "The civic shortcomings of Chicago are so widely notorious abroad and so deeply deplored at home that there is little need to linger upon them, even for the purpose of throwing into relief the worthier and more attractive features of the local life" (534). He then clarifies the plight of the Chicagoan who cares about art: "We are obliged to fight—determinedly, unremittingly—for those desirable, those indispensible things that older, more fortunate, more practiced communities possess and enjoy as a matter of course" (534). For Fuller, Chicago does not know how to create this higher life that seems to come so easily to older, more established cities. The city's artists must fight for recognition against the naive and unsophisticated sentiments of the Chicago patrons of the arts, whose conception of culture was overwhelmingly utilitarian.

Fuller's ideas about the negative aspects of Chicago's push for the higher life play out in his earlier novel *The Cliff-Dwellers* (1893). The novel describes the inhabitants of the fictitious Clifton Building, who struggle with business and domestic failures as they attempt to raise themselves up against Chicago's oppressive and hostile atmosphere. Ann Massa has shown that "the presence at the Fair of a Cliff Dweller exhibit, and the exposure it gave to that culture's problematisation of issues of evolution and progress, convinced Fuller of the aptness of the Cliff Dweller analogy to express his reservations about the modern cliff dwellers" (80). She concludes that "Fuller was less interested in the Cliff Dwellers per se than in the critical light they allowed him to shed on what Chicago and America had achieved by 1893" (84).

Fuller's novel used the cliff dwellers as a metaphor for the elite Chicagoans who occupied skyscrapers and worked high above the city's immigrant hordes. He may have derived the metaphor from earlier versions of the ideas about the Anasazi Indians contained in the catalog put out by the H. J. Smith Exploring Company to accompany the cliff-dweller exhibits at the World's Fair of 1893. The catalog describes the cliff dwellers as "by far the most highly civilized representatives of the 'stone age,' antedating the Aztecs and the Toltecs, and exhibiting almost as high a degree of civilization. . . . They are a mythical race, exhibiting in the relics found, rare powers and refined tastes at variance with the common idea of aborigines" (1). The legend continues, "They were not a warlike people—their fighting was simply done in defense. Arrows of reed . . . were their chief implements of war, and the small number of these found is indicative of their naturally quiet and peaceable natures, which only rose up to defend themselves against the attacks of their foes" (7–9). The catalog concludes with an interpretation of part of the exhibit that repeats the ideas of its first pages: "Several fine specimens of feather-cloth and buckskin garments denote their fondness for ease and comfort, and the rare stone axes, bows, arrows, and slingshots found give additional proof to their peaceful pursuits and may also give a cue to the mysterious disappearance of this once great nation, which was possibly annihilated by more warlike tribes surrounding it" (19).[2]

The catalog draws the Anasazi Indians' position on the high cliff as a reminder of the cliff dwellers' cultural superiority to the surrounding, newer tribes bent on attacking the more peaceful, artistic civilization. The catalog transcribes the cliff dwellers' physical location into a cultural position: they took up a defensive position to protect their culture not just physically, but culturally. The legend of the cliff dwellers, then, demonstrated to Chicagoans that climbing upward serves as a form of cultural self-protection.

Guy Szuberla observes that, "Like many of his contemporaries, Henry Blake Fuller frequently paired his ideas and fears of the 'new immigrant' with the spectre of a declining or dispossessed 'native American stock'" (246). He argues that Fuller's novel expresses his grave concerns that if the cliff dwellers uplifted too many immigrants to join the ranks of the elite members of cultural circles, their numbers would overwhelm and eventually deplete those who raised them in the first place (250–52). The cliff-dwelling conceit in the novel also serves as a warning to the elite citizens of Chicago, who, like the Anasazi, may become extinct if they continue to participate in the futile project of using art to uplift others to their position.

Chicago's struggle with and self-conscious examination of the "higher life" explains why Chicago patrons, artists, and the artgoing public embraced The Eight, a group of New York urban realists known derisively in the New York art scene as the Ashcan painters. First shown at the Macbeth Gallery in New York in 1908, their paintings portray immigrant city street life, rendered in broad, spontaneous brushstrokes and vivid colors intended to give a vivacious and celebratory cast to the gritty scene. Patrons of the New York art scene considered the paintings' subject and presentation too crude and inappropriate, but in Chicago, the Art Institute, the Renaissance Society at the University of Chicago, and the Arts Club of Chicago all held regular exhibits of the group (Weininger 54). George Bellows, a student of the original Eight, painted *The Cliff Dwellers* (1913) using bright colors to illuminate immigrant tenements and life on New York's Lower East Side. The painting succeeds in transforming the cliff dwellers from Fuller's Europeans perched at the top of Chicago's downtown buildings into immigrants hanging out of windows in the Bowery. Susan S. Weininger asserts: "After 1910 George Bellows exerted the strongest direct influence of any contemporary American artist on Chicago's progressive painters" (54). By 1919 he was made a temporary professor at the Art Institute, and in 1922 he was offered a permanent position, which he kept until his death in 1925 (Moser 202). *The Cliff Dwellers*, as a statement about immigrants in urban populations, spoke directly to a Chicago, rather than a New York, sensibility, because it employed the metaphor of cliff dwelling in a way already legible to Chicagoans.

Cather, too, uses the metaphor of cliff dwelling in a way that would have been legible to turn-of-the-century Chicagoans, as a way of informing Thea's upward trajectory in *The Song of the Lark*. Initially, Cather uses the idea of uplift to demonstrate how exposure to art will better Thea and ultimately allow her to escape the provincial world of Moonstone. Before giving a piano lesson, Wunsch "conducted her at once to the piano in Mrs. Kohler's sitting-room. He twirled the stool to the proper height, pointed to it, and sat down in a wooden chair beside Thea" (26). He elevates her seat so that she will sit at the proper height during her exposure to European classical music, in turn suggesting the heightening effect of the music on this little girl. His conducting connects him to two other important conductors in her life: Ray Kennedy and Theodore Thomas. Ray's money allows her to travel to Chicago, and she sees Thomas conduct at a crucial moment in her artistic development in Chicago. Both men will help raise her to greater heights as well by allowing invisible currents to conduct through them. However, Wunsch and Ray do not want anything from Thea in return and do not believe her singing talents will raise the profile of Moonstone, separating Moonstone's ideas about raising artists from Chicago's idea about using them to achieve the higher life.

When Thea moves to Chicago, Mr. Harsanyi makes an important discovery: Thea should train to be an opera singer. The discovery changes Thea's relationship to Chicago's creation of its higher life and allows the novel's critique of the Chicago art world to begin. Loretta Wasserman notes: "After finishing *The Song of the Lark*, Cather had more to say about opera singers. What fascinated her was the difference between performing artists, who must please and charm the public, and artists such as herself—writers or painters—who work in private or even anonymously" (9). Uplift does not apply to solitary pursuits such as writing or painting, but only to those activities that may elevate a considerable portion of the population. Thea thinks her fate is hers alone, but when she becomes a performer, an opera singer, she has the potential to lift up large audiences who hear her, in turn, raising others around her to a higher plane.

The Song of the Lark does not echo the anxiety expressed by Fuller, who is unable to assess whether the immigrants who are lifted up through introduction to European culture are a good thing for Chicago's art and culture or if their uplift will destroy the very culture that did the heavy lifting. The novel addresses Fuller's issue with one line: "She had often heard Mrs. Kronborg say that she 'believed in immigration,' and so did Thea believe in it" (186). Instead, the novel turns the concern inward onto its artist and asks whether the particularly Chicagoan model of uplift is good for its artists, a question that also troubled Fuller. Cather uses the metaphor of cliff dwelling, in the post-fair Chicagoan's sense, to examine the ways in which cultural uplift threatened an artist's spirit and in turn predicted extinction for the artist.

The cliff dwellers make their first appearance in the novel imagistically. Ray, who will be the first to tell Thea about the Anasazi Indian cities, takes her family out to the desert where she sees heifers. The young cows "were magnified to a preposterous height and looked like mammoths, prehistoric beasts standing solitary in the waters that for many thousands of years actually washed over that desert;—the mirage itself may be the ghost of that long-vanished sea" (44). Thea sees for the first time how the females of a species can be raised up to heights larger than the role into which they are cast because of their gender. The passage invokes the "prehistoric" Anasazi Indians, who "vanished" because of their upward movement according to Chicago lore. Thea's observation casts an ominous gloom over the novel's discussion of her upward trajectory and artistic growth. The passage warns against reaching "preposterous heights" that will result in extinction for those who reach them. Thea later declares she only wants "impossible things" (205), a signal that the heights to which she will be lifted will guarantee her destruction.

When Thea moves to Chicago, her metamorphosis into an uplifted Chicago artist begins and the novel continues to employ and expand the metaphor of cliff dwelling to indicate the complexity of her transformation. One night, she leaves the Auditorium Theater and a man accosts her. The Chicago wind racing off of Lake Michigan balloons up her cape and almost lifts her into the sky (171). The strong wind, a uniquely Chicago phenomenon, forces Thea upward violently and against her will, as if she is meant to glide upward onto the tops of the skyscrapers that surround her as she stands on lower Michigan Avenue. If she ascends, she may develop into, in one sense, one of Fuller's cliff dwellers, the uplifted immigrant who has become a resident of Chicago's skyscrapers.

At the same time, she wants to hold on to what she has learned and gained from hearing the symphony, and directs her anger at those who want to steal the new knowledge from her. She "glared round her at the crowds" (171) and thinks: "All these things and people were no longer remote and negligible; they had to be met, they were lined up against her, they were there to take something from her. Very well; they should never have it. . . . As long as she lived that ecstasy was going to be hers. She would live for it, work for it, die for it; but she was going to have it, time after time, height after height" (171–72). In her anger, Thea employs the same metaphors used by the

H. J. Smith Exploring Company catalog produced for the Columbian Exhibition to describe the Anasazis' defensive position. She has learned that she must ascend the heights in order to defensively guard against those other, less civilized people who want to destroy what she has now found: the higher culture she obtained at the symphony. Thea seems to embrace the idea of the higher life that Chicago art patrons believe will elevate its immigrants.

Thea's metaphorical uplift transpires because she just heard one of Theodore Thomas's "heavily symphonic programs" (Miller 409). The conductor of the Chicago Symphony believed fervently in the project of uplift and participated by bringing classical European music to Chicago. Donald L. Miller writes: "As Rose Fay wrote to him on the occasion of his death in 1905: 'He not only disciplined his musicians, but he disciplined the public, educating it sometimes perhaps against its will'" (409). Thea's uplift also takes place because on the next page, Harsanyi asks Thomas who Thea's next teacher should be for voice training (173). By juxtaposing Thea's experience outside the Auditorium Theater with Harsanyi's request to Thomas inside the same building, the novel skillfully ties together the idea of Thea's cultural uplift with the Chicago businessmen's manipulation of the art world through contacts and money.

Thea's angry reaction to being accosted by the man and the upward thrust of wind can be read as her reaction to being uplifted by Theodore Thomas's baton against her will. It is at this point that the novel begins to articulate the damage done to an artist when she must defend herself against those who want to use her, including Chicago's art patrons who will mold her for the purpose of uplifting others. The novel's paradox emerges here. Thea has benefited from being exposed to Western art and to those engaged in the project of uplifting her, but she suffers from those same contacts that construct her talents as useful, and her art as engaging in public service.

When Thea meets Fred Ottenburg, he continues to manipulate the Chicago business scene for her artistic career. Through her involvement with Fred, Thea becomes introduced to the cliff dwellers and their dwellings: the Anasazi Indians and Fuller's cultural elite of Chicago. While Fred and Thea are "waiting for their tea at a restaurant in the Pullman Building, overlooking the lake" (241), he tells her that his family owns "a whole canyon of cliff dweller ruins" (242). The conversation draws attention to their perch at the top of the Pullman Building, one of the earliest steel-framed skyscrapers in what was called the business canyon of Chicago. Thea and Fred are now Chicago cliff dwellers, in the sense used in Fuller's novel.

Mark A. Robison observes that from the high altitude, Thea gazes at the Art Institute and at "a lumber boat, with two very tall masts . . . emerging black and gaunt out of the fog" (241). Her gaze links the Art Institute with a symbol of Chicago commerce, the lumber boat, and Robison declares that "in one perceptive moment, Thea's urban present and rural past merge with her artistic future" (207). The trajectory promised by her gaze from the heights contains the seed of her own downfall, the merging of art and commerce. The appearance of the boat foreshadows Thea's dreadful appearance to Dr. Archie at the end of the novel, dressed in black, "deeply lined," and looking "forty years old" (344–45).

The novel suggests that Thea's angry, defensive posture against the attacking hordes will crumble as it does for forty-year-old Madame Necker, whom Thea replaces on the stage: "Her voice was failing just when her powers were at their height. Every fresh young voice was an enemy, and this one was accompanied by gifts which she could not fail to recognize" (389). The future threatens extinction for the artists who reach the top, just as it did for the Anasazi cliff dwellers and Fuller's skyscraper inhabitants who climbed up the high cliffs to ward off their enemies. Ann W. Fisher-Wirth notes that "Cather's writing has always betrayed a keen sense of loss. At the center of her fiction . . . is the story of the Garden and the Fall. The lives of most of the major characters enact a recurrent tragic pattern, a sense of dispossession, exile and longing" (37). In *The Song of the Lark*, the cliff-dweller metaphor deepens the sense of loss by showing how the artist gains and loses simultaneously, which causes the tragic pattern Fisher-Wirth identifies playing out in Cather's later novels.

In *The Song of the Lark*, Thea will lose because she learns how to be an artist and receives her fundamental training in Chicago. The novel suggests that those who stand at the highest levels in the Chicago art and business scene cannot raise themselves to a higher cultural level because they expect their art to be useful in some way, whether as social realism or to raise the city's higher life. The novel draws this ambivalence about Chicago from Fuller's novel and replicates his doubts about whether Chicagoans can achieve the higher life. The cliff-dweller conceit operates as a double-sided metaphor that at once allows the wealthy and cultured citizens of Chicago to stand above the masses, as Thea does at the top of the Pullman building, and simultaneously allows for the wrongheadedness of their ideals to use art to accomplish the business of raising Chicago.

In order to accomplish its critique of the Chicago art scene, *The Song of the Lark* relied on an intrinsic understanding of the 1890s Chicago club scene and the knowledge that the Cliff Dwellers was also a men's club, started in 1907 by Hamlin Garland. In 1890s Chicago, two kinds of clubs existed: the men's clubs, at which businesses were built, bought, and sold, and the women's clubs, which were interested in the project of social uplift. The contacts and power provided by the men's clubs allow Thea to continue her work and her ascent. The novel shows her commodification beginning in earnest at the Chicago Club, the most prominent of all the Chicago men's clubs. Fred reveals that he belongs to the club, as befits his status and wealth, when he takes Bowers there to discuss Thea. She overhears "the young brewer ask Bowers to dine with him at his club that evening, and she saw that he looked forward to the dinner with pleasure" (228). Thea, oblivious to the machinations of the Chicago art scene, wonders: "If he's such a grand business man, how does he have time to run around listening to singing-lessons?" (228). For her, art stands apart from business, so her question highlights her ignorance as to the relationship between art and business in Chicago. Bower's boasting and excitement over Fred's invitation makes it evident that the invitation is to the Chicago Club and that Thea is a worthy topic of business. The invitation also underscores that Bowers does not have his own membership to the club, further illustrating his place in Chicago's business world. Fred's place is indicated by the fact he does not sit at the millionaire's table with Potter Palmer, George Pullman, and Marshall Fields, but does belong to the same club. It was said that all business done in Chicago happened at this table, and perhaps Fred's friendship with the extraordinary Nathanmeyers has allowed Thea to be brought to this table.

The millionaire's table had an established interest in the business of art. The club first housed the Art Institute, before it moved across the street into the building designed after the Columbian Exhibition. They brought Theodore Thomas to Chicago to conduct the music program at the fair, and then brought him permanently to Chicago with the prospect of his own symphony and the construction of Orchestra Hall. Business discussion at the club traditionally happens in the dining room, over a meal, just as Fred invites Bowers to discuss Thea. When Thea thinks about the men later that night, "she looked up from her grammar to wonder what Bowers and Ottenburg were having to eat. At that moment they were talking of her" (228). Melissa Homestead has demonstrated that "The language of finance and investment permeates the thoughts and speech of both Dr. Archie and Fred Ottenburg" (xi), and the passage implies that their topic, Thea, will be consumed right along with their food. The novel condemns the way Chicago's men's clubs treat art as business and artists as a commodity to be chewed up and swallowed.

Fuller's cliff-dweller conceit warns that Chicago's temperament and attitudes toward art would result in the cultural destruction of the city. He wrote *The Cliff-Dwellers* while a member of the loose group of artists who first met in Bessie Potter's top-floor studios in the Fine Arts Building, next to the Chicago Club, the Auditorium Building, and across from where the Art Institute would be when it moved out of the Chicago Club. He designed his club to be like a salon, a place that sheltered artists against the harshness of the Chicago business world. The club formalized around the name "The Little Room" and derived their name from a short story by Madeline Wynne that appeared in *Harper's Monthly* in 1895. Membership included Jane Addams, Lorado Taft, Allen B. and Irving K. Pond, Anna Morgan, Ralph Clarkson, Hamlin Garland, and others interested in creating a literary and artistic club in Chicago.

When Thea tells her teacher, Bowers, "I have to hunt a new boarding place," and Bowers asks, "What's the matter with the Studio Club? Been fighting with them again?" (213), she reveals her temporary stay in the Fine Arts Building. Even Fuller's club causes Thea to become angry and demoralized as she fights with the other members of the club, who, it turns out, buy into the Chicago belief that art has a use-value to raise the artistic standards of Chicago. She answers, "The Club's all right for people who like to live that way. I don't." When Bowers asks, "Why so tempery?" (213), her reply provides further evidence that she may be staying with members of this uniquely mixed gendered club: "I can't work with a lot of girls around. They're too familiar" (213).

In 1907, Garland started a formal men-only club that would deliberately drain away the male members of the Little Room.[3] He made it new club business to "tender an invitation to join the new club" to all Little Room male members.[4] According to Henry Regnery, a Cliff Dweller Club member who published the club's history in 1990, at the first gathering of interested and like-minded men, including most of the male members of the Little Room, Garland laid out the plan: "This club will bring together men of artistic and literary tastes who are now widely scattered among the various social and business organizations of Chicago and unite them with artists, writers, architects, and musicians of the city in a club whose purposes are distinctly and primarily aesthetic" (9). Garland's club would bring together artists and businessmen with artistic tastes in a union that made formal the alliance that characterized Chicago's art scene to Fuller's and Cather's displeasure. Because it was perched at the top floors of the newly constructed Orchestra Hall, the members called the new club the Attic Club. The group would decide on the name the Cliff Dwellers Club two years later.

As the members of the Attic Club anticipated, Fuller declined to join the Cliff Dwellers Club. The minutes of the 27 June 1907 meeting reveal: "Henry B. Fuller asked to serve as temporary secretary. Mr. A. B. Pond to act in case of the refusal of Mr. Fuller to serve." Fuller scholarship has made much of Fuller's refusal to join the club that bore the name of his most popular novel. Most recently, Massa argues that Garland's arrogance and insensitivity caused Fuller to "boycott" the club (73–74). Her interpretation is highly plausible, given Garland's deliberate destruction of Fuller's club and his later boasting that he, not Fuller, was a founding member. The Attic Club minutes also show that Fuller's attitude toward the club and presumably its founder was well known even before the Attic Club changed its name to the Cliff Dwellers Club.

Cather, who disliked Garland and was "irritated" by his work, was probably not surprised by his utter disregard for Fuller. In the 26 January 1896 *Nebraska State Journal* she wrote a review of James Lane Allen's "The Butterflies" that turns into one of many attacks she made on Garland: "It is just the sort of thing that poor Hamlin Garland is always trying and failing to do. And the reason thereof is that Mr. Allen has just two things that Mr. Garland has not, imagination and style. . . . Art is temperament and Hamlin Garland has no more temperament than a prairie dog" ("Passing Show" 331). When Cather wrote *The Song of the Lark*, Garland's Cliff Dwellers Club was well established, and Chicago readers, hearing that the novel made use of the cliff-dweller conceit, would think immediately of Garland's club. Because Garland was the president of the Cliff Dwellers Club, he would have represented Chicago's worst sins regarding art for Cather: social realism, the blending of art and business, the commodification of the artist. Cather seems to be writing specifically against Garland each time the novel suggests that the Chicago cliff dwellers have worn Thea out with their consumption of her art.

The names of the clubs—Little Room, Attic Club, and Cliff Dwellers Club—correlate with the significant rooms that Thea moves through in the novel. She "was allowed to use the money—her pupils paid her twenty-five cents a lesson—to fit up a little room for herself upstairs in the half-story" (51). She moves from her little room or attic room through a series of very unsatisfactory rooms, until she has the opportunity to also fit up the Cliff Dwellers room. Sharon O'Brien notes, "In her attic retreat Thea begins to discover the voice or self that is her own" (85), and she traces the discovery in a line that culminates in Thea's epiphany in Panther Canyon. But Homestead points out: "Even Thea's nonproductive months alone in Panther Canyon are entangled in Fred's finances. The canyon is part of a ranch owned by his father, so proceeds from the family beer empire underwrite her artistic awakening" (xii). If the rooms Thea moves through as she discovers her own voice are metaphorically Chicago businessmen's clubrooms, then the novel shows the art and business worlds woven together so tightly that the entire trajectory of her spiritual awakening has also been underwritten by the Chicago business world.

In Chicago, Fred manages to introduce Thea to the one character who wishes Thea to hone her own voice: Mrs. Nathanmeyer. He tells Thea, "You'll be all right with her so long as you do not try to be anything that you are not" (231). Cather based Mrs. Nathanmeyer on Bertha Palmer, who, with her husband, Potter Palmer, was "so rich and great that even" someone like

Thea would have "heard of them" (230). The Palmers built a road to the northern section of Chicago, which would become Lake Shore Drive, and built "The Castle" at its end. The Palmer House, the largest and most modern hotel in Chicago, was her husband's wedding present to her. She was the only Lady Manager at the World's Fair, was known for her Parisian tastes in art and clothing, and with her husband she acquired a magnificent art collection through annual trips abroad. In Paris she met Mary Cassatt, who introduced her to Manet and the other impressionist painters in his group (Miller 414–15).

Fred stops Thea to admire the "Rousseaus and Corots" hanging on the Nathanmeyers' walls, and in the hall he stops her "before a painting of a woman eating grapes out of a paper bag, and had told her gravely that there was the most beautiful Manet in the world" (232). Though Polly P. Duryea has identified the painting Fred points out as Manet's *Street Singer* (1862), which Bertha Palmer never owned, Palmer was a friend of Manet's and was known for her large collection of his work (Museum of Fine Arts, Boston). A reading public that knows 1890s Chicago society would easily recognize Mrs. Nathanmeyer as a version of Mrs. Palmer, the only woman in Chicago who owned Corots, and who could own Manets too, if she chose.

Mrs. Nathanmeyer's "standards . . . that have nothing to do with Chicago" are also those of Bertha Palmer, whom Fred seems to be describing (231). She "would not confine herself to established standards, but rather visited artists' studios and current exhibitions, consulted with experts and subscribed to the major magazines in order to explores recent developments" (Germer 177). Her standards, as well as her strong feminist ideas, led Palmer to create salons for young artists, particularly female artists who did not fit into the more realistic and gritty Chicago art scene. It is at one of these salons that Thea first meets her, "and this seemed a remarkable opportunity" (230). It certainly is, because Mrs. Nathanmeyer/Palmer has the status and connections to orchestrate Thea's training and career in New York and abroad, as well as her disgust with the Chicago way of coupling business and art together.

While at the canyon, Fred recalls Mrs. Nathanmeyer, to whom he had introduced Thea in Chicago (268), and on the next page "an eagle, tawny and of great size," flies directly over the canyon and inspires Thea to rise to her feet with the realization that the Anasazi Indians, though a "vanished race," have left behind "fragments of the their desire": their art (269). Fred's recollection makes even more explicit the link between the eagle and Mrs. Nathanmeyer, the "heavy, powerful old Jewess, with . . . an eagle nose, and sharp, glittering eyes" (232). While Mrs. Nathanmeyer's eagle nose is an anti-Semitic caricature, the image of the eagle soaring far above the canyon replicates her position in relation to the cliff dwellers perched at the top of Chicago's skyscrapers. She soars far above them with superior standards "that have nothing to do with Chicago" (231). Cather's representation of this Jewish character is deeply marked by an ambivalence that Susan Meyer has shown as being at work in the representation of Louie in *The Professor's House.*

The Palmers were not Jewish, so Cather made a deliberate choice in making Mrs. Nathanmeyer Jewish. Many scholars, most recently Loretta Wasserman, have cited the character as an example of anti-Semitism in Cather's writing. However, Wasserman claims that the Nathanmeyers "are not significant in Thea's fate" (8) and concludes her longer reading of "The Diamond Mine" by suggesting that the Jewish characters in that narrative are present because Cather "needed an image to convey the dangers of human commodification, and she chose that cartoon figure" (13). The novel frames Mrs. Nathanmeyer in a repulsive stereotype because her power comes from her relationship to her husband's money and the Chicago businessmen's dealings in the art world. However, in *The Song of the Lark*, Fred's description of Mrs. Nathanmeyer's standards makes them sound like Cather's own: that art was a "search for something for which there is no market demand . . . where the values are intrinsic and have nothing to do with standardized values" ("Art of Fiction" 103). Cather constructs the character through her salons, attitudes, connection to Bertha Palmer, and metaphorical appearance in the canyon as a positive force in Thea's career. The novel's ambivalence toward the character of Mrs. Nathanmeyer sharpens the critique of the relationship between art and commerce in Chicago by containing the tension in one character.

The eagle's presence indicates that, symbolically, Mrs. Nathanmeyer watches Thea from behind the scenes and is most likely pulling strings at that moment to allow her to rise to even greater heights in the art world far beyond the limited vision of those businessmen who control the art scene in Chicago. This is the second time Mrs. Nathanmeyer has caused Thea to rise up, inspired, and not angry or feeling used from being raised into Chicago higher life. The first was when she supplied her with a low dress for singing. Thea "laughed and drew herself up out of her corsets, threw her shoulders high and let them drop again" (235). The gift allows Thea to breathe deeply in while singing, providing inspiration, giving life to her spirit, and releasing her from the drudgery of corsets. If the novel ends, as it does in its first version, after Thea's experience in Panther Canyon, Mrs. Nathanmeyer's presence as the eagle might be a sign that Thea will escape the clutches of the male, Chicago business art scene.

Yet even the eagle must struggle against the boys who try to snare it in nets. Thea sees "a watch-tower upon which the young men used to entice eagles and snare them with nets. Sometimes for a whole morning Thea could see the coppery breast and shoulders of an Indian youth there against the sky; see him throw the net, and watch the struggle with the eagle" (253). Because the novel does not end with Thea's stay in Panther Canyon, her time spent there is not an escape from the Chicago clubs. Instead, it serves as a reminder of just how fully enmeshed her awakening is with her participation in the business of constructing a higher life for Chicago.

At the novel's end, Dr. Archie notices that Thea has been successfully become a cliff dweller. He gazes at her top-floor apartment in New York: "the fourteen stories of the apartment hotel rose above him like a perpendicular cliff" (341). He also notices in the next paragraph that inside the Metropolitan Opera House, "the height of the audience room, the rich color, and the sweep of the balconies were not without their effect upon him" (341). Even though Thea makes her debut in New York and has been trained in Europe, the particularly Chicagoan use of the metaphor of cliff dwelling cloaks her success and indicates that she has succeeded because of the Chicago business world: Theodore Thomas, the Nathanmeyers, the Chicago Club, and Fred, who had the entry into Chicago's club scene to orchestrate it all. The metaphor also promises that Thea, like Madame Necker and the Anasazi Indians, will eventually disappear.

It is unclear whether Thea recognizes the significance of the Chicago phase of her training and whether she even understands the multiple connotations of the phrase "cliff dweller" in Chicago. But for Cather, the multiple meanings of the phrase allow her to construct a subtle yet biting critique of the Chicago art scene. She pushes back against their belief that art and artists are commodities to be bought, sold, and traded. In doing so, Cather examines the threat of extinction for the artist contained in the notion of cultural uplift.

NOTES

The seed of this essay was written in response to Guy Reynolds's call for papers for the Twelfth International Cather Seminar on Cather, Chicago, and Modernism. I would like to thank the conference organizers for the inspiring theme. Thanks are in order to John Swift, Ann Romines, and Michael Schueth for their positive feedback and encouragement.

1. See Whyte for a current reassessment of the European idea of the city from 1880 to 1960.

2. I wish to thank the Chicago Historical Society for granting me access to the official catalog of the Cliff Dwellers exhibit at the Columbian Exhibition.

3. I wish to thank Alison Hinderliter, Manuscripts and Archives Librarian in the Roger and Julie Baskes Department of Special Collections at the Newberry Library, for her help and for granting me access to the records of the Attic Club and the Cliff Dwellers Club.

4. Minutes of the Attic Club, 3 July 1907.

WORKS CITED

Cather, Willa. "On the Art of Fiction." *Willa Cather on Writing: Critical Studies on Writing as Art*. Lincoln: U of Nebraska P, 1988. 99–104.

———. "The Passing Show." *Nebraska State Journal* 26 Jan. 1896: 9. Reprinted in *The Kingdom of Art: Willa Cather's First Principles and Critical Statements, 1893–1896*. Ed. Bernice Slote. Lincoln: U of Nebraska P, 1966. 330–31.

———. *The Song of the Lark*. 1915. Ed. Sherrill Harbison. New York: Penguin, 1999.

Duryea. Polly P. "Paintings and Drawings in Willa Cather's Prose: A Catalogue Raisonné." Diss. U of Nebraska. 1993.

Fisher-Wirth, Ann W. "Dispossession and Redemption in the Novels of Willa Cather." *Cather Studies 1*. Ed. Susan J. Rosowski. Lincoln: U of Nebraska P, 1990. 36–54.

Fuller, Henry Blake. *The Cliff-Dwellers*. 1893. Rpt. New York: Hardpress, 2008.

———. "The Upward Movement in Chicago." *Atlantic Monthly* Oct. 1897: 534–47.

Germer, Stefan. "Traditions and Trends: Taste Patterns in Chicago Collecting." *The Old Guard and the Avant-Garde: Modernism in Chicago, 1910–1940*. Ed. Sue Ann Prince. Chicago: U of Chicago P, 1990. 171–91.

H. J. Smith Exploring Company. "The Cliff Dwellers/The H. Jay Smith Exploring Company, World's Columbian Exposition, 1893." Official Catalog. 1–19. Chicago Historical Society. Chicago IL.

Homestead, Melissa. Introduction. *The Song of the Lark*. Ed. Melissa Homestead. New York: Signet Classics, 2007. v–xiii.

Massa, Ann. "Henry Blake Fuller and the Cliff Dwellers: Appropriations and Misappropriations." *Journal of American Studies* 36.1 (2002): 69–84.

Meyer, Susan. "On the Front and at Home." *Cather Studies 6: History,*

Memory, and War. Ed. Steven Trout. Lincoln: U of Nebraska P, 2006. 205–27.

Miller, Donald L. *City of the Century: The Epic of Chicago and the Making of America.* New York: Simon and Schuster, 1996.

Moser, Charlotte. "'In the Highest Efficiency': Art Training at the School of the Art Institute of Chicago." *The Old Guard and the Avant-Garde: Modernism in Chicago, 1910–1940.* Ed. Sue Ann Prince. Chicago: U of Chicago P, 1990. 193–208.

O'Brien, Sharon. *Willa Cather: The Emerging Voice.* New York: Oxford UP, 1987.

Papers of the Cliffdweller's Club. Roger and Julie Baskes Department of Special Collections. Newberry Library. Chicago IL.

Regnery, Henry. *The Cliffdwellers: The History of a Chicago Cultural Institution.* Evanston: Chicago Historical Bookworks, 1990.

Robison, Mark A. "Transcending the Urban-Rural Divide: Willa Cather's Thea Kronborg Goes to Chicago." *Regionalism and the Humanities.* Ed. Timothy R. Mahoney and Wendy J. Katz. Lincoln: U of Nebraska P, 2009. 190–210.

Shikoh, Jane Allen. "The 'Higher Life' in the American City of the 1890's: A Study of Its Leaders and Their Activities in New York, Chicago, Philadelphia, St. Louis, Boston, and Buffalo." Diss. New York U, Oct. 1972.

Szuberla, Guy. "Henry Blake Fuller and the 'New Immigrant.'" *American Literature* 53.2 (1981): 246–65.

Wasserman, Loretta. "Cather's Semitism." *Cather Studies* 2. Ed. Susan J. Rosowski. Lincoln U of Nebraska P, 1993. 1–22.

Weininger, Susan S. "Completing the Soul of Chicago: From Urban Realism to Social Concern, 1915–1945." *Chicago Modern 1893–1945: The Pursuit of the New.* Ed. Elizabeth Kennedy. Chicago: The Terra Foundation for American Art, 2004. 53–65.

Whyte, Iain Boyd, ed. *Modernism and the Spirit of the City.* New York: Routledge, 2003.

6 Willa Cather and Henry Blake Fuller

More Building Blocks for *The Professor's House*

RICHARD C. HARRIS

In his study of the making of *The Professor's House*, David Harrell asserts that the influence of Mesa Verde "accounts for more of the novel's final form and meaning" than any other material. He concedes, however, that there were clearly many influences on the novel and that *The Professor's House* apparently derived, "more thoroughly than other works, from disparate origins whose separation in both time and place were no doubt a challenge to the creative power that finally brought them all together" (5). In the historical essay to the Scholarly Edition of *The Professor's House*, James Woodress, drawing on Harrell, notes written sources as diverse as Gustav Nordenskiöld's 1893 archaeological study *The Cliff Dwellers of the Mesa Verde*, Anatole France's 1897 novel *Le mannequin d'osier*, and Cather's 1902 short story "The Professor's Commencement," adding that because Cather "had a very retentive memory, the hundreds of books she read lay in the deep well of her consciousness, to use William James's phrase, as a literary source to be drawn upon" (302). I would suggest that several of the works of Chicagoan Henry Blake Fuller were among the sources that Cather re-

trieved from that "deep well" in creating *The Professor's House.*
In particular, at a time in her life when Cather was most concerned with the human consequences of modern material culture
and with the passing of what she increasingly came to see as a
nobler past, Fuller apparently provided themes, plots, and characters that enabled her to articulate her own fictional response
to that modernized commodity-driven culture and to generation-
al conflict and change.

Though little known today, Henry Blake Fuller was the leading Chicago novelist of the late nineteenth century. He originally
established his literary reputation in the early 1890s with the
publication of two Italian romances. His two major "realistic"
novels of the 1890s—*The Cliff-Dwellers*, published in 1893,
and *With the Procession*, published in 1895—both deal with
the successful business and social classes of Chicago. William
Dean Howells and other eastern critics praised the latter two
books highly. Although he continued to write fiction, in the first
two decades of the twentieth century Fuller spent much of his
time writing book reviews and essays for the *New York Times,*
the *New York Evening Post*, the *New Republic*, the *Nation*, the
Dial, and other important periodicals. During this period, Harriet Monroe invited him to be an advisory editor for *Poetry: A
Magazine of Verse*. He was considered by his contemporaries
an excellent critic and interesting conversationalist; at the same
time, however, a rather enigmatic and very reticent personality
(perhaps a result of his homosexuality) contributed to a kind of
social isolation. In 1919 he made a brief reemergence as a writer
of fiction with his novel *Bertram Cope's Year*. Poor health and
his disappointment at the negative reaction to *Bertram Cope's
Year* apparently limited Fuller's attempts to publish his fiction in
the 1920s, although he published two novels in the six months
before his death in 1929.[1]

Theodore Dreiser declared Fuller "the father of American realism" (1), but by 1954 the author of a scholarly article on Fuller's career in *American Quarterly* characterized him as "only a

footnote in the history of American writing" (Lawrence 137). Edmund Wilson's lengthy 1970 *New Yorker* article seems to have done much to revive interest in Fuller, whom Wilson identified as one of America's undeservedly "neglected" artists. He declared Fuller "a unique and distinguished writer" whose Chicago novels are characterized by an admirable "precision and elegance" of style (112, 114). Wilson, in fact, judged Fuller superior to Howells as a novelist of manners, an opinion that Howells himself had voiced. Three book-length biographies followed within a decade of Wilson's article; since then, however, Fuller has again largely been ignored.[2]

So, then, what is the possible connection between Fuller and Cather, and, specifically, what influence might Fuller have had on *The Professor's House*? Although there is no mention of him in Woodress's biography or in Andrew Jewell and Janis Stout's *Calendar of the Letters of Willa Cather*, it seems highly likely that Cather would have heard of Fuller, especially during the 1890s, when his Chicago novels occasioned widespread comment in both the Midwest and the East. *The Cliff-Dwellers* was serialized in *Harper's Weekly* from June to August 1893, and the novel appeared in book form in the late fall of that year. A starkly realistic condemnation of Chicago's business world and of its upper middle class, the novel was found objectionable by writers of the genteel tradition.[3] However, Hamlin Garland declared that Fuller "had beaten the realists at their own game" (266), and Howells praised *The Cliff-Dwellers* as "a work of very great power" ("Cliff Dwellers" 863). *With the Procession*, published in March 1895, two months before Cather made her first trip to Chicago,[4] evoked Howells's praise of Fuller's "perfect intelligence" (M. D. Howells, *Life in Letters* 508) and James Huneker's declaration, "In Fuller we have at last met the American novelist. . . . He has culture, courage, conviction, [and] sees his country from the objective viewpoint" (18). Moreover, once Cather herself became a novelist, she was likely aware of Fuller's comments on her and her work. As Kenneth Scambray notes in his study of him, Fuller "promoted the works" of a number of writers, including Cather, in his reviews and essays (7–8).[5] Cather and Fuller also shared aesthetic ideas. In August 1917 the *Dial* published Fuller's essay "A Plea for Shorter Novels," which argues for an approach to fiction writing strikingly similar to that expressed by Cather in "The Novel Démeublé." "The long novel," Fuller says, "too often suggests the unpacked trunk—the contents have never been compactly brought together at all, but are spread loosely, and often at random, over bed, chairs, and floor" (140). Like Cather, who criticizes the realist's tendency toward "mere verisimilitude" (40), Fuller admonishes the writer of fiction to "abolish set descriptions of places" and to "sweep away" all the "stuff" that too often "is dragged in because someone will think it 'ought to be there'" (140). Criticizing the "swollen novels" of the late nineteenth and early twentieth centuries, Fuller asserts that "construction" in a novel "is the art of leaving out"; lack of "discipline" in fiction writing "makes for diffuseness and formlessness" (139). In 1918 Fuller published *On the Stairs*, which put his theory of the "shorter" or "unfurnished" novel into practice.

These facts, of course, suggest only that Cather might have been familiar with Fuller and his work. Fuller's fiction itself, however, provides the strongest evidence that Cather indeed had read his work and had been influenced by it. Major sources and background material for the middle section of *The Professor's House* have generally been agreed upon and are discussed in detail in Harrell's *From Mesa Verde to "The Professor's House."* Cather evidently began working on a southwestern story titled "The Blue Mesa" in 1916, which she seems to have finished in late 1922 or early 1923 (Harrell 323). At some point she had renamed the piece "Tom Outland's Story," and that story, "a turquoise set in dull silver" (epigraph, *The Professor's House*), became the middle section of Cather's novel.

Backgrounds for parts 1 and 3 of *The Professor's House* have also been identified. John Hinz long ago pointed to Cather's

early story "The Professor's Commencement" as a forerunner
of *The Professor's House* (79), and subsequently both David
Stouck and Bernice Slote noted similarities between Cather's story "Her Boss" (written in the latter part of 1917 and published
in *The Smart Set* in 1920) and the first and third parts of the
novel (Stouck 98; Slote, Introduction xv). Cather's reading of
Viola Roseboro's novel *Storms of Youth* (1920) may also have
piqued her interest in telling the story of a college professor: she
wrote to Roseboro from Paris that she had read the book on
her voyage to France, had found one of the characters, a professor, particularly interesting, and would like to have had a whole
book on him (Cather to Roseboro, 5 June [1920]).

Fuller's works, however, may have been even more important
than these other sources to Cather's development of parts 1 and
3 of *The Professor's House*. Fuller's title "The Cliff-Dwellers"
suggests an obvious connection, but his cliff dwellers are not
the Anasazis of the Southwest but the Chicagoans who live and
work in the city's new skyscrapers. (In the late nineteenth and
early twentieth centuries the term "cliff dwellers" became widely used to designate anyone living in high-rise dwellings.) Although cliff dwellings in his novel are modern structures, Fuller
nevertheless begins his book with an elaborate ironic juxtaposition of the southwestern landscape and the Chicago cityscape.
In the modern city, "towering cliffs"—manmade structures—
look down upon "great cañons" filled with "rushing streams of
commerce"—"shoppers, clerks, and capitalists"—and "the confused cataract" of Chicago's diverse citizenry (1, 54).[6]

From this description Fuller turns to the business and social
life of Chicago and delivers a scathing attack on the crassly materialistic, superficial, manipulative, and dishonest society of the
day. (Needless to say, to a city congratulating itself on the overwhelming success of the Columbian Exposition, the novel was a
great shock.) The opening allusion to the Southwest in *The Cliff-
Dwellers* reminds one of Cather's juxtaposition in *The Professor's House* of the Anasazi cliff dwellers and the office workers

of Washington DC. In his study of Fuller, John Pilkington comments that Fuller's "complaint against Chicago" was his belief that "the basic assumptions or premises upon which life rested in Chicago were destructive, or at least inimical, to the qualities which he considered requisite for satisfactory living" (91). Fuller's "complaint," of course, resembles Professor Godfrey St. Peter's view of the world in which he lives and prefigures a number of comments Cather herself made in the 1920s about life in modern America.

The business theme is a major element in *The Cliff-Dwellers*, but Fuller himself declared in his essay "My Early Books" that his real intention had been to examine fundamental questions about marriage (Scambray 87), a topic that Cather also explored in *The Professor's House* and other works. In this vein Fuller clearly set out to attack the depictions of happily married couples so prevalent in the popular "genteel" and sentimental fiction of the day. There are thirteen married couples of different ages in *The Cliff-Dwellers*; in all but one of the marriages, one or both of the partners feels dissatisfied or unfulfilled (Scambray 87–88). Lives of "quiet desperation" fill the novel, and Fuller skillfully examines the problematic situations and unsatisfactory relationships created by those who strive for and even achieve success (another topic Cather repeatedly examined in her works of the 1910s and 1920s).

At the center of these problems are the women, the wives and daughters, for whom the material success of the husband or father is clearly a mixed blessing. In both *The Cliff-Dwellers* and *With the Procession*, Fuller depicts strong-willed women who too often measure their own and their families' worth largely in material terms. The same acquisitive spirit that typifies St. Peter's wife, Lillian, and his older daughter and the same envy that haunts the relationship between Rosamond and her sister Kathleen in Cather's novel appear repeatedly in *The Cliff-Dwellers*. As one critic has said, the wives and daughters in *The Cliff-Dwellers* "divert their considerable nervous energies into the channel of social rivalry. Their husbands [however] are not expected to follow them into this world, merely to pay the bills" (Bowron 135). In one relationship after another, the characters question whether they had married the right person. Godfrey St. Peter's bemused statement about Euripides might as well have come from the mouths of several of the male characters in *The Cliff-Dwellers*: "when he [Euripides] was an old man, he went and lived in a cave by the sea, and it was thought queer, at the time. It seems that houses had become unsupportable to him. I wonder whether it was because he had observed women so closely all his life" (154).

These obvious thematic similarities between *The Cliff-Dwellers* and *The Professor's House* are intriguing, but specific plot and character parallels between *The Professor's House* and *With the Procession* strongly suggest Cather drew on the novel, consciously or unconsciously, as a source. In *With the Procession* (1895), Fuller softened his tone and produced a study less stark, less bitter, and less uncomplimentary to Chicago and its ruling class. The world of modern business and the social and domestic dramas are still important, but Fuller here explores a theme that he saw as fundamental to the America of the late nineteenth century: an older generation's being passed by and its values being ignored or rejected as the world changes. In this case, Chicago's effort at "uplift," the popular term for the attempt to create a positive environment for "culture," is rendered difficult because the older, moneyed, upper class finds itself engaged in an apparently futile struggle with the emerging, uncultured nouveau middle class. One critic explains that in this second Chicago novel Fuller "now determined to focus his attention upon those whose allegiance was to the old Chicago but who were forced to live in the new era" (Pilkington 97).

The chief representative of that older culture is Mrs. Granger Bates,[7] but the focus of the narrative is the Marshall family, in particular David Marshall, a sixty-year-old businessman. The Marshalls had earlier withdrawn from "the procession," the continual march to make more money and to move higher in society. However, the Marshall women—David's wife and two daughters—now discover that they, unfortunately, have fallen behind their contemporaries and have slipped down the social ladder. The question for the women in the family is how to reestablish themselves, how to rejoin the "procession" or "caravan."

Doing so requires first that David Marshall's two daughters be accepted into Chicago high society. For Rosamund, the dark-haired, very attractive, self-willed daughter, who "was teaching her father how to spend [his] money," this is no problem. Her looks, confidence, and superior air make her a natural in that social world. Godfrey St. Peter also has two daughters. The dark-haired, more confident and assertive of his daughters is also named Rosamond—a mere coincidence, or a tip of the hat to Fuller? Notably, while Cather's Rosamond receives a bracelet with "a turquoise set in dull silver" (106), Fuller at one point describes his Rosamund as looking "like a garnet set in dull gold" (106). The other Marshall daughter, Jane, certainly cannot match her sister's looks or confidence. She is, however, her father's favorite, just as Kathleen, her counterpart in Cather's novel, is *her* father's favorite. Like the Professor, David Marshall constantly hears the "hubbub of female voices" from another room (*With the Procession* 22), but he is generally uninterested in and largely uninvolved in the "domestic drama" (*The Professor's House* 100) that goes on in the house. He is immersed in his own affairs and is "altogether alien to the amenities of the great world" (89). As he says, "There are lots of other things to think about" (152).

Having achieved great success—that is, having made a great deal of money—David realizes that though he is growing older, he is still useful: he writes checks to finance the social and domestic activities of his wife and daughters. The biggest check he is preparing to write is one for a new house. Frustrated that her home does not measure up to those of the people she now knows, Rosamund asks her mother, "Are we going on forever living in this same old place?" (156). Rosamund and her mother finally decide that the family must move to a new house in a better neighborhood. Plans are developed and Mrs. Marshall and her daughters spend hours discussing the various details of architecture, furnishings, and decorations.

As mother and daughters discuss plans for the new house, David, resigned to a move he does not want to make, responds to their project with "unillumined indifference" (176). In *The Professor's House* we see the same attention to constructing and decorating two houses—the Professor's own new house and Louie and Rosamond's new house, "Outland"—and Godfrey St. Peter is similarly resigned and indifferent to both. Fuller's Rosamund, like Cather's Rosamond, will have her ideal house, "a palace and a show-place" (*With the Procession* 233), but Jane sums up her father's feeling about new houses when she remarks, "It may be a nice house, but it will never be home . . . our dear old home" (209).[8]

The prospect of surrendering his old home and a series of problems with his business take a heavy toll on David Marshall. As his son Roger observes, "Father is not the man he used to be" (226). David has long felt alienated from his family, and he feels increasingly alienated from the new generation he now confronts. He has vowed to try to get to know and come to like Rosamund's fiancé, but he finds a disturbing distance in their relationship. David is too inexperienced in the drama of modern business to detect or to respond successfully to the materialism, insincerity, hypocrisy, and unethical practices of those around him. Obviously lacking the consumer mentality and concern with social standing of the other members of his family, he clearly is not "with the procession." With a "pathetic pride," Fuller says, he insists on "standing at his post" (251), as a representative of an older world that has given way to a "new and careless public" (273). Like Godfrey St. Peter, David Marshall is "tired." With a bitter irony, Fuller tells us that on "a chilly day in early November . . . wrapped in shawls and bolstered up with pillows," David is moved from his old house to the new house. Lying in bed in that cold, unfurnished structure, he prepares to die. Whether Cather had read *The Cliff-Dwellers* and/or *With the Procession* when they first appeared in the mid-1890s, or at a later point, Fuller's examination of modern American society would no doubt have seemed particularly relevant to Cather in the early 1920s. She, like any number of other American writers at the time, had cause to question the less than positive consequences of "progress" (as does Godfrey St. Peter) and certain negative values and attitudes that had come by this time to be seen by many as distinctly "American." As Honor McKitrick Wallace notes in her essay on Cather and commodity culture, a broad shift occurred circa 1900 with the transformation from a society "emphasizing production and property to one emphasizing consumption and spending" (145). Interested in much older New World cultures and events, Godfrey St. Peter might not have fit well into the pre-1900 world; the world of the early twentieth century is even more foreign to him.

The influence of Thorstein Veblen and the relevance of his work to *The Professor's House* have been clearly demonstrated by Guy Reynolds (124–49) and others. In 1920 and 1922 Sinclair Lewis lambasted American materialism in *Main Street* and *Babbitt*. In Cather's *One of Ours* Claude Wheeler is appalled by his brothers' fascination with "mechanical toys" (35); the cluttered Wheeler cellar symbolizes an end result of the American desire to own "things." In the same year in which *The Professor's House* was published, F. Scott Fitzgerald's Nick Carraway would lament the corruption of Gatsby's dream and, implicitly, of the original American Dream as well. The modern consumer mentality, they all recognized, often encourages much of what is worst in mankind, breeding anxiety and disappointment for those who embrace it as well as for those who disdain it. Jay Gatsby's pride in the number of shirts in his closet and George F. Babbitt's satisfaction with his alarm clock, bathroom towel rack, and toothbrush holder are paralleled in *The Professor's House* by the desire of the St. Peter women (encouraged by Louie Marsellus) for beautiful furs and showy jewelry, a painted Spanish bed, the right faucets, and glass doorknobs. Their fascination, if not obsession, with material goods, exemplified in a trip to Chicago that becomes "an orgy of acquisition" (152), is presented as typical of a modern America whose values both the Professor and Tom Outland, rightly or wrongly, find far different from and disappointingly inferior to those of the simple and noble cliff dwellers described in the middle section of the novel.

The attempt to come to terms with, or the tendency to react against, the emphasis on commodity and consumerism is, of course, fundamental to modernist philosophy. The complex consequences of having money and therefore being able to purchase and possess "things" would also, no doubt, have interested Cather in the early 1920s, for it was with the commercial success of *Youth and the Bright Medusa* and especially *One of Ours* that she finally achieved financial success. Sales of those two volumes in 1923 brought her over $19,000 (Lewis 115), equivalent in today's (early 2010) terms to almost $240,000. As both Janis Stout (Introduction) and Mary Ann O'Farrell have argued, Cather's attitude toward her own material success must have been ambivalent. While she long was seen as someone who was more interested in art for its own sake than in popular success and the financial rewards of authorship, more recent revelations about the extent to which she was directly involved in the marketing of her books (see Porter, for example) and the repeated references in her letters to various niceties—a comfortable apartment, good food, fine wine, tickets to the opera, nice clothes, the opportunity to travel—make it clear that those "things" and experiences that money could buy were central to her life.

For Cather, aesthetic appreciation and the emotions and memories associated with what she owned apparently were more important than the things themselves. During the early to mid-1920s, however, she seriously considered the costs and negative consequences of commercial success, concerns explicitly reflected in "Coming, Aphrodite!" (1920) and in what Patrick Shaw calls Cather's "conflict narratives": *A Lost Lady*, *The Professor's House*, and *My Mortal Enemy* (95). Shaw contends that Cather's use of unsatisfactory or broken marriages in these works also reflects her concern with a broken world (95), in which the traditional value system has been replaced by "quite another" otherwise grounded, modern system inferior to and incapable of providing a satisfactory sense of purpose and meaning. The same feeling is evident in a 1922 letter to Dorothy Canfield Fisher [17 June 1922]) in which Cather notes that the contemporary world is different from the world they had known earlier, and, of course, in Cather's well-known remark, "The world broke in two in 1922 or thereabouts" ("Prefatory Note" v). According to Stout, "Uncle Valentine," published six months before *The Professor's House*, makes clear the relationship between *A Lost Lady* and the two novels that followed it (*Writer and Her World* 204); all these works look back, to one extent or another, to "a bygone period of American life" around the turn of the century before those changes that "made all the world so different" ("Uncle Valentine" 3).

During the time Cather was working on what became *The Professor's House*, Fuller's previously mentioned 1917 essay "A Plea for Shorter Novels" might have interested her; during the late 1910s and early 1920s she herself was developing her ideas about the art of fiction. The publication of Fuller's *Bertram Cope's Year* in 1919 might also have caught her attention. Indeed, many striking parallels between *Bertram Cope's Year* and *The Professor's House* strongly suggest that Cather had read Fuller's novel.

Set in a midwestern university town, rather obviously Evanston, Illinois, the novel focuses on the various social adventures and problems of Bertram Cope, a twenty-four-year-old English instructor. One of the major themes in the novel is the relationship between the older and younger generations, a theme that Bernice Slote long ago saw as taking on "a kind of archetypal significance in [Cather's] imaginative world" (xiv). One of Bertram's acquaintances is Basil Randolph, a scholar in his mid-fifties, who is very much aware that he is growing older. Like Professor St. Peter, who bemoans the indifference and lack of graciousness of his students, Randolph finds most of the younger generation "commonplace," "noisy, philistine, glaringly cursory and inconsiderate toward their elders" (13). Despite his desire to teach them "civilized" ways and to help promote their careers, they clearly have little use for him.

A few of them, however, "he would have enjoyed knowing, and knowing intimately" (13). Bertram Cope is such a young man. Just as Godfrey St. Peter had found Tom Outland the most remarkable young man he had ever met, Randolph finds Cope a notable exception among the students at the university. Just as St. Peter's knowing Outland causes him to think of his youth, to rediscover his "original ego," "the original, unmodified Godfrey St. Peter" (265, 263), Randolph's relationship with Cope evokes much the same response: Randolph, we are told, "thought of his own early studies and of his own early self-sufficiencies. He felt disposed to find his earlier self in this young man—or at least an inclination to look for himself there" (41).

Bertram Cope's Year was perhaps the most important, if not the first, homosexual novel published in the United States in the early twentieth century. It deals frankly with the topic and addresses it with skill and grace. In 1922, Carl Van Vechten called Fuller's treatment of homosexuality "refined" and "studiedly refrained." He could not think of another American writer, he said, "who could have dealt with the subject so thoroughly, from so many angles, and yet have written it so discreetly" (295). Some critics have read St. Peter's relationship with Outland as homosexual or homoerotic. Doris Grumbach, for instance, says the novel "hints at a private, unconfessed, sublimated" homosexual relationship (339), and John Anders sees the relationship as "overtly eroticized" (99). Despite Van Vechten's comments about Fuller's "discreet" treatment of homosexuality in *Bertram*

Cope's Year, Fuller is nevertheless far more direct than Cather—if, indeed, Cather intended to portray a homosexual relationship indirectly. Whether or not Cather read *Bertram Cope's Year* and/or comments on it by Van Vechten and other critics, Fuller's novel provides a crucial context for interpreting the meaning and significance of Cather's portrayal of a cross-generational friendship between a younger and an older man in a university setting. One might argue that *Bertram Cope's Year* gave her the idea of at least inviting readers to entertain the idea of a homoerotic attraction between St. Peter and Outland in her own novel, as she continued to examine gender and sexuality issues reflected in a number of her previous works.

Fuller's fiction, then, apparently provided fictional material that Cather appropriated for her own uses, a common tendency for a writer who admitted late in her career that she had "invented" very little (Cather to Carrie Miner Sherwood, 29 April 1945). As can be seen in studies of influences on many of Cather's works, her fictional creations generally were imaginative collages created from a variety of materials.[9] She, in fact, revealed the workings of her creative imagination in several interviews given in the early 1920s. In 1921, for example, she told Eleanor Hinman, "It happened that my mind was constructed for the particular purpose of absorbing impressions and retaining them (Bohlke 44). And in 1925, she remarked to Flora Merrill, "Your memories are like the colors in paints, but you must arrange them" (Bohlke 77). As David Harrell has made clear, *The Professor's House* was made up of many "disparate" elements. A number of striking similarities between Fuller's three novels and *The Professor's House* suggest that Cather, remembering or rediscovering elements from Fuller's fiction, likely drew upon and rearranged them in her own.

Shortly after the publication of *One of Ours*, Cather wrote to a reader who had discovered subtle allusions to the Parsifal legend in the novel, declaring that she thought she had "buried" the references so deeply that no one would detect them (Cather to

Orrick Johns, 17 November 1922). Might she have used much the same technique here? In his 1982 article "The Uses of Biography: The Case of Willa Cather," James Woodress asserted that literary analysis cannot "unlock the ultimate secrets of an artist's act of creation" (202). However, awareness of possible source material for Cather's novels, in this case her possibly having drawn upon Fuller's works, certainly can provide insight into her creative method.

NOTES

1. Edmund Wilson notes that Fuller was so disappointed by publishers' refusals to print the book that he had it printed privately. He later destroyed the manuscript and proofs (134).

2. In early 2010 the Broadview Press published a new edition of *The Cliff-Dwellers*, edited by Joseph DiMuro, and a new edition of *Bertram Cope's Year*, also edited by DiMuro.

3. This term was coined by George Santayana in *The Genteel Tradition in American Philosophy* in 1911 and was applied to certain nineteenth-century American writers (principally from New England) whose work exemplified conventional literary, social, religious, and moral values.

4. Cather visited Chicago at least eleven times between March 1895 and January 1925, the month she finished writing *The Professor's House* (Jewell, "Mapping"). There is no clear evidence in her known letters or in the collection of Fuller material at the Newberry Library that she knew Fuller personally. However, during a summer 1894 Chautauqua in Crete, Nebraska, she was especially impressed by the Chicago sculptor and art critic Lorado Taft, whom she heard lecture on European painting (Woodress, *Cather* 96). Taft, a close friend of Fuller's, might subsequently have introduced Cather to him. While living in New York, Fuller moved in the city's art and literary circles. Between 1898 and 1918 four of Fuller's seven books were published by Houghton Mifflin, which became Cather's publisher in 1912. Anthony Millspaugh has suggested that Cather might also have met Fuller through Elia Peattie, a Chicago clubwoman whom Cather came to know during this period (Millspaugh to Harris, 2 March 2000).

5. See Swanson for a bibliography of Fuller's writings, including his

criticism. For example, Fuller mentions Cather shortly before publication of *The Professor's House* in a 3 May 1925 *New York Times Book Review* article.

6. For an interesting discussion of Fuller, the cliff dwellings, and American society c. 1900, see Clarke.

7. Mrs. Bates may have been suggested in part by Bertha Palmer, wife of the Chicago financial magnate Potter Palmer. Mrs. Palmer, the leader of late-nineteenth- and early-twentieth-century Chicago society, is famous for her comment, "Keep up with the procession, is my motto, and head it up if you can. I do head it. And I feel that I am where I belong." From her mansion on Lake Shore Drive, Mrs. Palmer engaged in a number of activities, most notably as president of the Board of Lady Managers for the 1893 Columbian Exposition and later as the lone woman on the national board responsible for organizing the American exhibit for the Paris Exposition of 1900. She became good friends with a number of members of European royal families, as well as with French impressionist painters, whose work she championed in the United States. Many of the paintings from the Palmers' private collection are now in the Chicago Art Institute.

8. Cather's own feelings about losing houses (or homes) are clear in her letter to her Aunt Franc in late 1915 when she realized that with Isabelle McClung's marriage to Jan Hambourg she would lose the room she had had for fifteen years in Pittsburgh (25 December 1915) and also in her reaction to the loss of the Bank Street apartment in 1927.

9. For example, on evident borrowings in *A Lost Lady* see my "First Loves" and "Cather's *A Lost Lady*."

WORKS CITED

Anders, John P. *Willa Cather's Sexual Aesthetics and the Male Homosexual Literary Tradition*. Lincoln: U of Nebraska P, 1999.

Bohlke, L. Brent, ed. *Willa Cather in Person: Interviews, Speeches, and Letters*. Lincoln: U of Nebraska P, 1986.

Bowron, Bernard R. *Henry B. Fuller of Chicago: The Ordeal of a Genteel Realist in Ungenteel America*. Westport CT: Greenwood, 1974.

Cather, Willa. Letter to Franc Cather. 25 Dec. 1915. George Cather Ray Collection, Archives and Special Collections, U of Nebraska–Lincoln.

——. Letter to Dorothy Canfield Fisher. [17 June 1922]. Special Collections, Bailey/Howe Library, U of Vermont, Burlington.

——. Letter to Orrick Johns. 17 Nov. 1922. Alderman Library, U of Virginia, Charlottesville.

——. Letter to Viola Roseboro. 5 June [1920]. Alderman Library, U of Virginia, Charlottesville.

——. Letter to Carrie Miner Sherwood. 29 Apr. [1945]. Willa Cather Pioneer Memorial, Red Cloud NE.

——. "The Novel Démeublé." *Willa Cather on Writing: Critical Studies on Writing as an Art.* Lincoln: U of Nebraska P, 1988. 35–43.

——. "Prefatory Note." *Not Under Forty.* New York: Knopf, 1936. v.

——. *The Professor's House.* Willa Cather Scholarly Edition. Ed. James Woodress and Frederick M. Link. Lincoln: U of Nebraska P, 2002.

——. "Uncle Valentine." *Uncle Valentine and Other Stories: Willa Cather's Uncollected Short Fiction, 1915–1929.* Ed. Bernice Slote. Lincoln: U of Nebraska P, 1986. 3–38.

Clarke, Michael Tavel. "Lessons from the Past: The Cliff Dwellers and the New Historicism." *Western American Literature* 42 (Winter 2008): 395–425.

Dreiser, Theodore. "The Great American Novel." *American Spectator* 1 Nov. 1932: 1–2.

Fuller, Henry Blake. "America's Coming of Age." *New York Times Book Review* 3 May 1925: 2.

——. *Bertram Cope's Year.* Chicago: Ralph Fletcher Seymour, 1919.

——. *The Cliff-Dwellers.* 1893. Ridgewood NJ: Gregg, 1968.

——. *On the Stairs.* Boston: Houghton Mifflin, 1918.

——. "A Plea for Shorter Novels." *Dial* 30 Aug. 1917: 139–41.

——. *With the Procession.* 1895. Chicago: U of Chicago P, 1965.

Garland, Hamlin. *Roadside Meetings.* New York: Macmillan, 1930.

Grumbach, Doris. "A Study of the Small Room in *The Professor's House.*" *Women's Studies* 3 (1984): 327–45.

Harrell, David. *From Mesa Verde to "The Professor's House."* Albuquerque: U of New Mexico P, 1992.

Harris, Richard. "First Loves: Willa Cather's Niel Herbert and Ivan Turgenev's Vladimir Petrovich." *Studies in American Fiction* 17 (Spring 1989): 81–91.

——. "Cather's *A Lost Lady* and Schubert's *Die schöne Müllerin.*" *Willa Cather Newsletter and Review* 52 (Fall 2007): 39–43.

Hinz, John. "*A Lost Lady* and *The Professor's House*." *Virginia Quarterly Review* 29 (Winter 1975): 70–85.

Howells, Mildred, ed. *Life in Letters of William Dean Howells*. Vol. 2. New York: Doubleday and Doran, 1928.

Howells, William Dean. "The Cliff Dwellers." *Harper's Bazaar* 18 Oct. 1893: 863.

Huneker, James. "Raconteur." *Musical Courier* 19 June 1895: 18.

Jewell, Andrew. "Mapping a Writer's World: A Geographical Chronology of Willa Cather's Life." *Willa Cather Archive*. Ed. Andrew Jewell. 8 May 2010. http://cather.unl.edu/geochron.

Jewell, Andrew, and Janis P. Stout, eds. *A Calendar of the Letters of Willa Cather: An Expanded, Digital Edition*. *Willa Cather Archive*. Ed. Andrew Jewell. U of Nebraska–Lincoln. 8 March 2011. http://cather.unl.edu.

Lawrence, Elwood P. "Fuller of Chicago: A Study in Frustration." *American Quarterly* 6.2 (1954): 137–46.

Millspaugh, Anthony. E-mail to Richard Harris. 2 Mar. 2000.

O'Farrell, Mary Ann. "Words to Do with Things: Reading about Willa Cather and Material Culture." Stout, *Willa Cather and Material Culture* 207–17.

Pilkington, John. *Henry Blake Fuller*. New York: Twayne, 1970.

Porter, David. *On the Divide: The Many Lives of Willa Cather*. Lincoln: U of Nebraska P, 2008.

Reynolds, Guy. *Willa Cather in Context: Progress, Race, Empire*. New York: St. Martin's, 1996.

Scambray, Kenneth. *A Varied Harvest: The Life and Works of Henry Blake Fuller*. Pittsburgh: U of Pittsburgh P, 1987.

Shaw, Patrick. *Willa Cather and the Art of Conflict: Re-Visioning Her Creative Imagination*. Troy: Whitson, 1992.

Slote, Bernice. Introduction. *Uncle Valentine and Other Stories: Willa Cather's Uncollected Short Fiction, 1915–1929*. Lincoln: U of Nebraska P, 1986. ix–xxx.

Stouck, David. *Willa Cather's Imagination*. Lincoln: U of Nebraska P, 1975.

Stout, Janis P. Introduction. Stout, *Willa Cather and Material Culture* 1–14.

———, ed. *Willa Cather and Material Culture: Real-World Writing, Writing the Real World*. Tuscaloosa: U of Alabama P, 2005.

———. *Willa Cather: The Writer and Her World*. Charlottesville: U of Virginia P, 2000.

132

RICHARD C. HARRIS

Swanson, Jeffrey. "A Checklist of the Writings of Henry Blake Fuller."
American Literary Realism 7 (Summer 1974): 211–43.
Van Vechten, Carl. "Henry Blake Fuller." *The Double Dealer* May
1922: 289–99.
Wallace, Honor McKitrick. "'An Orgy of Acquisition': The Female
Consumer, Infidelity, and Commodity Culture in *A Lost Lady* and
The Professor's House." Stout, *Willa Cather and Material Culture*
144–55.
Wilson, Edmund. "Henry Blake Fuller: The Art of Making It Flat."
New Yorker 23 May 1970: 112–16, 120–39.
Woodress, James. "The Uses of Biography: The Case of Willa Cather."
Great Plains Quarterly 2.4 (1982): 195–203.
———. *Willa Cather: A Literary Life.* Lincoln: U of Nebraska P, 1987.

7 Cather's "Office Wives" Stories and Modern Women's Work

AMBER HARRIS LEICHNER

"Miss Willa Cather, the editor of the *Home Monthly*, is . . . such a thoroughly up-to-date woman she certainly should be mentioned among the pioneers in woman's advancement" (2), wrote Jeanette Barbour in an 1897 interview with the up-and-coming young editor. Barbour's short interview appeared in the *Pittsburg Press* and placed Cather's profile alongside those of other notably employed women, including architects, an embalmer, a dentist, and a real estate dealer (Bohlke 1). Although Cather was less than a year into her position at the *Home Monthly*, her editorial work was already celebrated as a predictor of her future professional success: "Miss Cather is just beginning her career, but she is doing it with the true progressive western spirit, that fears neither responsibility nor work, and it will be a career worth watching. To go off, when one is but twenty-one, into an entirely new part of the country and undertake to establish and edit a new magazine requires plenty of 'grit'—a quality as valuable in a business woman as in a business man" (Barbour 2–3).

Barbour's brief profile documents how Cather's early success fit into a wider context of female achievement and highlights her outsider persona as a westerner in the urban East. Notions of Cather's "western spirit" and "grit" would become staples of her public persona as an American writer. In addition to forecasting Cather's professional success, Barbour's article also provoked its subject to undertake her own editorial revision of the article, a revision that reveals how Cather understood herself in relation to the wider advancement of women. Rather than clipping the entire article from the newspaper to send to her family in Red Cloud, Nebraska, Cather removed its accompanying Gibson girl–style caricature of a woman editor, as well as the introductory two and a half sentences. The omitted lines contain a brief history of the young editor's Virginia roots, her childhood relocation to Nebraska, and her father's foreclosure on their town's only newspaper (Bohlke 2).[1]

Cather may have purposefully clipped the article so as to omit fictionalized claims about her and her family's past. Nonetheless, it is significant that, so early in her life and career, her cutting also eliminates a description of herself as "a thoroughly up-to-date woman" who ought to be cited with other "pioneers in woman's advancement" (Barbour 2). Cather's lifelong reluctance to construct her own accomplishments in relation to her gender—to point toward her career as exceptional at a time when critically acclaimed and financially successful women writers *were* exceptional—has become an easy justification for ignoring how her work directly engages issues associated with the turn-of-the-century feminist movement. In recent decades, feminist scholarship has contended with Cather's complex relationship to her own gender and the larger "woman question." As part of that feminist project, this essay specifically addresses three of Cather's short stories from the 1910s portraying women office workers and situates them within Cather's career and era in order to illuminate her skepticism about such women workers' chances for "having it all" in the New Woman era.

Cather's small body of office fiction dramatizes the tensions and ironies of a modernizing workplace in need of women workers to fill low-paying clerical positions. The contested territory of the urban office was ample enough material to compel her to propose to the *Century* that she write a series of stories titled "Office Wives." Ultimately, however, Cather's expectations for this series and its subsequent collection into a book yielded only three published magazine stories never collected by Cather: "The Bookkeeper's Wife" and "Ardessa" appeared in the *Century* in 1916 and 1918 respectively, and "Her Boss" appeared in the *Smart Set* in 1919.[2] No other fictional representations of Cather's "office bohemia" are currently known to exist, in either print or manuscript form.[3]

Cather's three extant office stories do at times mirror her professional experiences in newspaper and magazine offices, but they also pointedly depart from her perspective as a middle-class, college-educated woman from the Midwest to focus instead on women with working-class, "business school" backgrounds, whose goals are generally more practical than artistic. These stories resist autobiographical narrative and its attendant authorial perspective(s), instead engaging more directly with issues pertinent to common workingwomen of Cather's day and participating in a contemporaneous discussion about women's place in America's modernizing labor market. Specifically, they grapple with sex-specific workplace standards shaping the modern office.

In contrast to most of Cather's other early short fiction, her office stories have garnered less critical attention.[4] Francesca Sawaya and Ellen Gruber Garvey have analyzed Cather's office fiction as part of their (re)examinations of Cather's work as an editor and journalist. Their analyses map the larger cultural forces that shaped not only Cather's journalism and editing but also her sense of professionalism in those fields. This essay builds on Sawaya's and Garvey's efforts by looking beyond what the stories suggest about Cather's editing work to explore instead how they undermine optimism about female secretarial employment at a time of rapid growth in women's participation in the labor force. I argue that Cather's office fiction is an experimental space in which Cather tests a variety of models for women workers who are very unlike herself and, in so doing, exposes the depersonalized and morally perilous position these women occupy in the modern American workplace.

During the years just before and well after the start of the twentieth century, young women, particularly those who were white and middle class, crossed many of the educational, professional, and social boundaries that regulated the lives of earlier generations of American women. With their increasing individuality and independence, these "New Women" were the subject of much interest and debate. For example, magazine advertisements adopted imagery of New Women as early as the 1890s by featuring hearty, active American women, such as illustrator Charles Dana Gibson's Gibson girls. Concurrently, writers developed New Woman figures in the plotlines of popular fiction, often following a formula in which a heroine's unconventional life and desires challenge the nineteenth-century "True Womanhood" ideal.[5] Since the historical New Woman was generally dependent upon the resources afforded by white, middle-class privilege, fictional representations of her often reflect this perspective.[6]

Cather's own background and social position correspond with that of the New Woman, including her middle-class upbringing, college education, fulfilling urban career, economic independence, frequent travel, and unmarried status. She eventually left a successful editorial career at the offices of one of the most influential magazines of her day to devote herself more fully to her art, a fitting story arc for a New Woman heroine of popular fiction. Yet Cather, like other modern women of the early twentieth century, defies easy categorization; one might expect a successful professional woman to support women's rights, but she was ambivalent about women's suffrage. Nonetheless, by examining how Cather depicts modern women workers in their urban office spaces, we can see her preoccupation with the ways in which the ideals of modern womanhood merge with the ideals of the urban American office. She depicts a new space in which women's clerical service is as crucial as the individual women who perform it are dispensable. Notably, Cather's office stories do not strictly follow any of the typical New Woman narratives because they focus on the experiences of working-class women, whose class status and more limited educational opportunities excluded them from the idealized New Woman paradigm. Because she focuses on these women rather than depicting educated middle-class women like herself, Cather depicts working-women characters who struggle to balance the economic benefits of office employment with the patriarchal attitudes of their male supervisors. Cather demonstrates that many women could only gain a modicum of economic self-sufficiency if they adhered to gendered codes of conduct—a misstep such as a change in marital status often meant dismissal—and also stayed competitive in ever more fast-paced and impersonal jobs. In her stories, then, Cather simultaneously draws on the material of her lived office experience as an editor and writer and resists a direct self-portrait. Her office women are not editors or writers, nor are they motivated by artistic expression. Instead they are pragmatically motivated and occupy more common, if less glamorous, pink-collar positions as stenographers, typists, and clerks. Through these female characters, Cather avoids the formulaic fantasy of popular stories of New Women and instead presents a realistic portrait of many an urban working woman's experience. These stories present scenarios in which women workers in both the office and the home navigate—with varying degrees of success—the boundary between their own ambitions and their employers' or husbands' beliefs about proper women's work. Ultimately, Cather's office stories are pessimistic about clerical work as a means for urban women to accomplish something more individually meaningful than an economic independence that may prove temporary.

At the turn into the twentieth century, Cather's urban, working-class "copyists" (a term she uses to encompass stenographers and typists) are relatively atypical, since manual factory labor and retail work were the two principal types of position available to urban women (Goldin 82). Secretarial service was still a relatively novel vocation for women during the years Cather published her office fiction, although women rapidly filled new clerical positions as jobs evolved. In fact, by 1930, women held 95 percent of all typist and stenographer positions (Brown 96). For publishing houses, as well as other office spaces in sectors such as insurance and banking, modern business and its attendant paperwork necessitated a large clerical staff. Despite the influx of females into the labor market, women workers were not replacing men; instead, women filled newly created positions as stenographers and typists—jobs that rarely offered promotion or advancement or a guarantee of economic independence or stability. Companies staffed these pink-collar positions at offices like those in Cather's stories mostly with single young women, many of them trained in business "colleges" (not institutions granting baccalaureate degrees) or technical high schools. Employers' patriarchal beliefs about the social conditions and economic value of women's work led them to view individual clerical workers as temporary and replaceable, expected to leave their positions as they married.[7] Despite these conditions, pink-collar jobs were preferable to factory or retail employment for women. In the big picture of women's employment, even a clerical worker with little job security represented "the elite of working-class women" (Schneider and Schneider 74).

Employment in magazine offices in particular meant a connection to literary production, which had real cultural value. The special enticement of jobs connected to publishing stems from a long-standing cultural belief that editorial work was closely aligned to reading, and women were well suited for it. As Garvey explains, "the earlier gentlemanly aura of magazine editing evidently seemed congruent with sheltered, ladylike work" (182). Consequently, middle-class, university-educated women like Cather found editing work a suitable alternative to that traditional staple of middle-class female employment, teaching. Certainly Cather's career complies with this model, though she and many literary scholars alike have customarily designated her editorial work as an inferior, if necessary, career stage. However, as Garvey has shown, Cather used her time as a single woman employed in the modern editorial office to advance her writing skills and career. While at *McClure's* she earned enough to live comfortably as well as save for her future as a full-time writer. She also developed her narrative technique by editing others' writing, learned the value and practice of literary research, created a national literary reputation, and forged connections with other writers (Garvey 190–91). These accomplishments are integral to Cather's development as a novelist. It is hardly surprising, therefore, that Cather situates the plot of her best-known office story, "Ardessa," in a magazine office, but she did not confine herself to this particular office workspace in her other two office stories.

Though Cather experienced office culture at the *Home Monthly*, the *Pittsburgh Leader*, and *McClure's*, this setting did not appear in her fiction while she was at work in these communities. In fact, she had already transitioned from managing editor of *McClure's* to full-time novelist when, in 1916, the *Century* published her first story featuring modern American office workers, "The Bookkeeper's Wife." The story's title, like the titles of Cather's other two office stories, suggests a focus on a central female character; however, the story is unique among Cather's office fiction because it largely unfolds outside office walls and focuses substantially on a male office worker, the titular bookkeeper. Through the portrayal of an unsuccessful marriage between the protagonist, Stella Bixby, and her husband, Percy, the story dramatizes the clash of competing ideals for women's personal and work lives. Stella's husband loves his desk, the books he keeps, and the regularity of his job (51). Despite his affection for these things, he risks them in wanting to marry Stella, a woman with tastes beyond his means whose exceptional beauty means she "could scarcely be expected to do poorly" in marriage (52). Favorable marriage prospects aside, Stella Brown already makes "good money" as a "capable New York stenographer" (52, 54). "[L]ike all girls," Stella has no desire to marry anyone whose projected income will not exceed her own, and, as the narrator explains, "[she] was the sort of girl who had to be well dressed" (54). The narrative revolves around Percy's choices—principally, his twofold deception, first in misrepresenting his salary to Stella and second in embezzling the money he needs to win her hand. As such, Cather reveals little of Stella's motivations; nonetheless, she imbues Stella with a great deal of agency. Stella is in many ways the most New Woman–like character to appear in any of Cather's office fiction.

Stella's independence is evident, for example, in her decision to marry Percy rather than his more affluent rival, Charley Greengay, who has better business prospects: "She knew that Charley would go further in the world. Indeed, she had often coolly told herself that Percy would never go very far" (54). Here Stella's matrimonial decision-making process demonstrates self-confidence. Her accurate predictions confirm Stella's shrewd ability to assess men's marketplace value. Her decision to marry Percy despite his lesser earning capacity indicates an internal tension between the calculating businesswoman in Stella and the impractical romantic. On the other hand, she is described as cold, materialistic, and emotionally remote, indicating Cather's ambivalence toward her strong New Woman heroine: "She would have been a little too remote and languid even for the fastidious Percy had it not been for her hard, practical mouth," states the narrator (54). Cather reinforces this characterization of Stella by following it with a similar assessment: "Her employers, who at first might be struck by her indifference, understood that anybody with that sort of mouth would get through the work" (54). In fusing Stella's shrewd indifference with one of her physical attributes, Cather positions Stella as unsympathetic even as she emphasizes how others objectify her. Similarly, when Stella and Percy encounter his employer, Mr. Remsen, and his wife in a theater lobby, Mrs. Remsen observes, "She's very pretty of her kind . . .

but rather chilling" (55). Mr. Remsen's opinion of Stella matches his wife's, so when seeing his bookkeeper at the office bent over his desk, Mr. Remsen frequently "remembered Mrs. Bixby, with her cold pale eyes and long lashes, and her expression that was something between indifference and discontent" (55–56). Cather uses these accounts of Stella's personality to call attention to the very qualities—perceived by others as calculating and unladylike—that make Stella successful in the working world. Cather creates a character who is ambiguous and compromised; her desire for finery and calculating views of what men are willing to pay for her favors compete with her softer side, "something left that belonged to another kind of woman" (54).

On the other hand, Cather imbues Stella with positive qualities as well. For instance, she exhibits traits of a born businesswoman who is confidently aware of her own capabilities and value in the modern urban landscape. Stella wants her own income and resists becoming the domestic helpmate Percy wants her to be. When Stella marries, she already intends to restart her career if Percy does not get a raise by the end of their first year together, and later, when he tells her his true salary and that he embezzled from his employer five years earlier, Stella resolves to get a job. In a gesture of support, she declares that her income will expedite Percy's restoration of the seven hundred dollars he still owes, but the idea affronts Percy's manhood: "I won't have you grinding in any office. That's flat," he protests (58). Ironically, it is Stella's desire to work rather than Percy's dishonesty that elicits his feelings of emasculation and failure. Once Stella knows her husband's actual salary and the reason he has never spent a day away from the office in all the years of their marriage, she responds clear-mindedly without self-pity, regret, or resentment: "You ought n't to have married a business woman; you need somebody domestic. There's nothing in this sort of life for either of us" (59). We can see in her stance the idea that female ambition and business sense are incompatible with a woman's traditional role as a wife. This conflict is driven home when Stella declares Percy's old-fashioned ways to be as tiresome as his meager earning power. I contend that by rebelling, Stella also undermines Percy's traditional patriarchal need for an appropriately dependent trophy wife. Percy feels the pressure of this cultural expectation strongly enough that he is willing to marry a woman whose expensive tastes are more than he can afford, while, simultaneously, he is unable to accept her capacity and willingness to help satisfy those expensive tastes with her own income. Moreover, Stella's attraction to qualities "in Percy that were not good business assets" (54) demonstrates a romantic side of her that is not cold and calculating. In other words, even if she is emotionally aloof and has expensive tastes, Stella still marries Percy primarily because of a romantic inclination, not because she calculates to gain financially and materially by the union.

Cather's story concludes six months after the pivotal scene of Percy's ultimatum; the couple is separated and Stella works for a ready-to-wear firm headed by Charley Greengay. In Stella, Cather creates a woman who, like many women workers of her day, leaves her job when she marries, reminding readers that marriage regulates most women's movement between the public and private spheres. But when Stella returns to work against her husband's wishes, effectively ending the marriage, Stella creates a new space for herself outside the moral codes of domesticity versus work. She and Charley would seem to be equals—he, too, is a person "who is out for things that come high and who is going to get them" (52). With Stella and Charley as characters, Cather draws a contrast between a new, less gender-defined business attitude and its attendant threat to traditional marital roles and the patriarchal attitudes Percy embodies.

Cather disputes the traditional rules of gender in the workplace. Consider, for example, that when Percy is at last honest with Mr. Remsen about his embezzlement, Percy's relief is tangible. He happily returns to his professional routine, free of a bored wife and her elegant tastes. It is unlikely that Percy will ever again take a personal or professional risk of the sort necessary to marry an ambitious woman like Stella. As a working man, Percy lacks the qualities of a determined risk taker that define Charley's success as the true "man of business." As one 1914 women's employment manual, *Vocations for the Trained Woman*, described, "the man engaged in business or a profession needs to be relieved of detail [by women office workers] in order that he may give his time and energy to matters of larger moment and broader reach" (Martin and Post 111). In other words, Percy is more like a woman office worker than a "man of business." Indeed, he is just like an expert female stenographer in Cather's final "Office Wives" story, "Her Boss": he shows "a strong feeling for office organization" (104). Percy relishes the routine of bookkeeping. His role in the office is as obligatory and marginal as that of the stenographers and copyists whose work enables successful magazines and law firms. The essential difference, of course, between Percy's professional situation and that of women employed in correspondingly subsidiary jobs is his professional resilience. Privileged by his gender, Percy retains his position even after his embezzlement comes to light. Cather's subsequent "Office Wives" stories evidence her recognition of women's vulnerability in offices where they are evaluated more stringently than the men who outrank them. By first depicting how Percy professionally bounces back from his act of workplace fraud and then following his story with later stories portraying women's vulnerable positioning in the office, Cather underscores the hypocrisy of a gendered moral double standard.

Similarly, Cather's characterization of Charley as the urbane new American businessman early in "The Bookkeeper's Wife" enables her to draw Stella as a variation on the new businessman—the New Business*woman*. Stella's sporty tastes, cool calculations, and assertiveness are traits more often associated with masculine success in modern American business. Indeed, Stella exhibits the sort of occupational courage and "grit" that the *Pittsburgh Press* profile of Cather deems "as valuable in a business woman as in a business man" (Barbour 3). Cather only limits Stella's achievement by assigning her to a job with so little room for advancement, and even this tactic highlights the absurdity of restricting women's full access to modern professions. To do this, Cather uses the seemingly competing aspects of Stella's personality—the businesswoman and the woman who marries (and relinquishes her job) for love—to call attention to Stella's feminine subjectivity, whether she is at work in her (male) employer's office or her husband's home. In both settings, Stella's agency is limited by her gender. Beauty and business sense are key to Stella's success, and yet neither can sustain her marriage. Nor does Cather imply that Stella's career—successful though it may be when she returns to the office—is unlikely to progress beyond stenography into a position truly equal that of a businessman like Charley Greengay.

Finally, in outlining how Stella moves back and forth across professional and domestic spaces—the office and home—Cather dramatizes a modern workingwoman's predicament. Whether Stella fulfills her husband's desire for a beautiful but inexpensive domestic helpmate or funds her extravagant tastes by going to work in Charley Greengay's office, she must choose between the domains of two men. The story's inherent conflict between old and new gender roles is finally resolved through a separation. Stella and Percy end their marital partnership when it becomes clear that each "partner" deeply values work—and for parallel reasons. For Percy, bookkeeping is simultaneously a source of pleasure and the means by which he can afford (or not) the domestic life he desires, and yet he fails to comprehend that Stella views her own career in much the same way. Through her work she can satisfy her stylish tastes and fondness for excitement; she gains reentry into the lifestyle she cultivated before assuming the ill-fitting role of Percy's wife. Percy is firmly grounded in the past, and Stella is pushing toward the future. In this way Cather juxtaposes old and new ways of thinking about gender and work, just as she does in all of her office fiction. Like the other two office stories Cather published in the following years, "The Bookkeeper's Wife" ambivalently responds to the problems it outlines. Cather slyly conveys through Percy's closing words in the story that the conditions of his marriage and its breakup are not unique: "I'm very comfortable. I live in a boarding-house and have my own furniture. There are several fellows there who are fixed the same way. Their wives went back into business, and they drifted apart" (59). Cather's ironic touch appears in Percy's reference to multiple men who prefer a boardinghouse (where, presumably, women who are paid for their work handle the domestic duties) to sharing a home with a happily employed wife.

In 1918, the next of Cather's office stories, "Ardessa," was published in the *Century*. The story features the staff of a muckraking magazine, *The Outcry*, the rising reputation of which parallels the early trajectory of *McClure's*. In addition, the character of the young new editor, Marcus O'Mally—a western transplant to the American East with an Irish surname and origins—resembles S. S. McClure. Despite these commonalities with Cather's professional experience at *McClure's*, the story is not a roman à clef. Cather situates her story in the magazine industry's great transitional period, when growing advertising revenues drove down subscription costs and enabled wider access and distribution to readers. Consequently, members of *The Outcry*'s office staff labor with mixed results in the undefined spaces between art and commerce. At greatest disadvantage in this new environment is Ardessa Devine, the editor's senior stenographer. Her employment at the publication predates O'Mally's arrival and his subsequent reinvention of the magazine that was previously edited by "a conservative, scholarly gentleman of the old school" (107). Over the course of the story Ardessa undertakes little clerical work, especially when O'Mally is out of the office. However, since the editor is a relatively recent western transplant, he relies upon Ardessa's institutional knowledge of the magazine to provide him "a background" on matters such as "editorial traditions of the eighties and nineties . . . antiquated as they now were" (107). She also helps him network with essential literary and business contacts, acting as "the card catalogue of his ever-changing personal relations" (107).

In this way, Ardessa's office comes to serve as gateway to the editor's desk, and under O'Mally she acts as an office hostess graciously mollifying the passé writers who linger, hoping to once again see their work in *The Outcry*. Though her familiarity with the magazine's history and the attentions of "people with whom O'Mally was quite through" (108) may seem to make Ardessa resemble an assistant editor more than a senior stenographer, vanity, rather than interest in the magazine, motivates her interactions with "ardent young writers and reformers" (108). When not hosting hopeful authors, Ardessa spends her time critiquing the office boy or young stenographers in her charge or working at the "ladylike tasks" of reading and embroidering (107). And although Ardessa is neither young nor pretty, when she is cloistered in her private office she imagines herself "a graceful contrast to the crude girls in the advertising and circulation departments across the hall" (107). She conspicuously fashions herself as "insinuatingly feminine" in response to the "cold candor of the new business woman" (105). Deluded by a sense of privilege acquired under her former boss, the previous editor, Ardessa is blind to her reputation for indolence in an office populated by "competent girls, trained in the exacting methods of modern business," who acutely feel pressure to exhibit speed and efficiency (107).

Cather draws a direct contrast to Ardessa in young Becky Tietelbaum, who is fresh out of a commercial high school with dreams of lucrative stenography work. In addition to chastising Becky's gum-chewing habit and inappropriate office attire, Ardessa foists her own work on the younger employee. When Becky covers for Ardessa, her proficiency starkly contrasts with Ardessa's inefficiency. O'Mally observes to his business manager that after working with Ardessa, working with Becky is "like riding a good modern bicycle after pumping along on an old hard tire" (114). With this stunning analogy, Cather highlights O'Mally's objectification of his female employees, who are only tools for their (male) boss's use. Additionally, O'Mally's metaphor suggests that Ardessa's ladylike qualities are outmoded (like an old-style nineteenth-century bicycle), even detrimental, in the fast-paced twentieth-century offices of *The Outcry*. Ardessa may write more elegant letters responding to authors' queries than Becky can, but this skill is increasingly superfluous at a modern sensational magazine driven by a revolving door of celebrity authors.

Eventually, Ardessa's approach proves too antiquated for O'Mally's taste, and her condescending attitude in the office brings her little sympathy. Near the story's conclusion, O'Mally endeavors to cure Ardessa of her complacency by transferring her into the business department across the "Rubicon" (112) from his editorial office.[8] In spite of Ardessa's faults, however, the story is not a ringing endorsement of the women who *do* succeed at the office, Becky and the business stenographer Rena Kalski. For instance, even though Becky is realistically motivated by the financial needs of her struggling parents and nine siblings, the exaggerated pace of her increasingly skilled work performance seems untenable in the long term. Further, Cather marks Becky's and Rena's otherness in the office through ethnic coding. For example, the third-person narrator uses Jewish stereotypes to describe Becky: she is "a thin, tense-faced Hebrew girl of eighteen or nineteen . . . gaunt as a plucked spring chicken . . . [in] her cheap, gaudy clothes" (109). Ardessa's reflections on the young woman's early days at *The Outcry* indicate her otherness as an immigrant "ignorant as a young savage" who knew little English and "fairly wore the dictionary out" (110). Drawing on similar anti-Semitic stereotypes, the narrator highlights Rena's materialism, as exemplified by her first appearance in the story polishing her diamond rings in the washroom during her lunch break. Rena, who at one point "serpentined" from a room, is also referred to as a "young Hebrew" (112).

Yet despite Cather's use of these stock stereotypes, Becky and Rena are nuanced characters to whom she assigns both positive and negative traits. Becky's impressive work ethic, for example, parallels Rena's success as "the right bower of the business manager" (112). Rena's aptitude has earned her a place in the bookkeeper's office for half of her workdays—presumably a promotion for the stenographer. Both women also exhibit admirable qualities specific to their membership in *The Outcry* office community. Becky is grateful rather than gloating in response to praise for her accomplishments, while Rena is conciliatory toward Ardessa after her unceremonious transfer to the business office. O'Mally and the business manager, Henderson, expect Rena to be unfriendly to Ardessa, but instead she demonstrates a collegiality visible nowhere else in the office. Henderson's surprise at Rena's munificence is apparent: "What interested and amused him was that Rena Kalski, whom he had always thought as cold-blooded as an adding-machine, seemed to be making a hair-mattress of herself to break Ardessa's fall" (116). Becky and Rena's friendship with one another and, particularly in Rena's case, compassion toward an unsympathetic co-worker make them the most admirable characters in the story. Despite the stock Jewish stereotypes Cather deploys, she also creates in Becky and Rena two sympathetic women clerical workers who navigate the patriarchal minefield of the office with their humanity intact.

It is instructive here to turn to Francesca Sawaya's astute reading of this story. By exploiting "anti-Semitic descriptions of mercenary Jews to describe the modernized business offices" (89), Sawaya argues, Cather precludes Becky and Rena from signifying acceptable approaches to professionalism—especially professional journalism—just as Ardessa's femininity and privilege describe the editorial offices (and preclude her from being a viable model for the New Woman). Sawaya argues that because none of these female characters employed at a magazine known for its new journalism can embody Cather's ideal, the third-person narrator offers a "normatively white and male" journalistic objectivity to avoid "gendered or racialized interestedness" and thus "compromised commercialism" (91). Sawaya links Ardessa's workplace behavior to an "obsolescent femininity" (90) indicative of traditional separate spheres and the Victorian gender boundaries they imply. Ardessa's private office resembles a home where she serves as hostess, and "Her femininity is inextricable from her obsolete, personalized, elitist work habits" (90). The magazine's division of labor between business (public sphere) and editorial (private sphere) work is an imagined one, and the characters that move between them are visible reminders that all employees—whether tethered to the business or editorial side—are dependent on advertising revenue.

As fruitful as Sawaya's interpretation is to understanding the story's setting at a magazine of the sort Cather knew so well, the disembodied (and thus ungendered) narrator fails to resolve issues the story raises regarding models of women's work. The fact remains that Ardessa, Becky, and Rena (and every other woman character in the story, named or unnamed) have negligible influence on *The Outcry's* new brand of journalism because they are clerical workers, working-class women who could work in any kind of office, not college-educated editors or writers with professional expertise tied to the magazine industry. For Cather's working-class women in "Ardessa," *The Outcry* office is a public workspace, and they cannot fully escape the gendered expectations of others—namely, male managers and editors who control professional access, promotion, transfer, and so forth. This is the attitude toward female labor plainly visible, for example, when O'Mally calls Ardessa—his former stenographer— "the bartered bride" (116); and, in the larger context of Cather's other office fiction, the message resonates in her proposed book title: "Office Wives." Ultimately, "Ardessa," the one story of the three set in an office space like the one Cather worked in at *Mc-Clure's*, resists suggesting to its contemporary readers that there is meaningful professional work for women in office spaces—including those connected to publishing—in spite of the author's own distinguished editorial work at a premier American magazine. Instead, the story illustrates how some women trained in vocational schools for clerical work, like Becky and Rena, can thrive by staying within the gendered bounds of the clerical side of the office space and acting as tools that ensure the productivity of the male managers and editors. Cather subtly refers to this system to emphasize its ubiquity, as when Henderson casually notes Rena at her desk, "where [her] lightning eye was skimming over the printing-house bills that he was supposed to verify himself" (114). Such a detail reinforces Rena's suitability for attending to the tasks on her manager's desk and, combined with her increasing bookkeeping responsibilities, suggests that a full realization of her potential to move into a professional position is inhibited by her employer's expectations for her sex. By juxtaposing the career paths of both an upwardly mobile stenographer and a discerning assistant to the business manager with the idle and outdated workplace femininity that costs Ardessa her job, Cather exposes the ways that office work could both empower and exploit women.

Becky and Rena may represent Cather's conscious revision of the popular New Woman story to more accurately reflect the female staff she saw every day during her many years in the office. By rewriting a popular fictional genre without a Cather-esque female editor—an unequivocal New Woman heroine—Cather "[wrote] herself out of a place at the magazine office" (Garvey 188).

In the 1919 story "Her Boss," Cather also mines her editorial work experience, but she locates her female clerical workers in a law office and diverges in her representation of them.[9] "Her Boss" illustrates how a combination of economic need, increasing demand for clerical staff, and cultural trends toward women's independence conflicts with the American business culture's need to regulate women's work through a gendered moral code. Annie Wooley, a young law office stenographer, has an easy and unassuming nature that makes her ill-prepared to navigate the moral perils of her office. Annie's story actually begins with her boss, prosperous lawyer Paul Wanning, who has been recently diagnosed with a terminal illness. The indifference of Wanning's family and law partners provokes him to compose a solace-seeking letter to an old college friend in the West. So dependent on stenographers that he feels unable to write down his own narrative using a pen and well aware that his own "expert legal stenographer," Miss Doane, is loath to stay after hours to take his personal dictation, Wanning asks a new office stenographer, "little Annie Wooley," to stay late and take down his letter, as she "had always been good-natured" on the "several times" he had already detained her to take his private letters in exchange for "a dollar to get her dinner" (101).

On this particular occasion, Wanning waxes nostalgic on his life, eventually observing that "Little Annie" has been "carried away by his eloquence, . . . fairly panting to make dots and dashes fast enough, and . . . sopping her eyes with an unpresentable, end-of-the-day handkerchief" (101). He clearly perceives Annie in a way that is self-serving, but the scene is nonetheless telling in its depiction of Annie as a generous and even empathetic listener moved by Wanning's storytelling. The invigorating experience of narrating his life for an interested audience—Annie—spurs Wanning to embark on the project of writing his autobiography. Annie's kindhearted and unguarded disposition may make her ideally suited for taking down Wanning's autobiography, but such a disposition will not advance her professionally. Cather signals early in the narrative that Wanning's own legal secretary would deem taking the autobiographical dictation of her boss a breach of proper professional conduct: Miss Doane is "scrupulous in professional etiquette, and Wanning felt that their relations, though pleasant, were scarcely cordial" (101). Here Cather implies that "a strong feeling for office organization" rather than the practice of workplace cordiality has earned Miss Doane both her seniority and "furs of the newest cut" (104, 101).

Lacking Miss Doane's appreciation for strict professional

boundaries, Annie consents to work as Wanning's personal secretary and "sort of companion" during the summer months
(105). Even though Annie is uninterested in earning money for
either present enjoyment or future security, in payment for her
assistance Wanning gives her an immediate pay raise and promises "a little present" in his will (105). The extra income from
the raise enables Annie's exhausted sister to quit her job for a
period. Like Becky in "Ardessa," Annie is in her late teens, but
unlike Becky, Annie lacks ambition to advance in the workplace.
Her carefree approach to money and work is reinforced through
other characters' impressions of her. For example, Wanning in-
fantilizes Annie by referring to her condescendingly as "Little
Annie," and throughout the story he emphasizes her childlike
enjoyment of the moment without regard to future consequences. Cather defines Annie's character by tracing her relationship
with money and work, including her difficult background as one
of four children to reach adulthood out of the eight her parents
had. "Girls like Annie," the narrator explains, "know that the
future is a very uncertain thing, and they feel no responsibility
about it" (105). Having this mind-set, it never occurs to Annie
that working alone after hours with her boss could have negative consequences for her future.

When Wanning dies, his law partners and son simply assume
Annie's relationship with him had been inappropriate and thus
feel free to ignore Wanning's codicil requesting a payment to Annie of one thousand dollars. They punish her for her perceived
immorality by blocking her inheritance and dismissing her from
her job. Annie's inexperience with office protocols is most apparent when one of Wanning's law partners, Mr. McQuiston, fires
her. "[Y]ou should have known what a girl in your station can do
and what she cannot do," McQuiston declares (107). Although
McQuiston assumes that Annie knows exactly how she has trans-
gressed the moral boundaries of her entry-level secretarial job,
she cannot identify her mistake and struggles to defend herself
against the reprimand. Explaining her arrangement with Wann-

ing, Annie underscores her solicitous naïveté: "Of course he was sick, poor man! . . . I wouldn't have given up my half-holidays for anybody if they hadn't been sick, no matter what they paid me" (104). Though Annie is the kind of person who "had the gift of thinking well of everything, and wishing well" (104), Cather shows how the law office converts such a positive human quality into a liability for the female clerical worker. Conveniently, they place all culpability on her, not on the dead man they believe to have been her partner in immorality, and by so doing they enrich themselves while impoverishing her.

For working-class women like Annie or Becky, the office is a desirable employment option; it can offer both a measure of personal independence and a way to contribute to their families' incomes. Cather's depiction of a handful of women employed at the lower rungs of the clerical ladder, however, exposes the underside of early-twentieth-century women's office work. Both "Ardessa" and "Her Boss" demonstrate how easily secretarial workers like Ardessa or Annie, whose personal attributes or abilities become more inconvenient than useful to her employer, can lose their positions after committing real or perceived infractions. In this way, Cather's office stories shrewdly expose the inhumane and exploitative conditions of the modern American office for the very women workers who enabled its growing influence on the broader culture.

Cather's professionalism developed in editorial offices and gave her financial independence, training in her craft, and a wide network of contacts. Her cynicism about women's secretarial labor is hardly surprising, given her divided feelings about her own work as a magazine editor. Four years before her first office story appeared in print in 1916, Cather had already left her "incessant, important, responsible work" as *McClure's* managing editor (Jewett 247). From this distance, she glanced back at offices she knew well, culling only the most useful material to channel into stories about characters quite unlike herself, a process perhaps less akin to "writing what you know" and more akin to "coming to know through what you write." Ultimately, then, Cather's three surviving office stories do more than fictionalize the daily realities of her editorial work. They serve as testing ground for a number of models of women's office work, and Cather's fictional clerical workers, I believe, represent the true working-woman in ways that the more overtly feminist New Woman heroine did not. Though Cather downplayed her editorial work and sought to represent her art as gender neutral, the women she actually writes into office settings are, like Becky, Rena, and Stella, marked by both their desire to excel at work and their hindrance by traditional roles. They cannot choose to conduct their clerical careers outside of the business prescriptions for their gender. And, in Stella's case, the movement from one gendered role (the wife) to another (employed wife) irreconcilably breaches her marital relationship. Despite ambivalent feelings about women's-rights activists, Cather contributes a feminist critique of America's patriarchal office culture by showing how its concurrent ideals of modern impersonal efficiency and old-fashioned domestic morality particularly victimize women.

NOTES

1. Barbour's article explains that Cather took over the paper as editor and business manager (earning salaries for both positions) over the course of three months. In his preface to Barbour's article in *Willa Cather in Person*, Bohlke suggests that inaccuracies and embellishments reflect "Cather's talent for fiction." He explains, "There is no other record of her father's foreclosure or of her three months of newspaper work. Her active work on the *Nebraska State Journal* and the *Lincoln Courier* was considerably less involved than is implied" (1).

2. As biographer James Woodress explains, the *Century*'s editor, Douglas Doty, only published one of the two stories included with Cather's original "Office Wives" series proposal. Accepting "Ardessa," he rejected "Her Boss" (then titled "Little Annie") because it "was too sad to run in wartime" (286). Cather's agent, Paul Reynolds, then sent Doty the draft of another story, "Explosives," which was never published and for which no manuscript survives (286).

3. The phrase "office bohemia" is drawn from a December 1908 letter from Sarah Orne Jewett to Cather, in which Jewett encourages Cather to leave her editing career in order to concentrate on her own writing.

4. One possible explanation for the relative neglect of the "Office Wives" stories in comparison to those included in *The Troll Garden* (1905), *Youth and the Bright Medusa* (1920), and *Obscure Destinies* (1932) is that they remained uncollected during Cather's lifetime. To date, the handful of critics to study one or more of Cather's office stories have been interested primarily in their relationship to her creative and professional development while at *McClure's*.

5. See Honey for a detailed overview of popular stories of the New Woman appearing in mass-market magazines from 1915 to 1930.

6. For a historical overview of the New Woman, see Schneider and Schneider 16–19. Despite the dominant image of the white, middle-class New Woman in American mass-circulation magazines, diverse women writers explored the New Woman theme in their fiction, including writers of the Harlem Renaissance era such as Jessie Fauset, Nella Larsen, and Zora Neale Hurston. Rich's recent critical study of non-white women writers' engagement with the New Woman ideal focuses on S. Alice Callahan, Mourning Dove, Pauline Hopkins, Sui Sin Far, María Cristina Mena, and Anzia Yezierska.

7. The marital status of women is significant in discussions of female labor in the Progressive Era. For example, in her study of economic and census data from the period, Goldin notes that in terms of U.S. women's labor market history, "the half-century from about 1870 to 1920 was the era of single women" (81). By 1930, however, even as single women made up 82 percent of the clerical workforce, the number of married women in the field had doubled (Brown 96).

8. The Rubicon is the Italian river over which Julius Caesar led his army when invading ancient Rome. Caesar's military action was a point of no return, ensuring civil war. Cather's figuring of the hall between *The Outcry*'s editorial and business departments as the Rubicon both implies that Ardessa cannot return to her former position outside the editor's office and underscores the irreversibility of the publishing industry's new advertising-dependent business model.

9. See Thacker for a reading of this story in relation to Cather's relationship with S. S. McClure and her collaboration with him on his autobiography.

WORKS CITED

Barbour, Jeanette. "A Woman Editor." *Pittsburg Press* 28 Mar. 1897. *Willa Cather in Person: Interviews, Speeches, and Letters*. Ed. L. Brent Bohlke. Lincoln: U of Nebraska P, 1986. 2–3.

Bohlke, L. Brent. "1897: Pittsburgh." *Willa Cather in Person: Interviews, Speeches, and Letters*. Ed. L. Brent Bohlke. Lincoln: U of Nebraska P, 1986. 1–2.

Brown, Dorothy M. *American Women in the 1920s: Setting a Course*. Boston: Twayne, 1987.

Cather, Willa. "Ardessa." *Century* May 1918: 105–16. *Willa Cather Archive*. Ed. Andrew Jewell. U of Nebraska–Lincoln. http://cather.unl.edu.

———. "The Bookkeeper's Wife." *Century* May 1916: 51–59. *Willa Cather Archive*. Ed. Andrew Jewell. U of Nebraska–Lincoln. http://cather.unl.edu.

———. "Her Boss." *Smart Set* Oct. 1919: 95–108. *Willa Cather Archive*. Ed. Andrew Jewell. U of Nebraska–Lincoln. http://cather.unl.edu.

Garvey, Ellen Gruber. "'Important, Responsible Work': Willa Cather's Office Stories and Her Necessary Editorial Career." *Studies in American Fiction* 36.2 (2008): 177–96.

Goldin, Claudia. "The Work and Wages of Single Women, 1870–1920." *The Journal of Economic History* 40.1 (1980): 81–88.

Honey, Maureen. Introduction. *Breaking the Ties That Bind: Popular Stories of the New Woman, 1915–1930*. Ed. Maureen Honey. Norman: U of Oklahoma P, 1992. 3–36.

Jewett, Sarah Orne. "To Miss Willa Siebert Cather." 13 Dec. 1908. *Letters of Sarah Orne Jewett*. Ed. Annie Fields. Boston: Houghton Mifflin, 1911. 3: 247–50.

Martin, Eleanor, and Margaret A. Post. *Vocations for the Trained Woman*. New York: Longmans, Green, 1914.

Rich, Charlotte J. *Transcending the New Woman: Multiethnic Narratives in the Progressive Era*. Colombia: U of Missouri P, 2008.

Sawaya, Francesca. *Modern Women, Modern Work: Domesticity, Professionalism, and American Writing, 1890–1950*. Philadelphia: U of Pennsylvania P, 2004.

Schneider, Dorothy, and Carl J. Schneider. *American Women in the Progressive Era, 1900–1920*. New York: Facts on File, 1993.

Thacker, Robert. "'It's Through Myself That I Knew and Felt Her':
S. S. McClure's *My Autobiography* and the Development of Willa
Cather's Autobiographical Realism." *American Literary Realism* 33
(2001): 123–42.
Woodress, James. *Willa Cather: A Literary Life.* Lincoln: U of
Nebraska P, 1987.

8 It's Mr. Reynolds Who Wishes It
Profit and Prestige Shared by Cather and Her Literary Agent

MATTHEW LAVIN

In the introduction to *My Ántonia* (1918), a fictionalized author, ostensibly an unnamed version of Cather herself, tells a story of soliciting and receiving a manuscript from her childhood friend Jim Burden, adding, "the following narrative is Jim's manuscript, substantially as he brought it to me" (xiii). This frame introduction situates Burden as the narrator of the novel, sets up the story's autobiographical mode, and establishes an unreliable narrator whose presence arguably inaugurates the experimental or modernist phase of Cather's career.[1] Notably, the introduction also depicts an established author passing an enthusiastic amateur's manuscript to the public with an endorsement of its authenticity and importance.[2] This exchange is also a useful point of entry for an analysis of what Aaron Jaffe identifies as "the complex economies of cultural prestige" and "secondary literary labor" fundamental to the U.S. literary marketplace in the early twentieth century (3). The unnamed author of *My Ántonia*'s introduction acts as an agent or mediator, passing Burden's work to the public with a brief word of context and an implicit endorsement of its content.

Cather's depiction of a private literary exchange at the outset of *My Ántonia* speaks to her awareness of how a range of personal, professional, and managerial figures mediated literary careers. Cather advocated powerfully for herself but also benefited from the support of several literary intermediaries, including but not limited to her domestic partner and collaborator Edith Lewis, her former employer S. S. McClure, and her agent Paul Revere Reynolds. Of these figures, Reynolds has probably received the least attention. He did not introduce Cather to the public, nor did he participate in the early crafting of her literary persona, yet his involvement in her career speaks to Cather's engagement with the issues of literary identity and credibility raised by scholars such as Jaffe. Reynolds took Cather on as a client once she had established herself, and he placed many of her short stories and novels in magazines from 1916 through the 1920s.[3] During this period, Cather also triangulated her decisions with Alfred and Blanche Knopf (president and vice-president of Alfred A. Knopf, Inc., respectively) and made individual efforts to sell her work.[4] Although some have framed Cather as the reluctant artist and Reynolds as the aggressive salesman, her relationship with the market as mediated by Reynolds was more complex than such a dichotomy suggests. In an essay published in 2000, Rebecca Roorda moves past the stereotype of Reynolds as "merely being an employee or a manuscript peddler" (72), providing detailed profiles of the magazines Cather published with and considering their significance to her career. Roorda also argues that "the inconsistencies of her magazine publications would seem to be a direct reflection of her ambivalence about the changing trends in what was becoming the writing business" (75). My analysis of Reynolds builds on Roorda's, providing a broader historical and theoretical context to emphasize the connection between Reynolds's work and the driving principles of the modern literary marketplace. Rather than viewing Cather as a figure "caught in the middle and pulled in opposite directions" by artistic and monetary concerns (Roorda 75), I document an association that was limited but mutually beneficial, with Cather and Reynolds consistently seeking a balance between profit and prestige. While their efforts sometimes seem adversarial, Cather made careful use of Reynolds's skills and crafted a convincing anti-commercial posture as a component of her strategic self-fashioning. Reynolds, in turn, developed a diverse client base: his most artistically credible authors ensured his cultural legitimacy in the eyes of editors, publishers, and clients, while his most commercially marketable authors allowed him to maximize his income.

I am less concerned with Cather's status as a literary modernist than with the distinctly modern cultural factors that enabled a diversity of literary communities and texts. Modernism is often defined by its most distinct stylistic or aesthetic features, especially experimental forms that did not conform to preexisting ideas of texts as commodities.[5] As Catherine Turner argues, modernism is defined by more than stylistic experimentation. Instead, it is an "integrative mode" that both encompasses stylistic differentiation and "describes the place . . . the moderns occupied within their culture" (6). Indeed, Turner argues, the idea of modernism as integrative mode accounts for the fact that modernists simultaneously held "a fascination with and opposition to mass culture" while "play[ing] a role in making their own artistic works into commodities" (7). In recent scholarship, Turner, Jaffe, and Loren Glass have all emphasized the complex relationship between modernists and the broader culture they framed themselves against. Many high modernists, either directly or through proxies acting on their behalf, worked hard to secure their popularity or ensure that their work had wide appeal.[6] Conversely, authors characterized as middlebrow or popular innovated stylistically or engaged philosophical ideas associated with modernism. Much of the work Cather published with Reynolds's help was not stylistically experimental, but her cultivation of a relationship with him suggests she was a modern author responding to the marketplace's evolution rather than an inconsistent or indecisive author resisting the market.

Critical to the reassessment of modernism and the market by

Glass, Jaffe, and Turner is the theorizing of sociologist Pierre Bourdieu. In *The Field of Cultural Production*, Bourdieu traces the emergence of "art for art's sake" in nineteenth-century France, where an interdependent opposition arose between the commercial market (the field of large-scale production) and the avant-garde (the field of restricted production). By rejecting financial profit, writers in the restricted field gained credibility, prestige, and authority (symbolic capital), even though they made little or no money (specific capital). That is, according to the ordinary rules of economics the field of restricted production is governed by a "generalized game of 'loser wins'" (39). Even though the two fields seem antagonistic to one another, the field of large-scale production may "renew itself" periodically by drawing upon the restricted field (Johnson 16).

Further, according to Glass, "the volatile passage from the restricted elite audience of urban bohemia and 'little magazines' to the mass audience of the U.S. middlebrow became a signature career arc for American modernist writers. Along this arc, the model of the author as solitary creative genius whose work goes unrecognized by the mainstream collides with the model of the author as part of a corporate publisher's marketing strategy" (6). This fundamental hierarchy structured the U.S. publishing marketplace in the first half of the twentieth century.

Bourdieu also provides a framework to explain how the different fields influence artistic form. He notes that in nineteenth-century France the rejection of historically rooted formal conventions coincided with the appearance of a "socially distinguishable category of professional artists or intellectuals who are less inclined to recognize the rules" (112). Paradoxically, then, the rise of the mass market led to the social construction of modernism, which in turn spurred modernism's most conspicuous stylistic features; subsequently, modernism secured elite status by appearing to be separate from the very system that helped give it meaning. Of course, the greater part of literary production fell somewhere between the artistic and popular extremes.

Intermediary professionals like Reynolds earned their pay based on their ability to navigate these complexities.

The existence of Reynolds's profession, in fact, resulted from the emergence of a national American readership with money to spend on magazines and the products advertised within them. Sometimes characterized as America's first literary agent, Reynolds was actually preceded by British agents operating within the United States. Furthermore, as early as the 1820s, many individuals in the United States functioned as literary agents well before the profession formally emerged (West 81). Born in Boston in 1864 and educated at Harvard, Reynolds wanted to be a writer but abandoned that pursuit after working as a reader for *Youth's Companion*. In 1891 he moved to New York, where he became a publisher's agent for Cassells, a British publisher, and helped place British titles for American publication and vice versa. He was responsible for offering newspaper publisher O. M. Dunham first refusal on British books that might interest them, and he served as a general intermediary between Cassells in England and American publishers or authors. Subsequently, he established similar relationships with Heinemann, Sampson Low, and Constable. By 1895 he represented authors as well as publishers and typically earned a 10 percent commission on material sold. Moving into the twentieth century, commissions from authors became his primary source of income (Hepburn 74). According to James Hepburn, Reynolds was the "most important early literary agent in America" and was of particular interest because "in a much more conspicuous way than his fellows he was a double agent, serving both publishers and authors" (73, 74–5).

Reynolds began primarily as a specialist in transatlantic copyright, benefiting from the expansion of the book trade enabled by the Chace Act of 1891 and the availability for the first time of reciprocal copyright between the United Kingdom and the United States. Christopher P. Wilson describes the way literature, as a result of the "initial spark" of the bill, "became defined as legal property," subject to "managerial collaboration and supervision," expanding, both directly and indirectly, the need for professionals like Reynolds (74). Within ten years, Reynolds was making most of his income by placing British and American authors' writings in commercial magazines (West 84). Frederick Lewis Allen, who penned a commissioned "biographical sketch" of Reynolds (published posthumously in 1944), dedicates an entire chapter to the so-called magazine revolution of 1893, when *Cosmopolitan*, *McClure's*, and *Munsey's* began to sell their product for five to ten cents. These new magazines relied on ad revenue as their major source of income, and each soon boasted between 500,000 and one million readers. Meanwhile, according to Allen, the shift "was furnishing to Paul Reynolds a new market and a profitable one; and by stiffening the editorial competition for the work of popular authors it was slowly fortifying the position of the literary agent in America" (39). Therefore the rise of the mass market, and specifically of commercial magazines, offered a new profession to figures like Reynolds. By the time Cather hired Reynolds, he was a well-known figure in the New York publishing world, with a dossier of clients that included Stephen Crane, Arthur Conan Doyle, Dorothy Canfield Fisher, Rudyard Kipling, Jack London, Frank Norris, Upton Sinclair, Booth Tarkington, and H. G. Wells (Allen 71).

In the face of a culturally constructed sense of opposition between the national mainstream and an avant-garde alternative, authors like Cather needed to find ways to reconcile financial gain with artistic status. While agents like Reynolds had been a part of the American publishing system since the late nineteenth century, the rising bifurcation between the most respected authors and the most profitable ones made an agent's job more difficult and important than ever before. Turner argues that those promoting modernism, "publishers' agents, patrons, and advertising men," performed a function "that is more complex than the role they have been assigned in the past" (7).[7] Reynolds's primary role was to sell his clients' work, but his strategies varied from client to client. For some authors he focused on maximizing their profit potential by selling their work at progressively higher rates to whatever venues would make both author and agent the most money. For others, such as Cather, he worked within a frame of respectability, following the authors' wishes, but simultaneously ensuring higher prices than the authors could have negotiated by themselves.

That Reynolds worked for Cather at all speaks to her appeal to a national, middle-class audience, since he refused to take on unproven talent and even said in a refusal letter to Upton Sinclair that he made his living "handling an author's work that has already made some place for himself" (29 September 1919). He worked exclusively on commission, so he only represented authors whose work he thought he could sell. He did not deal in poetry unless handling it as a small part of an author's larger body of work for sale. "The commission is so small," he said of poetry in another letter to Sinclair, "that it doesn't pay" (19 January 1905). Reynolds did not involve himself in the early stages of an avant-garde author's career; the unwritten rules of the restricted field of cultural production demanded that such authors reject consumer culture and produce experimental writing that would initially struggle to find an audience. Paul Revere Reynolds Jr., Reynolds's son and eventual successor at the helm of the family business, recalls in his memoir *The Middle Man: The Adventures of a Literary Agent* (1971) that Gertrude Stein once contacted Reynolds for representation but he turned her down: "He wrote to Miss Stein that he was unable to understand what she was trying to do with her writing, and hence he was not the person to handle her work" (28). Reynolds played a role in defining his clients' symbolic status. He used his understanding of the existing market to place short stories and serial novels. His choices affected his authors' exposure, the kinds of venues they would be associated with, and the kinds of readers they would be most likely to reach. The money authors received from publishing in magazines meant they could make less profitable (and possibly more reputation-driven) choices when publishing their books. The financial benefits of magazine publication are what initially led Cather to take Reynolds on as an agent; as she remarked in 1918, the extra money she made from Reynolds's salesmanship meant she could afford to "bone down on" the *My Ántonia* manuscript and finish it (Woodress 279).[8]

Like his other clients, Cather engaged Reynolds only after she had already established her national reputation. In June 1916, Ferris Greenslet of Houghton Mifflin wrote Cather reporting that Reynolds wanted to contact her because magazines were asking for her short fiction (Roorda 73).[9] Cather probably knew of Reynolds as far back as her days at *McClure's*; Reynolds sold to *McClure's* often and had a professional rapport with the magazine that went as far back at the late 1890s.[10] He sold Cather's short story "The Diamond Mine" to *McClure's* in 1916 and pressed her for more work thereafter, placing approximately two pieces a year with magazines for the next dozen years. Cather was initially pleased with Reynolds's abilities after he sold "The Diamond Mine" for six hundred dollars. According to biographer James Woodress, "She wrote Harry Dwight that she took the greatest satisfaction in Reynolds's conduct of her affairs. . . . [She] told Greenslet in June that Reynolds could sell anything" (278–79). While Cather had serialized *Alexander's Bridge* as *Alexander's Masquerade* in *McClure's* in 1912, she did not serialize another novel until she placed *A Lost Lady* with *Century* in 1923.[11] Previously, with *My Ántonia* (1918) and *One of Ours* (1922), she ruled out serialization with little consideration.[12] *A Lost Lady*, *The Professor's House* (1925), *My Mortal Enemy* (1926), and *Death Comes for the Archbishop* (1927), her entire book-length oeuvre of the 1920s, appeared in popular American magazines, which meant she would receive quick injections of capital shortly after finishing any given project.

Cather's potential as a source of profit paled in relation to Reynolds's highest-paid writers. This may strike some as evidence of an unsuccessful professional relationship, but it should instead call attention to the fact that Reynolds represented an assortment of authors with differing priorities. His highest-paid clients earned him the most commissions, but his best-known or most-respected clients helped him maintain professional validity, which contributed to his long-term success. Paul Revere Reynolds Jr. writes: "What is important for the agent and what takes years of experience is to discover how to handle oneself with authors and editors" (33). Because of her resistance to the commercial system, Cather would never make as much money as some other writers. Dorothy Canfield Fisher was able to command much higher prices for her work ($20,000 for a serial novel, $2,000 for a short story in the 1910s and 1920s), and Booth Tarkington in the 1910s was commanding up to $30,000 for a serial novel sight unseen, and up to $3,500 for a short story, which was more than Cather garnered for *Death Comes for the Archbishop*. In 1923 *McCall's* offered Tarkington $40,000 for his next novel and indicated a willingness to wait up to two years for the manuscript (Reynolds to Tarkington, 27 March 1923). Cather, in contrast, ruled out some publishing venues altogether and hesitated when pursuing other opportunities.[13] Comparing Cather with writers like Fisher and Tarkington suggests that Cather fulfilled a different market niche than either of these Reynolds clients.

An assessment of Cather's earnings should take into account how much she made relative to what kind of payment she was accustomed to receiving. The James R. and Susan J. Rosowski Cather Collection at the University of Nebraska, Lincoln, includes a financial ledger of Cather's earnings. This small black book (no bigger than a modern-day personal address book) shows the precision with which Cather kept track of profits from her books and magazine writings. Cather kept a separate page for serial novels, and notes her post-commission earnings for the serialization of *The Professor's House* in 1925 at $9,000. On a separate page, she lists profits from her publisher and royalties for the book at $20,305.10 by the end of 1929, indicating that she made about 30 percent of the book's total profits from one bulk sale of the novel, while it took another four years for the remaining two-thirds to accrue. Even though Cather made less than other writers, she made a substantial amount relative to her other income. Furthermore, Reynolds went to great lengths to accommodate her despite the relatively low commissions he earned placing her work compared with clients like Tarkington and Fisher. Not noted in Cather's ledger is the fact that Reynolds made special arrangements to deposit weekly checks in Cather's bank account while she traveled to New Mexico in June and July 1925. An internal memo from Reynolds to his staff indicates, "She wishes us when we get the receipt from the bank, to send such receipt to her. She says that the Garfield Bank often makes mistakes and she has to check them up" (Reynolds, Office Memo, 4 June 1925). Miss Magee was directed to see this done "in each case." At the end of the memo, Reynolds adds, "she seems to be fussy about these details and it is important we should carry them out because she is a valuable author." Reynolds's use of the term "valuable author" highlights the complexity of value for agent and author. Cather did not earn Reynolds as much in commissions as Tarkington or Fisher, but the prestige of being associated with her was nevertheless valuable to him.

Because Reynolds's job description varied from one client to the next, a proper understanding of the function of the agent requires a broader historical perspective and a willingness to engage in case-by-case interpretation. Literary agents in the first half of the twentieth century did not merely serve as financial representatives, and the scope of their duties steadily expanded between 1890 and 1945. Agents gradually took on handling film and other subsidiary rights, managed literary estates, and represented newcomers as they sought publishing contracts with book publishers (West 114). Comparatively, Cather limited Reynolds's role, only allowing him to place fiction in magazines and not granting him an exclusive right to perform this service for her. This constraint suggests that Cather resisted at least one aspect of the changing market, although she did rely on other intermediaries to perform much of this work for her. The Knopfs, for instance, handled the sale of film rights for *A Lost Lady* and subsequently helped her to fend off film offers when she became disillusioned.

Bourdieu's model, once again, is a useful interpretive tool to explain these kinds of maneuvers. His concept of "position-takings" accounts for the ways authors and secondary literary laborers construct literary meanings by defining themselves and each other "relative to other positions" (30). Artistic works, written pronouncements about art, and market choices all constitute "position-takings" in the field of cultural production. Cather may well have trusted Blanche and Alfred Knopf more than Reynolds. However, her rejection of Reynolds's attempts to do more work for her also operated as a series of "position-takings," which, within the context of Cather's entire career, helped define her as a commercially suspicious and, thus, artistically credible writer.

Less tangibly, though perhaps more significantly, secondary literary laborers like Reynolds could help convert past artistic success to financial profit and could act as buffers, allowing authors to accrue specific capital without losing symbolic capital. An exchange between Cather and Reynolds in the winter and spring of 1926 illuminates this aspect of their professional relationship. In the winter of that year, Cather spoke with Reynolds regarding the serialization of her most recent work, *Death Comes for the Archbishop* (1927). In February 1926 the two had already spoken about where it would appear. They discussed the *Forum*, as well as the *Atlantic Monthly* (Reynolds, Office Memo, 5 February 1926). Cather then received a direct query from *Atlantic* editor Ellery Sedgwick sometime that spring, asking why Reynolds had offered her manuscript to his magazine. In a 28 May 1926 letter she replied that it was offered because Mr. Reynolds wished it, that she never had any interest in the serialization of her books, and had never cared at all whether they were serialized. It was Reynolds who wished to serialize. She added that it was entirely Reynolds's decision, and she had merely mentioned Sedgwick as one of a few editors to whom she would allow him to show her work. Beyond that, she said, she would not interfere.

A superficial reading suggests that Cather hired Reynolds, set him loose on the magazine marketplace, and had little interest in what he did with her work except to collect payment, minus 10 percent. In this version of the story, Cather distanced herself from Reynolds because his profession was indicative of the dirty business side of publishing and she, a consummate artist, had no time for (or interest in) such things. According to Janis P. Stout, Cather has not, until recently, "been regarded as a person *or* a writer for whom the material world held much importance" (2). This version of Cather is not accurate, but her published pronouncements on the subject of art and the artist have contributed to a stereotype that persists to this day. Early in her career Cather wrote that "an artist should not be vexed by human hobbies or human follies" and "should be able to lift himself up into the clear firmament of creation where the world is not" (*Kingdom* 407). Later, she discouraged inexpensive editions of her books and worked to prevent cinematic adaptations of them after her negative experience with the adaptation of *A Lost Lady*. She railed against popular culture and said that "the modern novel, the cinema, and the radio" formed "an equal menace to human culture" (qtd. in Bohlke 155). Even though her expressions of distaste for various elements of consumer culture may have been sincere, her denouncement of the commercialization of literature must be placed within the context of her choices as an author and a businessperson. She verbally rejected the market while simultaneously enacting an individualized version of market engagement. The sincerity of her anti-market maneuvers is not at issue, but as Bourdieu argues, the field of cultural production itself offers writers like Cather a way to engage with the market in precisely this way, through position-takings that eschew commercialism but still engage in a "game in which the conquest of cultural legitimacy" is at stake (137).

In the case of *Death Comes for the Archbishop*, the magazine version ultimately appeared in the *Forum*, not the *Atlantic*, a fact that Reynolds Jr. traces back to the exchange between Cather and Sedgwick in May 1926. In his memoir, Reynolds Jr. refers to this exchange between Cather and Sedgwick, but he tells the story through the interpretive lens of a former agent:

> Sedgwick read *Death Comes for the Archbishop*. To circumvent my father Sedgwick wrote directly to Miss Cather. He told her that he much admired the novel but he asked two questions. Why was the novel offered to the *Atlantic*? What did Miss Cather think of the *Atlantic*? Miss Cather replied that her novel was offered to the *Atlantic* because Paul Reynolds so decided. She stated that she was sure the *Atlantic* was a fine magazine but did not have time to read any magazine regularly. Sedgwick then returned the manuscript to my father with a letter stating that "in view of Miss Cather's attitude," he would not buy it. (27)

The younger Reynolds's version adds detail to the extant archival record. If Sedgwick asked Cather what she thought of the *Atlantic*, she did not reply in the May 28 letter (his letter to her does not survive). Reynolds Jr. offers the anecdote as a way of explaining that "sometimes the outcome of a submission depended on my father's relationship with an editor" and that the entire interchange was a product of the animosity between Reynolds and Sedgwick (26). He also offers the story as an example of the rarely mentioned pact between author and agent, a silent complicity that formed the cornerstone of their functional business relationship. Cather articulated a lack of interest in Reynolds's work as a way of quashing Sedgwick's attempt to establish a direct line of communication between editor and author. Her letter to Sedgwick is performative: while she may express deeply internalized attitudes and values, her position-taking also served a generative purpose within the structure of the cultural field.

The Sedgwick anecdote points to a layer of confidentiality between Reynolds and Cather to which few would have had access. The limited volume of correspondence between author and agent as compared to that of some of his other writers tells a story of a resistant or an often uninterested author who acquiesced occasionally to her persistent agent. According to Roorda, Reynolds's "letters are full of advice and directions, prodding and suggestions to get his authors to do what was best for them" (73). In the case of Cather, she often refused Reynolds or ignored his requests. Reynolds regularly pressed her for more work, while Cather fairly consistently rebuffed his inquiries. Cather's private rejection of his advice, however, does constitute a kind of cultural work. The very act of exploring options for profit and eventually rejecting them is a kind of position-taking in the game of legitimacy. Many of the details of Reynolds and Cather's interactions are unrecoverable, since at least four internal memos refer to phone conversations between the two, and they also appear to have met in person. Reynolds as a rule made sure a paper record existed whenever he received instructions from a client, but his notations are restricted to actions he was instructed to take or not take, such as sending a manuscript to a specific magazine or relaying payment to specific address.[14] The existing archive suggests that the back-and-forth between figures like Reynolds and Cather was an essential ritual of the modern culture of letters, evidence that the publishing world was learning to incorporate anti-commercialism into its workings as a brand of artistic respectability.

Exchanges between Cather and Blanche Knopf, as well as between Cather and Reynolds, pertaining to the serialization of *Death Comes for the Archbishop*, suggest that although Cather was communicating individually with Reynolds and Knopf, Reynolds and Knopf were not necessarily communicating with each other. Reynolds's internal office memo dated 5 February 1926 expresses some confusion over Cather's discussions with the *Forum* regarding the serialization of *Death Comes for the Archbishop*. Cather told Reynolds "she had never made any promises to the Forum." The memo concludes, "It is evident that she has made no promise and they have written her a similar letter to the one they wrote us." In fact, Blanche Knopf had received a letter from the *Forum* and relayed it to Cather with an explanation on 2 February 1926. In her letter, Knopf says the *Forum* "called up and fussed about wanting you." In other words, Cather was making use of Reynolds's skills but not designating an entire sphere of labor to him exclusively. Instead, she consulted the expertise of other professionals, such as Knopf, and certainly did not set Reynolds loose on the market with little or no supervision. She made use of his skills but exercised restraint in how much she was willing to allow him to do on her behalf.

The circumstances under which Cather and Reynolds parted ways complicates the question of institutionalized market rejection, since it seems that Cather ultimately found Reynolds's professional style disagreeable or perhaps even personally encroaching. Reynolds's office memos from the 1910s and 1920s refer to a handful of private, face-to-face meetings or lunches between the two, but more often than not he had to work to communicate with Cather.[15] In at least four letters from the 1920s, Reynolds contacted Edith Lewis at 5 Bank Street to track Cather's travels or otherwise attempt to get in touch with her.[16] In 1928 he wrote to Lewis at her workplace, the J. Walter Thompson Company, stating that he had tried to call Cather but he "judged she has changed your address" (14 January 1928). In the fall of that year he documented by office memo that he had "talked with Miss Cather and she is always to be reached care of Knopf" (1 October 1928). He adds, "I suppose if we wrote to her care of Knopf, the letter wouldn't be opened so we would be perfectly safe in addressing her that way." However, a letter from Alfred Knopf to Reynolds the following winter states, "Miss Cather asked me to answer your letter of January 30 to her," suggesting that Cather had meant to consolidate her business affairs and cut Reynolds out of her professional life (15 February 1929). Reynolds provided Cather with a variety of incentives and benefits that she ultimately rejected, preferring to place her own work or rely on the assistance of Alfred and Blanche Knopf, whom she seems to have trusted more than Reynolds by the close of the 1920s.[17]

Understanding Cather's relationship with Reynolds in connection with the most important aspects of modern publishing culture requires a central reversal in thinking. Reynolds, like Cather, did not thrive merely on financial gain but depended on a respectable reputation. Between 1890 and 1945 the profession of literary agent was emerging, and the legitimacy of the job was a subject of some dispute. According to Allen, "the respectable publishers of the nineties . . . looked upon agents as pests, as contemptible interlopers" (90). Early distrust of agents is an issue that Reynolds's son addresses at length in his memoir. He spends an entire chapter early in his book describing his father's profession as he encountered it as a young apprentice. His overriding concern in this chapter is the respectability of the office and its performed service. "This was a formal age," he says, "and my father was a formal man. Air-conditioning for offices did not exist and on the hottest summer day my father would not remove his coat or unbutton his high starched collar" (16). Reynolds Jr. portrays his father's professional demeanor, his deference toward editors and writers, and his disrespect of hack agents who took fees from unknown amateurs. He explains, "The pseudo agents make their living by charging amateur authors a fee for the reading of each of their manuscripts. An amateur who pays the fee hopes the pseudo agent will sell his manuscript to a publisher" (18–19). His digression about pseudo agents points to a desire to differentiate the respectable work of the legitimate agent from the suspicious activities of hack pretenders. He tells a story of how his father showed discretion by writing a summary of payment to Eleanor Hallowell Abbott in code to protect her from her gossiping neighbors (23). He also recalls the case of Thornton Wilder, who, unprotected by a literary agent, naively signed an exploitive contract with a book publisher (28). As with all memoirs, the reliability of Reynolds Jr.'s narrative deserves a certain amount of skepticism. Regardless, the precise veracity of these descriptions is less important than the apparent concern Reynolds Jr. is responding to as he describes the agent's role in the publishing world. A sense of propriety was a deep-seated concern.

Likewise, Allen's "biographical sketch" of Reynolds dedicates a significant amount of attention to Reynolds's conservative salesmanship and overall decency. According to Allen, "Though his life work has consisted in selling, his technique is far removed from that suggested these days by the word salesmanship. There is no tub-thumping in it, no oratory, no frenzy of enthusiasm, no attempt to hypnotize the editor into signing on the dotted line" (85–86). Allen was hired by the Reynolds family to write this account, and he conducted the research for the book without ever explaining his intentions to Reynolds. The book was privately printed after Reynolds died. The document's bias is clear, but as with Reynolds Jr.'s memoir, its rhetorical goals are more significant than its accuracy. "The prices that he names are invariably high," Allen states, "but when he gets them it is not through high pressure methods. It is rather because editors know that through long experience he has gained an almost uncanny knowledge of his markets and of the sum which any particular manuscript can be expected to bring" (86). Allen's interest in describing Reynolds's conservative salesmanship, for example, shows how important the idea of respectability was to Reynolds and his family. Allen's eventual claim that "the feeling against agents . . . died because there were men acting as agents who were incorruptible" is equally loaded (93).

A 1916 letter to Wilbur Daniel Steele in which Reynolds tries to convince Steele to take him on as an agent exemplifies how Reynolds used salesmanship to craft himself as a trustworthy commodity: "I have sold stories of authors like Booth Tarkington, Mary Robert Rinehart, Mary Raymond Shipman Andrews, Richard Washburn Child, Fannie Hurst, Gouverneur Morris,

H. G. Wells, Henry Kitchell Webster, and so forth. I have only sold their work because I got them more money than they've got themselves. I am sure I could do this for you if you'd let me try!" (15 January 1916). At the heart of Reynolds's pitch is the promise of more money, but Reynolds knew all too well that his offer did not appeal exclusively to the greed of authors. By using the phrase "I could do this for you" he invites a prospective client to put something bothersome in his hands. In this sense he is selling liberation. Further, in order to convince authors to take him on, he had to convince them he was reputable and trustworthy. If authors had to spend as much time guarding themselves against sneaky agents, the appeal of a proxy would be lost. Hence the mention of his top clients, which subtly asserts his credibility.

The example of Cather and Reynolds points to the way modern American literature was framed, defined, evaluated, and edited—in essence, given meaning—by interactions between authors and intermediary professionals, including publishers, editors, and agents. The same cultural conditions that gave rise to these figures—in the United States, the emergence of a national, mass-market literature—created an environment in which avant-gardism and art for art's sake (i.e., stylistic modernism) had elite status. New hierarchies, however, affected literary figures at various points of the spectrum between avant-garde and mass popularity. In the modern marketplace, position-takings defined all parties in relation to both symbolic capital and financial profit. A range of authors enlisted middlemen like Reynolds to aid in that very process of negotiating both prestige and money. Though the work of literary agents was perhaps more subtle than that of editors who demanded manuscript revisions or publishers who marketed critically acclaimed masterpieces, their function was no less substantive.

These questions of the position-takings of authors and secondary literary laborers return us to the exchange in Cather's introduction to *My Ántonia*. The moment of exchange between an unnamed author and her childhood friend serves as an act of position-taking in relation to the secondary literary laborers Cather encountered repeatedly as a writer of the modern period. Cather's choice of narrative form in *My Ántonia* is itself an act of position-taking, since Cather complicates point of view in a way that aligns her with the modernists. The subject matter of the introduction further represents an act of position-taking, as estranged friends, former denizens of the West both living in New York, meet on a train and begin to talk of their old friend Ántonia. They agree, "more than any person we remembered, this girl seemed to mean to us the country, the conditions, the whole adventure of our childhood" (xi–xii). The two travelers form a pact: both will catalog their impressions of Ántonia. According to the fiction of the introduction, the frame tale's narrator—crucially an author figure—performs an act of secondary literary labor that is at once functional and intimate. On a pragmatic level, by acting as an intermediary, she enables Jim's story to cross over from manuscript to print and thus be accessible to readers. More importantly, the act of exchange requires a certain amount of credibility on the part of the intermediary. Only a secondary literary laborer who shares Jim's sympathies for the prairie, who is a member of "a kind of freemasonry," has earned the right to take possession of and disseminate Jim's narrative (10). This moment of exchange becomes a discursive meditation on the relationship between narrative and cultural legitimacy, a reenactment of the kind of position-taking Cather had repeatedly engaged in throughout her career. As a writer, Cather walked a middle path, triangulating with professionals like Reynolds and the Knopfs and others, to enact a strategy that balanced profit and respectability. Cather and Reynolds's relationship, with all its limits, exemplifies the intricate negotiations required by the modern literary marketplace.

NOTES

1. According to Jo Ann Middleton, "With *My Ántonia* Cather begins the series of experiments with point of view; *A Lost Lady* and *One of*

Ours are also technical masterpieces that resolve the issue of point of view. Indeed, Cather's experiments with point of view are one aspect of her work that ties her so closely with the twentieth-century modernists" (41). For more on the stylistics of Cather's modernism, see Middleton. For more on the significance of *My Ántonia*'s autobiographical mode, see Thacker.

2. The author figure of the introduction is never identified as such, but the implication is that the narrator is someone like Cather if not an imaginary version of Cather herself. "I can't see . . . why you have never written anything about Ántonia," Jim says "impetuously" (xii). The unnamed author enters into a contract with Jim to "set down on paper all that I remembered of Ántonia if he would do the same" (xii). According to the narrator, "My own story was never written" (xiii). The narrative is presented as Jim's half of this exchange, "substantially as he brought it" to the introduction's narrator.

3. Like many other authors of the period, Cather had an exclusive arrangement with her book publishers, first Houghton Mifflin and then A. A. Knopf. Reynolds did not play a role in the publication of her books.

4. Throughout the decade when she most actively enlisted Reynolds's services, Cather triangulated her efforts with the offices of Alfred A. Knopf, Inc. Blanche Knopf was vice-president of the company from 1921 until 1957, when she became president. Cather's letters to Blanche have the familiarity of a personal friend and professional confidant. A letter from Blanche dated 16 January 1923 refers to a lunch or dinner invitation at the Knopfs' home. Letters from February and April 1924 indicate that Blanche handled the licensing of the film rights of *A Lost Lady*. Cather had dealings the Knopf office pertaining to the serialization of *A Lost Lady*, *The Professor's House*, *My Mortal Enemy*, and *Death Comes for the Archbishop*. Thanks to Melissa Homestead for providing me with transcriptions of materials from the Knopf Archives.

5. Middleton's analysis of Cather's modernism, for example, is subtitled "A Study of Style and Technique."

6. Those often labeled "high modernists," whether it be Eliot, Hemingway, Mann, Stein, or Toomer, have been generally thought of as anti-market, but they all engaged in deliberate strategies to sell their work or legitimate it through institutions of prestige. According to Jaffe, the "prominent modernists . . . were canny about fashioning their literary careers—indeed, fashioning the very notion of a literary

career—than is often appreciated" (3). For more information on the blurred line between modernism and mass-market literature, see Glass, Jaffe, and Turner.

7. Turner examines how B. W. Huebsch, A. A. Knopf, Alfred Harcourt, and Scribner's created a commercially viable environment for modernism in America.

8. According to Woodress, Cather in 1917 was "frank to admit that she needed money, and the four hundred and fifty dollars she got for 'The Gold Slipper' helped offset the inflation that was accompanying the war" (282). Proceeds from the sale of "Coming, Aphrodite!" to *Smart Set* in 1920 financed a trip to Europe (315).

9. Roorda adds, "Lewis knew Reynolds at about this time from her work at *Every Week* magazine, so perhaps she seconded Greenslet's recommendation" (73).

10. Letters referring to this relationship include Garland to Reynolds, n.d., Reynolds to Wells, 2 May 1906, Reynolds to Tarkington, 14 October 1912, and Cather to Reynolds, 19 September 1917.

11. Reynolds participated in the sale of *A Lost Lady* to *Century* (Reynolds, Office Memo, 27 March 1923). However, Cather thanked Blanche Knopf for her efforts in placing the novel with *Century* and credited her with its ultimate acceptance (Cather to Blanche Knopf, 29 December 1922). Cather also indicated that she had sent the manuscript herself to other magazines (Cather to Blanche Knopf, 30 December 1922). Payment from the *Century* for *A Lost Lady* was sent through the Knopf office (Blanche Knopf to Cather, 16 January 1923).

12. According to Roorda, Cather told Reynolds "there was no chance of serializing *My Ántonia*" (73). Cather's close relationship with the Knopfs may begin to explain why Cather became more interested in serialization. In a letter to Alfred A. Knopf, Cather says that she would like to serialize *A Lost Lady* because of the money. She suggests that hiring a competent secretary would give her more time to write. Her tone suggests that her willingness to do so should have been self-evident (22 November 1922).

13. Cather wrote Alfred Knopf that magazines gave her a shudder, but she does not explain this prejudice (22 November 1922).

14. See Reynolds, Office Memos, 22 April 1924, 16 January 1925, and 5 February 1926.

15. See Reynolds, Office Memos, 11 May 1916 and 27 March 1923.

16. See Reynolds to Lewis, 8 November 1923, 16 June 1924, 29 September 1925, and 1 October 1925.

17. Throughout the 1920s, Cather seems to be more comfortable dealing with Blanche Knopf than with Reynolds. While Reynolds struggled to keep his contact information for Cather up to date, Cather addresses Blanche colloquially in several letters (18 September 1925; September 1926).

WORKS CITED

Allen, Frederick Lewis. *Paul Revere Reynolds: A Biographical Sketch.* Privately printed, 1944.

Bohlke, L. Brent, ed. *Willa Cather in Person: Interviews, Speeches, and Letters.* Lincoln: U of Nebraska P, 1986.

Bourdieu, Pierre. *The Field of Cultural Production.* New York: Columbia UP, 1993.

Cather, Willa. Financial Ledger. James R. and Susan J. Rosowski Cather Collection (MS 228). Archives and Special Collections, U of Nebraska–Lincoln Libraries, Lincoln.

———. *The Kingdom of Art.* Ed. Bernice Slote. Lincoln: U of Nebraska P, 1966.

———. Letter to Alfred A. Knopf. 22 Nov. 1922. Alfred A. Knopf, Inc., Records, 1873–1996. Harry Ransom Center, U of Texas, Austin.

———. Letters to Blanche Knopf. Alfred A. Knopf, Inc., Records, 1873–1996. Harry Ransom Center, U of Texas, Austin.

———. Letter to Paul Revere Reynolds. 19 Sept. 1917. Paul Revere Reynolds Papers 1899–1980. Butler Library, Columbia U, New York NY.

———. Letter to Ellery Sedgwick. 28 May 1926. Paul Revere Reynolds Papers 1899–1980. Butler Library, Columbia U, New York NY.

———. *My Ántonia.* Willa Cather Scholarly Edition. Ed. Charles W. Mignon with Kari A. Ronning. Lincoln: U of Nebraska P, 1994.

Garland, Hamlin. Letter to Paul Revere Reynolds, n.d. Paul Revere Reynolds Papers 1899–1980. Butler Library, Columbia U, New York NY.

Glass, Loren. *Authors Inc.: Literary Celebrity in the United States, 1880–1980.* New York: New York UP, 2004.

Hepburn, James G. *The Author's Empty Purse and the Rise of the Literary Agent.* Oxford: Oxford UP, 1968.

Jaffe, Aaron. *Modernism and the Culture of Celebrity*. Cambridge: Cambridge UP, 2005.

Johnson, Randal. "Editor's Introduction." Pierre Bourdieu. *The Field of Cultural Production*. New York: Columbia UP, 1993.

Knopf, Alfred A. Letter to Paul Revere Reynolds, 15 Feb. 1929. Alfred A. Knopf, Inc., Records, 1873–1996. Harry Ransom Center, U of Texas, Austin.

Knopf, Blanche. Letters to Willa Cather. Alfred A. Knopf, Inc., Records, 1873–1996. Harry Ransom Center, U of Texas, Austin.

Middleton, Jo Ann. *Willa Cather's Modernism*. Madison NJ: Fairleigh Dickinson UP, 1990.

Reynolds, Paul Revere. Letters to Edith Lewis. Paul Revere Reynolds Papers 1899–1980. Butler Library, Butler Library, New York NY.

———. Letters to Upton Sinclair. Paul Revere Reynolds Papers 1899–1980. Butler Library, Columbia U, New York NY.

———. Letter to Wilbur Daniel Steele. 15 Jan. 1916. Paul Revere Reynolds Papers 1899–1980. Butler Library, Columbia U, New York NY.

———. Letters to Booth Tarkington. Paul Revere Reynolds Papers 1899–1980. Butler Library, Columbia U, New York NY.

———. Letter to H. G. Wells. 2 May 1906. Paul Revere Reynolds Papers 1899–1980. Butler Library, Columbia U, New York NY.

———. Office Memos. Paul Revere Reynolds Papers 1899–1980. Butler Library, Columbia U, New York NY.

Reynolds, Paul Revere, Jr. *The Middle Man: The Adventures of a Literary Agent*. New York: Morrow, 1971.

Roorda, Rebecca. "Willa Cather in the Magazines: 'The Business of Art'" *Willa Cather Pioneer Memorial Newsletter* 44.3 (Winter–Spring 2000): 71–75.

Stout, Janis P. Introduction. *Willa Cather and Material Culture: Real-world Writing, Writing the Real World*. Ed. Janis P. Stout. Tuscaloosa: U of Alabama P, 2005. 1–12.

Thacker, Robert. "'It's Through Myself That I Knew and Felt Her': S. S. McClure's *My Autobiography* and the Development of Willa Cather's Autobiographical Realism." *American Literary Realism* 33 (2001): 123–42.

Turner, Catherine. *Marketing Modernism between the Two World Wars*. Amherst: U of Massachusetts P, 2003.

West, James L. W., III. *American Authors and the Literary
Marketplace since 1900.* Philadelphia: U of Pennsylvania P, 1988.

Wilson, Christopher P. *The Labor of Words: Literary Professionalism
in the Progressive Era.* Athens: U of Georgia P, 1985.

Woodress, James. *Willa Cather: A Literary Life.* Lincoln: U of
Nebraska P, 1987.

9　Thea at the Art Institute

JULIE OLIN-AMMENTORP

In an important scene in *The Song of the Lark*, Thea Kronborg finally goes to the Art Institute of Chicago—something she has been urged to do for months. Cather not only describes Thea's joy at her discovery of this museum but also tells readers which sculptures and paintings Thea finds particularly interesting. Although scholars have noted the importance of this episode in the novel and identified the paintings that draw Thea's attention (Duryea), the young singer's experience in the Art Institute merits closer analysis—an analysis not so much of the artworks themselves as of Thea's response to them. Through this short episode (it covers less than two pages in the novel), Cather conveys a good deal about this provincial girl who is in the early, still-inarticulate stages of turning herself into a sophisticated artist. Cather implies a progression in Thea's gradually growing understanding of beauty, with her experience in the Art Institute building on her childhood experiences in Colorado and laying the groundwork for her later insights into art in Panther Canyon. Further, reflection on the painting central to Thea's experience in the Art Institute, Jules Breton's *The Song of the Lark*, suggests that that artwork may have influenced Cather's technique in the novel's concluding pages, and, perhaps, her later shift from the "full-blooded method" of *The Song of the Lark* (Cather, "My First Novels" 96) to a sparer, more modernist style.

When Thea arrives in Chicago to study piano, she is unaware that she needs an education not only in music but in the arts in general. As her teacher Andor Harsanyi observes, she is strangely "incurious" about the opportunities Chicago offers (463). Her landlady, Mrs. Lorch, and her landlady's daughter, Mrs. Anderson, different as they are from Harsanyi, also remark that Thea has "so little initiative about 'visiting points of interest'" (464). When Mrs. Lorch asks Thea over dinner one evening if she has been to the Art Institute, Thea asks her if that is "the place with the big lions out in front? I saw it when I went to Montgomery Ward's. Yes, I thought the lions were beautiful" (464). For the still-provincial Thea, the Art Institute is initially notable only for its lions and its location—on the route to the "big mail-order store" which, with Chicago's meat-processing plants (464), are the two "points of interest" that most intrigue the Colorado native. As part of her effort to be sociable "without committing herself to anything" (464), Thea "reassure[s]" Mrs. Lorch and Mrs. Anderson that she will go to the Art Institute "some day" (465).

When Thea does finally take herself there one "bleak day in February" (465), the museum is a revelation to her; she leaves it chastising herself for not having gone sooner and promising herself that she will return regularly. This is a pledge she keeps; Cather implies that Thea develops a regular pattern at the Institute, always visiting certain artworks when she is there. With one exception, Cather is quite specific about the works to which Thea turns her attention. But despite her later remark that in this novel she "told everything about everybody" ("My First Novels" 96), Cather leaves it largely to the reader to discern why these particular works are so important to Thea. In doing so Cather puts her readers in Thea's position: if Thea is drawn to these works repeatedly by some quality she cannot quite define, so we, too, are drawn back to this passage to wonder exactly how each work contributes to Thea's growth as an artist.

Thea always visits the casts first, finding them both "more simple and more perplexing" than the paintings; they also seem to her "more important, harder to overlook" (465). Cather mentions four casts (i.e., copies of famous sculptures, widely found in American museums of that era), three of which Thea examines only briefly. She almost dismisses *The Dying Gladiator* (or *Dying Gaul*) because she is already familiar with it from Byron's "Childe Harold," a poem she has pored over while ill in bed; for her, the cast is "strongly associated with Dr. Archie and childish illnesses" (466).[1] Although her reaction to the Venus di Milo is not as strong as Paul's in "Paul's Case" (he makes "an evil gesture at the Venus of Milo as he passed her on the stairway" [470]), Thea is baffled by her: "she could not see why people thought her so beautiful" (464). Similarly, she does "not think the Apollo Belvedere 'at all handsome'" (466).

The very familiarity of these casts leads Thea to notice them but also to dismiss them. As works apparently already known in Moonstone, they are examples of merely conventional beauty—something against which Thea has rebelled since her first intimation that her own abilities were superior to those of the popular Lily Fisher. Indeed, Thea also rejects Moonstone's admiration of Lily Fisher's good looks. Cather both conveys Thea's attitude and subtly endorses it when she describes Lily as looking "exactly like the beautiful children on soap calendars" (348). From Thea's point of view, perhaps the young Venus di Milo or Apollo Belvedere would have been suitable models for advertisements geared to a broad, bland public.

In contrast, a fourth cast—the only one Cather does not identify by name—fascinates Thea: "Better than anything else she liked a great equestrian statue of an evil, cruel-looking general with an unpronounceable name. She used to walk round and round this terrible man and his terrible horse, frowning at him, brooding upon him, as if she had to make some momentous decision about him" (466). This is probably Andrea del Verrocchio's statue of Bartolomeo Colleoni (fig. 1).[2] Part of the attraction of this sculpture may be its novelty to Thea: unlike the other casts mentioned, Thea is not already familiar with it. Moreover, the statue's expression—cruel, not calm or composed—is notably different from that of the other casts. But clearly there is more to it than that. Cather's description of Thea "walk[ing] round and round this terrible man" suggests the extent to which Thea is drawn to this cast, as does her sense that "she had to make some momentous decision about him." Thea is in the early stages of her education as an artist; Harsanyi thinks of her as one of the most "intelligent" but also one of the most "ignorant" of his pupils (446). It is not surprising, then, that Thea cannot explain her own fascination with this statue, and does not even try to.

Her interest in the "evil, cruel-looking general" is, however, a further manifestation of Thea's interest in powerful leaders. Earlier in the novel Cather recounted Thea's purchase of a photograph of a bust of Julius Caesar for her room at Mrs. Lorch's—a purchase that baffles her landlady but is an extension of Thea's interest in "Caesar's 'Commentaries.' . . . [S]he loved to read about great generals" (442). Within this context, her fascination with the equestrian statue suggests her recognition and admiration of power, which in turn suggests that she may recognize—if only subconsciously—that power, and even a certain ruthlessness, are also elements in herself that she will need to come to terms with in order to succeed in her profession. Thus her feeling that she needs "to make some momentous decision about" the general, though on its surface illogical, makes sense at a deeper level: she may already intuit that she will someday need to make some difficult decisions, not about him, but about herself. The fact that the leaders who fascinate her—Caesar and the "cruel-looking general"—are men is also significant; both exhibit power she does not associate with women. Although she will never, of course, become a military or political leader, her career will require her to make difficult decisions, occasionally decisions that will cause others to see her as hard.

For instance, in a scene Cather implies rather than depicts, Thea decides not to leave her career at a crucial moment to re-

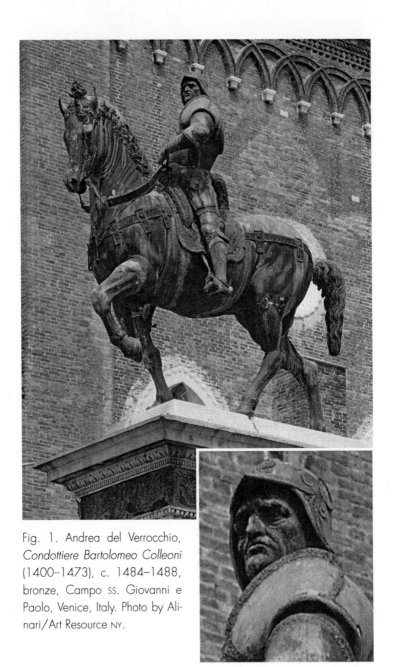

Fig. 1. Andrea del Verrocchio, *Condottiere Bartolomeo Colleoni* (1400–1473), c. 1484–1488, bronze, Campo ss. Giovanni e Paolo, Venice, Italy. Photo by Alinari/Art Resource NY.

turn to Colorado to see her dying mother. Although Thea was in Germany at the time and the trip to see her mother would have taken her half a year (632), even Dr. Archie fails to understand her decision; afterward, he may or may not be swayed by Fred Ottenburg's explanation that "she positively couldn't [leave Dresden]. . . . In that game you can't lose a single trick. She was ill herself, but she sang. Her mother was ill, and she sang" (628). Fred's remark emphasizes the cost of this decision to Thea herself, both physically (she was ill) and emotionally (her mother was dying). Thea's only direct testament to what this decision cost her comes late in the novel, when she tells Fred that she can, if she needs to, give up his friendship: "I've only a few friends, but I can lose every one of them, if it has to be. I learned how to lose when my mother died" (688). Circling the equestrian statue, she may well be intuiting the cost, both to herself and to others, of power and success.

Such a possibility would also explain why Thea eventually finds the casts "gloomy"—and why she is so glad to "r[u]n up the wide staircase to the pictures. There she liked best the ones that told stories" (466), Cather notes. The first is Jean-Léon Gérôme's *The Grief of the Pasha* (fig. 2, p. 189), a colorful Orientalist[3] painting that probably would have appealed to Thea not only because of its implied narrative—the Pasha's beloved pet, a handsome tiger, has died—but because of its extravagant beauty. Cather describes the painting in detail: "The Pasha was seated on a rug, beside a green candle almost as big as a telegraph pole, and before him was stretched his dead tiger, a splendid beast, and there were pink roses scattered about him" (466). As with many passages in the novel, Cather selects language that reflects the prairie girl's perspective, particularly the comparison of a candle to a telegraph pole. She also hints that Thea, though she is old enough to be on her own studying music in Chicago, is still a girl in some ways. Cather's observation in *O Pioneers!* that "There is often a good deal of the child left in people who have had to grow up too soon" (23) helps to explain why Thea is drawn by this painting, which conveys, regardless of its exotic setting, the relatively simple heartbreak of losing a pet. Gérôme's painting would be quite appealing to a girl who, having put the provinces behind her, simultaneously wants to see the world and longs for home, as Cather suggests through Thea's wish that her little brothers Gunner and Axel were there with her to see the painting.[4] Further, this painting is also, like the *Bartolomeo Colleoni*, a portrait of power—both the Pasha and his tiger—though in this case of power subdued and sympathetic.

The second painting, Jean-François Millet's *Peasants Bringing Home a Calf Born in the Fields* (fig. 3, p. 191), is summarized in a single sentence: "She loved, too, a picture of some boys bringing in a newborn calf on a litter, the cow walking beside it and licking it" (466). This painting also tells a story about an animal, but a simpler, happier one, a story of birth rather than death. At a deeper level, the painting may appeal to Thea because of its portrait of a harmonious family, one that works together: while the mother or older sister looks on, two young men carry the calf toward the barn, where two small children hover in the doorway. Thea's perception of the two figures carrying the calf as "boys" rather than men (they are adult-sized figures) may suggest that she misses her older brothers, who (at this point in the narrative) have not yet alienated themselves from her; the small children may remind her of the younger siblings of whom she is so fond. Even the cow licking her calf may be a subtle reminder of maternal love (albeit in bovine form) and of all the support Thea has received from her mother. Consciously, however, the implied narrative and the familiarity of the scene are no doubt what appeal to Thea; she feels at home in front of the painting.

In her choice of these paintings, Cather tells us much about Thea's character at this point in her development: both seem exactly what might appeal to a young and unsophisticated girl from Moonstone. The exotic setting of the Gérôme probably attracts her by its portrayal of a world far from the one she knows, as well by its expression of a strong but simple emotion; the Mil-

Fig. 2. Jean-Léon Gérôme, *The Grief of the Pasha*, 1882, oil on canvas on masonite panel, 36 3/8 x 29 in., Joslyn Art Museum, Omaha, Nebraska. Gift of Francis T. B. Martin. Used by permission.

let may attract her with its homey familiarity. In both, the narrative element is so strong that the paintings function almost as illustrations to the "stories" they tell, perhaps not that different from the "oil-chromos" Thea has seen in Moonstone (cf. Duryea 18), the painting of Napoleon's retreat, re-created in cloth, that she admires at the Kohlers' (317), or the "large colored print of a brightly lighted church in a snowstorm, on Christmas Eve," which, along with her photograph of the bust of Caesar, hangs in her boardinghouse room (442). Moreover, the glowing colors of the Millet, along with its depiction of a family that appears to function more harmoniously than the rather divided Kronborg family, may encourage Thea to cast a warm glow over her childhood years, allowing her (or even encouraging her) to miss her family during her first year away from home. On a more objective level, both paintings use intense colors; they also emphasize human figures, placing them in the foreground, perhaps reflecting Cather's statement in 1894 that "We want men who can paint with emotion. . . . We haven't time for pastels in prose and still life; we want pictures of human men and women" (*World and Parish* 1: 131; qtd. in Duryea 6). In short, they have an immediate appeal for Thea.

As with the casts, Thea dismisses—even ignores—some of the great paintings in the museum. Immediately after describing the Millet painting of the calf, Cather tells us that Thea "did not like or dislike" the Corot hanging next to it because "she never saw it" (466). To some extent, she may not "see" the Corot because Mrs. Anderson, whom Thea dislikes, has waxed enthusiastic over the painter's work (465); ignoring the painting is a way of distancing herself from Mrs. Anderson. An even stronger reason, however, may be the fact that much of Corot's work also differs significantly from the paintings that draw Thea's attention. Unlike the Millet and the Gérôme, most Corot paintings do not tell definite stories. Neither do they use the intense color palette of the Millet and Gérôme; instead, the colors are more delicate and atmospheric—Thea would probably say "dull"—and of-

Fig. 3. Jean-François Millet, *Peasants Bringing Home a Calf Born in the Fields*, 1864, oil on canvas, 81.1 x 100 cm, Henry Field Memorial Collection, 1894.1063, The Art Institute of Chicago. Photography © The Art Institute of Chicago.

tentimes, figures are small and set in the middle distance.[5] Even in her disregard of some art, however, Thea begins to find herself as an artist: she is learning to trust herself and her own impulses. She has begun to change; like Lucy Gayheart during her months in Chicago, "the changes were all in the direction of becoming more and more herself. She was no longer afraid to like or to dislike anything too much. It was as if she had found some authority for taking what was hers and rejecting what seemed unimportant" (*Lucy Gayheart* 698). Thea's response to art is, as Susan Rosowski has remarked, "unsophisticated but genuine" (58); finding her genuine self is one part of Thea's larger education.

After ignoring the Corot, Thea goes on to the painting that arrests her attention, which is, of course, Breton's *The Song of the Lark* (fig. 4). This is the painting that Thea feels is "her picture. . . . That was a picture indeed. . . . She told herself that that picture was 'right'" (466). Cather then throws down the gauntlet to readers by adding, "Just what she meant by this, it would take a clever person to explain. But to her, the word ["right"] covered the almost boundless satisfaction she felt when she looked at the picture" (466). Yet in issuing a challenge, Cather is also inviting the reader to speculate about why Thea feels so strongly that this is "her picture[,]" a painting that is "right," and why she takes "almost boundless satisfaction" in it.

To some extent, Thea's admiration of this painting is on a continuum with her admiration of the other two paintings; like them, it is a narrative—though one even simpler than Millet's narrative about the calf. In Breton's, a peasant girl is on her way to the fields at daybreak when she is arrested by the beautiful music of a lark's song. Yet although it implies a narrative, the Breton differs from the Millet and the Gérôme in an essential way: the two previous paintings depicted their subjects, but here the putative subject is not portrayed. A bird's song cannot be shown in a representational canvas like this one; the lark itself also goes unportrayed. Instead, the bird and its beautiful song are implied by the girl's riveted attention, by her stance and her raised face. In short, this brief narrative is a lyrical moment— much like a lyric poem or, for that matter, an aria in an opera, which springs from the opera's narrative but often freezes time for the duration of a song.

As in the other paintings, in the Breton Thea finds much that is familiar. Like the Millet painting, the Breton depicts a scene with which Thea, given her background, is generally familiar: the sunrise over a rural agricultural countryside. As Rosowski has written, the scene "involve[s] a character's possession of her own region" (58); the painting helps Thea claim her native landscape, much as Cather herself claimed it in writing *O Pioneers!* ("My First Novels" 93–94). Even more importantly, Thea may

Fig. 4. Jules Adolphe Breton, *The Song of the Lark*, 1884, oil on canvas, 81.1 x 100 cm, Henry Field Memorial Collection, 1894.1033, The Art Institute of Chicago. Photography © The Art Institute of Chicago.

see herself in the girl. Throughout the novel Cather has made it clear that Thea is not beautiful in a conventional way, if she is beautiful at all; when she is in her late teens, for instance, her mother thinks that "She would make a very handsome woman . . . if she would only get rid of that fierce look she had sometimes" (488–89). Similarly, Mrs. Nathanmeyer remarks to Fred Ottenburg when Thea is nineteen that "in ten years she may have quite a regal beauty, or she may have a heavy, discontented face, all dug out in channels" (533). Although Thea is not consciously thinking of her own face as she looks at the girl in Breton's painting, she sees the peasant girl's face as "heavy" (466), making her, one might think, an unlikely candidate for a portrayal in art; she is no Venus di Milo, nor even a Lily Fisher. At this stage it may be hard for Thea, much as she loves music, to imagine she has either the appearance or the ability to become "Kronborg," an internationally known singer. In fact, at this point in her development she has not yet accepted that her greatest potential is not as a pianist but as a vocalist.

But visual art, like literature, has a potentially validating and affirming effect. As Thea stands lost in front of "her picture," the seeds of that acceptance may be germinating within her. Like the Colorado minister's daughter, the plain French peasant girl is a provincial "nobody," yet she has been elevated to the status of art; why should Thea not also be worthy of art? The peasant girl is the focus of many eyes in a museum; looking at her may help Thea imagine that, despite her lack of conventional beauty, she will eventually become the center of the audience's gaze as she stands upon the stage of an opera house. Thea may divine that she has something superior to conventional beauty; Mrs. Harsanyi sees Thea's potential "to look strikingly handsome" (450), and Mrs. Nathanmeyer sees "great possibilities" in her appearance (533). (In contrast, Lily Fisher's conventional beauty dwindles into mediocrity, with Cather describing her in the epilogue as a "fair-haired, dimpled matron" [700]—not unattractive, but decidedly lacking Thea's ability to be the cynosure of all eyes.)

Yet Thea surpasses the peasant girl, becoming, in terms of Breton's painting, both the listening girl and the singing lark, functioning not only as the object of the audience's gaze but also as the creative, active subject—the singer who rivets their attention. The painting evokes the last lines of Percy Bysshe Shelley's poem "To a Skylark" so strongly that it is hard not to wonder if those lines were echoing in Cather's mind as she wrote this passage, and perhaps in Thea's (well read as she is in the romantics) as she stands in front of Breton's painting:

> Teach me half the gladness
>> That thy brain must know,
> Such harmonious madness
>> From my lips would flow
> The world should listen then—as I am listening now. (1035)

Surely Shelley's lines, or even the hint of them in Breton's painting, would inspire any young singer.

Thea's experience in the Art Institute, and in particular in front of Breton's painting, suggests that her trips to the museum provide an important stage in her education. Cather emphasized the need to seize an education in the arts, believing that "the individual can possess the treasure of the world's great music, literature, and art as his own" (Peck 109–10). In this view she seems very much aligned with those who were, in the period, building and laying out many of the country's great museums; they believed that the public could educate itself through a study of well-displayed objects (Conn 4). Yet Cather's portrayal of Thea in the Art Institute implies that such an education does not always mean "going hard at it," as Fred says of Thea. Sometimes the opposite is true: the most valuable education a museum can offer is for the visitor to wander at will, soaking in the objects that attract him or her and ignoring those that do not. In the Art Institute Thea finds not a school but rather "a place of retreat, as the sand hills and the Kohlers' garden used to be; . . . a place in which she could relax and play" (465). While the equation between an art museum, a garden, and a geological feature might seem peculiar on its surface (much like Thea's sense that she needs to make a decision about the general on horseback), it too falls into place. Cather had contemplated calling this novel *Artist's Youth* ("Preface" 433); writing a *künstlerroman* almost necessitates describing the artist's earliest introduction to the beautiful, which, for Thea, includes the Kohlers' garden and the sand hills. Her experience in the Art Institute takes her love of beauty another step; Thea is now seeing and selecting among works that are (unlike the garden or the sand hills) not only beautiful but which, by their very inclusion in the museum, carry the cultural cachet of being designated "art."

Thea's fascination with Breton's painting, her sense of its "rightness" and her sense that it is "her painting," also lays the groundwork for the next stage in her artistic development: her conscious awakening to the very concept of art in Panther Canyon. In an often-quoted passage, Thea stands in the stream on the floor of the canyon, thinking of the pottery the ancestral puebloans had made to contain the running water: "what was any art but an effort to make a sheath, a mould in which to imprison for a moment the shining, elusive element which is life itself,—life hurrying past us and running away, too strong to stop, too sweet to lose? The Indian women had held it in their jars. In the sculpture she had seen in the Art Institute, it had been caught in a flash of arrested motion" (552). In this passage Cather makes extraordinary connections across time, space, culture, and medium, drawing parallels between Italian Renaissance sculpture, American ancestral puebloan ceramics, and twentieth-century opera singing, and in doing so suggests that there are structures common to very different arts from very different cultures. Although Cather does not mention the Breton painting in this passage, it too possesses this quality; the peasant girl in *The Song of the Lark* is, like the cruel general, "caught in a flash of arrested motion." There is much, in short, to account for Thea's "boundless satisfaction," her sense that Breton's canvas is "her picture."

Imagining the scene that Cather suggests but does not actually describe—Thea frozen in admiration of Breton's painting, much as the girl in that work is frozen by her admiration of the lark's song—puts the painting in relation to Cather's own technique in the final pages of her novel; indeed, if the painting did not serve as an actual inspiration for Cather's conclusion, it certainly serves as a visual correlative for it. Breton, as we have seen, implies the beauty of the skylark's song by portraying the peasant girl's reaction; late in the novel, in her only depiction of Thea's performance in a major opera production, Cather conveys Thea's artistry by depicting the reactions of two of her listeners. When the opera begins, Thea's teacher Harsanyi is impatient, his fingers "fluttering on his knee in a rapid tattoo" (694). Cather keeps her readers wondering, like Mrs. Harsanyi, what he is thinking about the performance of his "uncommon" student; he ignores his wife's comment that Thea is a "lovely creature" and then "bow[s] his head" and covers his single eye for much of the act (694–95). It is as if the girl in Breton's painting were unsure about the lark's song. Only when the curtain goes down does Harsanyi express his enthusiasm, praising Thea's performance: "At last . . . somebody with *enough*!" (696). Cather employs the same technique with another member of the audience, Thea's old friend Spanish Johnny. During the performance he is deeply involved in the music, "praying and cursing under his breath" and "shouting 'Bravó! Bravó!' until he was repressed by his neighbors" (698). Cather doesn't describe Thea's singing; instead she conveys its beauty through Johnny's reaction.

Cather may adapt the painting to her own purposes in another way as well. In the penultimate paragraph of the novel proper[6] she describes Johnny as part of the "little crowd" that waits for Thea outside the theater; although the exhausted Thea does not see Johnny, he walks away "wearing a smile which embraced all the stream of life that passed him and the lighted towers that rose into the limpid blue of the evening sky" (699). It is a painterly moment in the text, one in which Cather gives us her own version of Breton's *Song of the Lark*—a version in words instead of paint, in which it is evening instead of morning, and in which, in place of the girl enraptured by the skylark, we have Spanish Johnny who has been listening rapturously to Thea's song. The effect of both songs is the same; and like Breton's oil painting, Cather's painterly description draws the inward eye upward, "into the limpid blue of the . . . sky."

Breton's *Song of the Lark*, along with other artworks Cather saw while she was composing her *Song of the Lark*, may also have influenced Cather's changing sense of literary aesthetics. As mentioned earlier, Cather came to believe that in *The Song of the Lark* she told too much ("My First Novels" 96) and that writers, instead of proliferating details, needed to select and simplify ("Novel Démeublé" 37–40). Paradoxically, what a writer creates is not the words on the page but rather "[w]hatever is felt upon the page without being specifically named there . . . . the overtone divined by the ear but not heard by it, the verbal mood, the emotional aura of the fact or the thing or the deed" ("Novel Démeublé" 41–42). Breton's painting invites the viewer to hear what cannot be depicted, much as Cather's developing aesthetic was to make the reader "fe[el]" certain things "upon the page without . . . specifically nam[ing]" them. There are notes of this aesthetic much earlier in her work; in 1898, for instance (twenty-four years before the publication of "The Novel Démeublé"), she argued that the nature of English as a language was such that the "Anglo-Saxon . . . learned to mean more than he said, and to make his reader feel it" (*World and Parish* 2: 583). But it may have been her contemplation of Breton's canvas that helped her to articulate this principle fully.

An avid viewer and critic of art, particularly painting, Cather saw that although the painting and writing are significantly different media, technique in one could carry over to the other. As a devoted reader of Henry James, she may have well been aware of his remark that "style for one art is style for another, so blessed is the fraternity that binds them together, and the worker in words may take a lesson from the picture-maker" (qtd. in Duryea 17). Certainly Cather was comparing the techniques of literary and visual arts herself by 1900, commenting that Henry Ossawa Tanner's "insistent use of the silvery green of the olives, of the yellow of the parched clay hills of Palestine . . . reminds me of Pierre Loti's faculty of infusing absolute personality into environment, if one may compare two such dissimilar mediums as prose and paint" (*World and Parish* 2: 762). Merrill Maguire Skaggs has remarked on Cather's association with the American impressionists, noting that from them she may have learned "techniques for capturing motion, mood, color and light that, translated to fiction, helped make her stories so startlingly memorable" (48).

Although Cather only implies Thea standing frozen in front of the Breton (though in doing so she is, of course, demonstrating her ability to create "the thing not named"), and although the notion that Cather herself may have learned from Breton's canvas is speculative, Elizabeth Shepley Sergeant gives us a concrete example of Cather soaking in a new aesthetic from a painting. When Sergeant returned to New York from France in late June 1913, Cather met her at the boat and "began at once to study with interest" some "canvases and drawings by the *Fauve*"—even as the customs inspector was still examining Sergeant's luggage, so intrigued was Cather with this "new way of *seeing*" (111). Conversations in the visit that ensued took, as one of their topics, one of the newest developments in painting, cubism (119). It was in this period that Cather was writing "Three American Singers," her important article on Louise Homer, Geraldine Farrar, and Olive Fremstad, and beginning to contemplate writing *The Song of the Lark*, which she would begin in October 1913 (Woodress 255).

The Cather who wrote *The Song of the Lark* may have been like Thea in front of the painting—not quite ready to move on to

JULIE OLIN-AMMENTORP

a different style, but taking in concepts of visual art that would eventually shape her own art. Five years after *The Song of the Lark* she published the short story "Coming, Aphrodite!" One of the two central characters in this story, the artist Don Hedger, has worked with the French painter "C——," probably a reference to Cézanne, whose postimpressionist experiments with composition moved him in the direction of cubism. When Don shows the aspiring singer Eden Bower some of his own sketches in "C——s" style (perhaps something like Cézanne's *The Bay of Marseilles*), she is baffled: "to Miss Bower . . . these landscapes were not at all beautiful, and they gave her no idea of any country whatsoever" (372)—a response that is not surprising in someone who had previously looked only at strictly representational art. Yet Eden's lack of comprehension and lack of curiosity about this "new way of *seeing*" are, like her unabashed materialism, a sign of her limitations as an artist. Her attitude suggests that she is the antithesis of Thea in the Art Institute, lost in thought in front of a canvas—or, for that matter, of Cather herself, standing on the dock at New York, staring at the fauvist canvases and beginning to divine the novel that would become *The Song of the Lark*—absorbing images and concepts that would help her reconceptualize her idea of fiction.

NOTES

1. Due to space restrictions I have not been able to include images of all the artworks discussed in this essay. Many of these may, however, be familiar to readers; most are easily available through an online image search. For art (including sculpture) between 1000 and 1850, the Web Gallery of Art (www.wga.hu) is informative, thorough, and easy to navigate. The website of the Art Institute of Chicago (www.artic .edu) is also an excellent resource and includes images of the Millet and Breton paintings discussed here, as well as several Corots and Cézannes (referred to later in this essay) in its collection.

2. Thanks to Warren Olin-Ammentorp for identifying this equestrian statue from Cather's description, as well as for various consultations

on art, artists, and art websites mentioned in this paper. The equestrian statue is also identified as the *Bartolomeo Colleoni* in the notes to Harbison, ed., *The Song of the Lark* (421). I suspect that Cather did not identify this work by name because it was not in the Art Institute, which did, in fact, house the other works she names in her novel. As indicated in the text, the paintings are identified in Polly P. Duryea's dissertation; taking a clue from her work, I consulted the Art Institute's *Catalogue of Objects in the Museum, Part I: Sculpture and Painting* (1896) to verify the casts which the Art Institute held at that time. Cather may have seen the statue of Colleoni during her July 1908 trip to Venice (see Jewell).

3. I use the term "Orientalist" advisedly. Many readers will be aware of Edward Said's landmark work *Orientalism* and its insightful analysis of the Western perspective on "Eastern" or "Oriental" cultures, including the derogatory aspects of this perspective. Thea's viewing of this painting participates in that perspective, though in a limited way. Gérôme's painting—at least taken on its own, as Thea seems to take it—does not convey the rather mocking attitude toward the Pasha conveyed by Victor Hugo's poem "The Grief of the Pasha," on which the painting is based.

4. It is possible, as Duryea notes (168), that Thea associates the painting with her brothers because she has read them Victor Hugo's poem "The Grief of the Pasha."

5. A comparison of Cather's attitudes with Thea's reminds us that Thea is not wholly autobiographical. Cather herself admired Corot's paintings, for instance (see Duryea 137–39), and understood the limitations of the notion that all "Orientalist" paintings "mean[t] crimson and ultramarine" (*World and Parish* 2: 762).

6. The paragraph referred to became the last paragraph of the chapter (and thus of the novel proper) in Cather's 1932 revision, clearly an improvement from the overly journalistic paragraph she included in the 1915 book version (the basis of the Library of America edition cited here).

WORKS CITED

Breton, Jules. *The Song of the Lark.* 1884. Oil on canvas. Art Institute of Chicago.
Catalogue of Objects in the Museum: Part I: Sculpture and Painting. 2nd ed. Chicago: Art Institute of Chicago, 1896.

Cather, Willa. "Coming, Aphrodite!" 1920. *Willa Cather: Stories, Poems, and Other Writings*. New York: Library of America, 1992. 357–96.

———. *Lucy Gayheart*. *Willa Cather: Later Novels*. New York: Library of America, 1990. 645–774.

———. "My First Novels (There Were Two)." *Willa Cather on Writing: Critical Studies on Writing as an Art*. Lincoln: U of Nebraska P, 1988. 91–97.

———. "The Novel Démeublé." *Willa Cather on Writing: Critical Studies on Writing as an Art*. Lincoln: U of Nebraska P, 1988. 35–43.

———. *O Pioneers!* 1913. Willa Cather Scholarly Edition. Ed. Charles W. Mignon, Susan J. Rosowski, and David Stouck. Lincoln: U of Nebraska P, 1992.

———. "Paul's Case." *Willa Cather: Stories, Poems, and Other Writings*. New York: Library of America, 1992. 468–88.

———. "Preface [to the 1932 edition of *The Song of the Lark*]." *The Song of the Lark*. Ed. Sherrill Harbison. New York: Penguin, 1999. 433–34.

———. *The Song of the Lark*. 1915. *Willa Cather: Early Novels and Stories*. New York: Library of America, 1987. 291–706.

———. *The World and the Parish: Willa Cather's Articles and Reviews, 1893–1902*. Ed. William M. Curtin. 2 vols. Lincoln: U of Nebraska P, 1970.

Cézanne, Paul. *The Bay of Marseilles, seen from Estaque*. c. 1885. Oil on canvas. Art Institute of Chicago.

Conn, Steven. *Museums and American Intellectual Life, 1876–1926*. Chicago: U of Chicago P, 1998.

Duryea, Polly P. "Paintings and Drawings in Willa Cather's Prose: A Catalogue Raisonné." Diss. U of Nebraska, 1993.

Gérôme, Jean-Léon. *The Grief of the Pasha*. 1882. Oil on canvas. Joslyn Art Museum, Omaha NE.

Jewell, Andrew, ed. "Mapping a Writer's World: A Geographic Chronology of Willa Cather's Life." *Willa Cather Archive*. Ed. Andrew Jewell. U of Nebraska–Lincoln. http://cather.unl.edu/geochron.

Millet, Jean-François. *Peasants Bringing Home a Calf Born in the Fields*. 1864. Oil on canvas. Art Institute of Chicago.

Peck, Demaree. *The Imaginative Claims of the Artist in Willa Cather's Fiction*. Selinsgrove PA: Susquehanna UP, 1996.

Rosowski, Susan J. "Willa Cather and the French Rural Tradition of Breton and Millet." *The Rural Vision: France and America in the Late Nineteenth Century.* Ed. Hollister Sturges. Omaha: Joslyn Art Museum, 1987. 53–61.

Sergeant, Elizabeth Shepley. *Willa Cather: A Memoir.* Lincoln: U of Nebraska P, 1963.

Shelley, Percy Bysshe. "To a Skylark." David Perkins, *English Romantic Writers.* New York: Harcourt Brace Jovanovich, 1967. 1033–35.

Skaggs, Merrill Maguire. "Young Willa Cather and the Road to Cos Cob." *Willa Cather's New York: New Essays on Cather in the City.* Ed. Merrill Maguire Skaggs. Madison NJ: Fairleigh Dickinson UP, 2000. 43–59.

Verrocchio, Andrea del. *Bartolomeo Colleoni.* 1480s. Gilded bronze. Venice, Italy.

Woodress, James. *Willa Cather: A Literary Life.* Lincoln: U of Nebraska P, 1987.

10 Art and the Commercial Object as Ekphrastic Subjects in *The Song of the Lark* and *The Professor's House*

DIANE PRENATT

Although we often note Willa Cather's devotion to high art and the frequency with which she depicts art and aesthetic experience in her fiction, we do not seem to have identified her use of ekphrasis as such—ekphrasis being the rhetorical figure that is most simply defined as "the verbal representation of a visual representation" (duBois 45).[1] I do so here in order to illuminate the different values Cather assigns to the work of art and the commercial object as cultural products in *The Song of the Lark* (1915) and *The Professor's House* (1925). In the former, Chicago serves as a setting for the display of what Cather affirms as authentic art; in the latter, the city is a source for the commercial object, which, however aestheticized, Cather views as only a poor substitute for authentic art, mistakenly valued by a society that has lost its artistic integrity. Cather's use of such a classical rhetorical device as ekphrasis is consistent with her characteristic reliance on traditional literary forms and canonical standards of aesthetic judgment, but it also suggests her operation within a new, modernist aesthetic. As Janis Stout argues, modernists (including Cather) expressed an antipathy to com-

204

modity and consumption while simultaneously expanding the function of reading and interpretation to include the world of physical (art) objects (3). Indeed, as I suggest at the conclusion of this essay, Cather uses ekphrasis to advance a critique of modern commodity culture akin to Walter Benjamin's in "The Work of Art in the Age of Mechanical Reproduction." Ekphrasis, with its origins in the classical pastoral tradition, meaningfully echoes the interweaving of the artistic and agrarian worlds in Cather's fiction. Its presence in *The Song of the Lark* and *The Professor's House* also underscores the extent to which the aesthetic was for Cather the primary portal of human experience.

Ekphrasis: "the verbal representation of a visual representation"—as in, for example, Keats's description of a Grecian urn in the eponymous ode or William Carlos Williams's description of Bruegel's painting in "Landscape with the Fall of Icarus." The Western origins of the device are located in ancient Greek literature: Homer's description of the highly decorated shield of Achilles in the *Iliad* is often cited as one of the earliest known examples of ekphrasis. Ekphrasis was cataloged as one of the exercises in the *progymnasmata*, the elementary rhetoric taught in the classical Greek world, formulated in the first century BCE and, adopted by Roman writers, was summarily defined in Horace's dictum *ut pictura poesis* ("as the picture, so the poetry"). It was used most often in pastoral poetry beginning with Theocritus around 300 BCE and in prose narratives of the second century CE, also largely pastoral, such as Longus's *Daphnis and Chloe* (c. 200 CE). Ekphrasis was used as the starting point for a poetic or prose narrative, as it is in Achilles Tatius's *Kleitophon and Leukippé* (c. 150 CE), for example, in which the narrator begins an account of his amorous misadventures with an ostensible description of a painting of Europa riding the back of the Cretan bull; or in Robert Browning's "My Last Duchess" (1842), perhaps a more familiar example, in which the speaker tells the story of his late wife to a viewer of her portrait. Ekphrastic passages were sometimes extended to provide the foundation for

DIANE PRENATT

an entire narrative, the narrator or speaker returning repeatedly to the details of the picture to move the plot forward, as is the case in *Daphnis and Chloe*. Ekphrasis may also "still" the narrative while offering us information to enhance our understanding of a character or situation without moving the plot forward, as it does in the *Aeneid*, when Virgil describes the sorrow Aeneas feels upon seeing the frieze of Trojan War scenes on the temple of Juno in Carthage.

Ancient or modern, the ekphrastic subject is a physical object—a painting, a piece of sculpture, an architectural structure or feature, or a decorated artifact like Achilles's shield. It might be what John Hollander calls a "notional" or imagined subject in distinction from an actual one (209), as Browning's portrait and even Keats's generic vase are, in contrast to the Bruegel painting of Williams's poem, which hangs in the Musée des beaux arts in Brussels. Whether real or imagined, the material reality of the ekphrastic subject must be apprehended visually (as opposed, say, to being heard or tasted), and its verbal description likewise allows the reader to imagine it visually.

Like Keats's poem, Cather's *The Song of the Lark* takes its title from the work of art featured in it, the Jules Breton painting young Thea discovers in the Art Institute of Chicago and for which she comes to feel such an affinity. In an ekphrastic passage, the painting is described in terms of what Thea notices about it: "the flat country, the early morning light, the wet fields, the look in the girl's heavy face" (197). As an ekphrasis, the passage adds to our understanding of Thea's characterization and her situation in the novel as well as the painting itself: the narrator states that Thea felt those elements in the painting "were all hers, anyhow, whatever was there. She told herself that that picture was 'right.' Just what she meant by this," the narrator goes on to say, however, "it would take a clever person to explain" (197).

Cather's passage, like ekphrasis in general, is primarily interpretive, although ekphrasis may also appear merely decorative.

Margaret Anne Doody argues in her study of early narrative that ekphrasis insists upon the viewer's and the reader's duty to interpret—not only the ekphrastic subject, but the entire literary work in which it is included. "A good painter," Doody states, "includes allegorical and encoded meanings; the art of knowing a painting"—and reading the significance of a painting in ekphrasis—"is hermeneutic" (137). By insisting upon interpretation, ekphrasis challenges mimesis; it suggests that the truth of literature transcends mere realism (137); we do not read either Browning's "My Last Duchess" or Keats's "Ode on a Grecian Urn" as a *catalogue raisonné* of portraiture or Greek vase painting. Furthermore, as Page duBois states in her study of the use of ekphrasis in Hellenistic epigrams, the reader of an ekphrasis often figures in a "productive triangulation" as he or she is "drawn into judgment in relation not just to the work of art, but also toward the contained viewer and toward the narrator himself" (47), sometimes becoming a "foil for irony" (46)—as in Browning's poem, which invites the reader to judge the character of the murderous duke, the speaker of the poem who does not seem to realize how much he reveals to the contained viewer and to us when he reports, "I gave commands; / Then all smiles stopped together" (ll. 45–46). Ekphrasis, in other words, is normative; it forms the viewing—and reading—subject (Goldhill 2).

As an ekphrasis, then, Cather's scene in the Art Institute challenges the reader to be "a clever person," a competent interpreter, in order to discern the relation of Breton's painting to the novel. The described rural landscape of the painting may remind us a little of Thea's hometown of Moonstone, Colorado—and even more of the Nebraska landscapes of *O Pioneers!* (1913) and *My Ántonia* (1918). But it is the inclusion of the girl's face in the description of the landscape that delineates what Doody would call the novel's allegory or code. Just as Williams's ekphrastic poems on Bruegel's paintings delineate, as Christina Giorcelli observes, his "poetic program," matching the poet's emphasis on the local, the landscape, and common people, and his rejection of foreign models to the painter's (200), Cather's ekphrastic passage delineates the "program" of *The Song of the Lark*. The novel's program/allegory/code has much to do with the relationship between Thea as an artist and her own local landscape. It stands as an early iteration of the Virgilian theme that will become more explicit in *My Ántonia*, reflecting Cather's interest in what David Stouck has defined as "an aboriginal relationship to place" (204), and resonates in the juxtaposition of landscape and girl's face in the description of the Breton painting. As a *künstlerroman, The Song of the Lark* is a study in the ways in which a brilliantly talented but culturally isolated girl finds access to the people and experiences that can develop her artistry. The novel muses upon the unlikely value of the people and experiences found in Thea's indigenous environment, an apparent cultural wasteland featuring small-town characters like an alcoholic piano teacher and a Mexican mandolin player, and experiences like a Sunday-school concert and a train ride to Denver. It is a major contention of the novel that art in fact springs from improbable sources. Even after Thea begins her formal training in Chicago, she "got almost nothing that went into her subconscious self and took root there" (301). The "recollections [that] were a part of her mind and personality" appear common and ordinary and are specific to Moonstone: "the moonflowers that grew over Mrs. Tellamantez's door, . . . memories of light on the sand hills, of masses of prickly-pear blossoms . . . , of the late afternoon sun pouring through the grape leaves and the mint bed in Mrs. Kohler's garden" (301). Thea is inspired by the things that mean "home" to her, like the typical French painter Cather spoke of in a later interview, who "doesn't talk nonsense about art, about self-expression. . . . His house, his gardens, his vineyards, these are the things that fill his mind. . . . When a French painter wants to paint a picture, he makes a copy of a garden, a home, a village. The art in them inspires his brush" ("Restlessness" 11).

In her belief that the domestic and the local are the sources of artistic inspiration and that the ordinary objects associated with those environments are the stuff of art, Cather is consistent with the strain of modernism defined by William Carlos Williams and Robert Frost as opposed to that of T. S. Eliot and Ezra Pound. In important ways (e.g., her admiration of European models), Cather is decidedly outside the Williams/Frost tradition, but in her endorsement of the aesthetic value of the local and domestic, her work has much in common with those poets of Paterson, New Jersey, and New Hampshire. And while Breton's painting, dated 1884, is not exactly a modernist work, it is related to the paintings produced by members of Barbizon school, whose humble agrarian scenes were precursors to the modernist re-envisioning of the familiar made even more startling by painters like Paul Cézanne. The poet Rainer Maria Rilke, who spent several weeks in 1906 in an ekphrastic thrall repeatedly visiting an exhibition of Cézanne's paintings in Paris, wrote that Cézanne "lays his apples on bed covers which [his landlady] will surely miss some day, and places a wine bottle among them or whatever happens to be handy. And he makes his 'saints' out of such things; and forces them—*forces them*—to be beautiful, to stand for the whole world and all joy and all glory" (*Letters* 40).

Moonstone's prickly-pear blossoms and Mrs. Kohler's mint bed are for Thea the equivalent of Cézanne's apples and wine bottles. Although Chicago is the site of significant developments in Thea's life—her lessons with Harsanyi, the discovery of her operatic voice, her friendship with Fred Ottenburg—Moonstone is the landscape that sustains her imaginatively. The novel depicts Chicago's harsh economic realities as they affect Thea's increasing self-consciousness: the "wretchedly conducted" boardinghouses (260) and the cheap clothes to which her finances limit her contrast with the generous comfort of restaurants and carriage rides shared with Fred. But the city, particularized by the novel's references to the northside neighborhood populated with Swedes, to Lake Michigan and the Pullman Building and the Art Institute, does not impress itself specifically on Thea; it does not take on the qualities of a character in her life, as Moonstone had. It is a "rich, noisy city, fat with food and drink," "a spent thing" (265), an almost prototypical turn-of-the-century metropolis; with its successful industrialists and businessmen, wealthy art patrons, and struggling workers, it is interchangeable with Pittsburgh, St. Louis, or Cleveland. In Thea's experience, the city does not ask to be known, does not invite relationship; it remains "simply a wilderness through which one had to find one's way" (193).

In her response to Breton's painting, Thea seems to register an enlarged understanding of the importance of the vernacular, the ekphrasis allowing Cather to use what John Hilgart sees as a consistent and typical strategy of "develop[ing] her characters through their perceptual habits" (377). We infer that Thea marks the painting as "hers" for the qualities we, too, discern; we are drawn into a judgment of the painting that coincides with Thea's, as well as a judgment of Thea herself and of the novel's meaning. The ekphrasis is proleptic, foreshadowing the next stage in Thea's perceptual development, which will take place in Panther Canyon, itself a profoundly vernacular landscape. At this point in the novel, Thea, too, realizes that developing her perception is important to her own artistic formation. After her first visit to the Art Institute, "she had a serious reckoning with herself. . . . She remonstrated with herself severely. She told herself that she was missing a great deal. . . . She was sorry she had let months pass without going to the Art Institute. After this she would go once a week" (196). As the fragment of sculpture tells the speaker of Rilke's ekphrastic poem "Archaic Torso of Apollo," the art has told Thea, "You must change your life" (l. 15).

Thea had finally taken herself to the Art Institute at the urging of the boardinghouse owner, Mrs. Lorch, who thinks of it as one of the city's "points of interest" (194), an opinion that "triangulates" the reader and Thea, who understand (or will, very shortly) that the museum is much more than a tourist site. However, it is also more than a repository of art—it is a social and political space. Ekphrasis, even in the ancient world, very often implies such social and political space. In her examination of third-century BCE epigrams, duBois highlights ekphrastic passages that exhibit a high degree of historical knowledge and consciousness of ethnic difference, gender, and class. She makes the point that an ekphrasis often suggests the social and political factors—slavery, women's restricted roles, and imperialism, among others—that affect the making of a work of art, as well as its display. Doody similarly argues that the ekphrastic subject "is located in a social space," and that we are always made aware of "the commodification of art" and "what kind of social space the gazing viewer is occupying" (140–41). In modern literature, the ekphrastic encounter typically takes place in a museum or gallery, as it does in *The Song of the Lark*, because that is where works of art in the modern world—as opposed to the world of Browning's duke, for example—are most commonly displayed. Cather's novel does not especially challenge the cultural economy that built the Art Institute on the shores of Lake Michigan, but it does acknowledge the social and political implications of entering that museum. When Mrs. Lorch and Mrs. Andersen, avid readers of the Sunday art column in the decidedly middlebrow *Inter-Ocean*, urge her to visit the museum, Thea explains that she did not do so the day she first noticed it because "The sign outside said it was a pay-day" (195). Michel Foucault, who defines the museum (along with the cemetery, garden, and library) as a "heterotopia," "a kind of effectively enacted utopia . . . outside of time," observes that the individual gains access to such spaces by submitting "to rites and purifications" (n.p.). In Thea's time and in ours, the rite is most blatantly a financial transaction, and with "no city consciousness" and a nervousness about being parted from her money (193), Thea is reluctant to submit to that rite.

Disciplined and decorous behavior in a gallery or museum serves as an additional rite required for gaining access and is thus another social or political context for an ekphrasis. The demands of classical ekphrasis are consistent with the teachings of philosophers like the Sophist Lucian, who tells us that when we stand in front of a work of art we are not to gasp and gesticulate, but to stand firm and speak as a display of our cultivation (Goldhill 18). Thea, no practiced museumgoer, does not buy a catalog of the collections and so makes up names for the artwork she sees. Uninformed as she might be, she nevertheless responds strongly to the casts and paintings on display: she likes or dislikes them for very specific and clear reasons, and they evoke for her childhood memories and the absence of her beloved brothers. In the Art Institute, Thea begins to see—and, importantly, begins to remember what she has seen before.

In the home of the Nathanmeyers, Thea enters the same nexus that is formed between the art object and viewer in a gallery or museum, where it is often constructed on social class and the market value of art. The Nathanmeyers, a wealthy Chicago family of art collectors and music connoisseurs, will pay Thea fifty dollars to sing at one of their "musical evenings." She thus gains access to this particular "heterotopia" by virtue of her own talent and Fred's friendship, but she still must be "purified" by exchanging her "broadcloth church dress" (273) for a more suitable evening dress belonging to one of the Nathanmeyer daughters; Selma, a maid, will assist her. Paintings by Rousseau and Corot, "which the old banker had bought long ago for next to nothing" (276), hang in the Nathanmeyer home, and the music room houses two Steinways (277). Fred directs Thea's attention to a painting displayed in the hall that he describes as "the most beautiful Manet in the world," depicting "a woman eating grapes out of a paper bag" (276).[2] This brief ekphrastic passage enforces the "allegory" of the Art Institute passage, the relationship between art and the vernacular. The opening pages of *The Song of the Lark* featured young Thea, bedridden, recovering from scarlet fever, eating grapes from a paper bag brought to her by a doting Dr. Archie. The ekphrasis thus juxtaposes the domestic space occupied by the sick child enjoying a rare treat and the heady world of Manet, Manet viewers, and Manet buyers. It casts an ironic light upon the social distance between a maid named "Selma"—surely Scandinavian—and the Swedish Norwegian artist Thea, earning her own money in the Nathanmeyer home. And it highlights the way in which Thea enlivens her rendition of "Tak for dit Räd" by informing it with a folktale from her Norwegian grandmother—in other words, making an intuitive connection between the canonical music of Edvard Grieg and the vernacular material transmitted through family, which allows her performance to attain the level of artistry. In so doing, she reminds the sophisticated Nathanmeyers and the reader that the origins of art are often local and domestic. Just as, when Thea hears a performance of Dvořák's *New World* symphony, she remembers the "high tableland above Laramie; the grass-grown wagon-trails, the far-away peaks of the snowy range, the wind and the eagles" (198–99), Mr. Nathanmeyer, when he hears Thea sing, thinks of "*Svensk sommar*. . . . She is like a Swedish summer" (280).

Thea's experience of the cliff dwellings in Panther Canyon parallels the more conventional ekphrasis of the Art Institute passage—and indeed that is its point. In Panther Canyon, Thea is led into further perceptual development, a deeper understanding of the sources and nature of art. In the same way that she had claimed as her own imaginative territory the simple, workaday landscape of Breton's painting, Thea inhabits the remnants of the cliff dwellers' civilization. Enacting that "fusion of people and place" (Trout 275) that marks the aboriginal landscape, she "found herself trying to walk as they must have walked, with a feeling in her feet and knees and loins which she had never known before. . . . She could feel the weight of an Indian baby hanging to her back as she climbed" (302). *The Song of the Lark*, as well as *The Professor's House*, derives its presentation of aboriginal culture from Cather's romantic view of history as a series of heroic conquests, which allowed her to "ignore some of its harsher realities, such as the displacement of the region's native peoples" (Stouck 203). The novel provides no critique of the Euro-American imperialism that rewards Fred's wealthy father with "a whole canyon full of Cliff-Dweller ruins" (289). Nor is Thea interested in that critique; Cather constructs her stay at Panther Canyon as a celebration of her relation with aboriginal culture as it had been foreshadowed by the ekphrasis in the Art Institute.

Thea's empathy with what she understands of the cliff dwellers' lives and her admiration of their pottery, which had been developed for ceremonial and religious use "far beyond any other crafts" (303), leads her to an epiphanic insight that equates the potsherds with the objects displayed at the Art Institute and with her own artistry. Her leap in perceptual development is evident in Cather's framing of these ordinary items as ekphrastic subjects, which allows the reader, too, to understand why these objects of everyday use can be considered art. Cather's representation of the jars as art objects is consistent with the aesthetic she outlines in "The Novel Démeublé": these jars are not extraneous objects; they exist in Thea's "emotional penumbra" (40). As she bathes in a canyon pool, a bath that had come "to have a ceremonial gravity" (304), it occurs to Thea that art is but "a mould in which to imprison for a moment the shining, elusive" stream of life: "The Indian women had held it in their jars. In the sculpture she had seen in the Art Institute, it had been caught in a flash of arrested motion. In singing, one made a vessel of one's throat and nostrils and held it on one's breath, caught the stream in a scale of natural intervals" (304).

The ritualistic origin of the jars and the "ceremonial" nature of Thea's daily bath contribute to the newly perceived artistic quality of the jars. In his essay "The Work of Art in the Age of Mechanical Reproduction," Walter Benjamin argues that the "aura" of a work of art, its relation to history and to ritual, is essential to its artistic integrity. Art, he writes, "begins with ceremonial objects destined to serve in a cult" (224). In the modern age, the capacity to reproduce the work of art compromises its integrity by distancing it from those origins. The physical survival of the abandoned cliff dwellings allows Thea rare access to an ancient culture in which art was not removed from its origins. Cather thus expands the ekphrastic mode to frame not only received works of art displayed in the museum and in the collector's home but the structures and artifacts of the cliff dwellers. The ekphrasis forms us as viewing subjects as Thea's experience has formed her. Although the aesthetic estimation (and the market value) of such artifacts appreciated significantly throughout Cather's lifetime, it had not yet reached the canonical status of, say, Roman sculpture or even nineteenth-century French painting. *The Song of the Lark* reveals its modernist program in Cather's expansion of ekphrasis to insist (with Picasso, among others) that these ancient artifacts, domestic and indigenous, be valorized equally with classical and more modern art.

In *The Professor's House* (1925), Cather complicates her use of ekphrasis, eliding it rather than expanding it, to include a wider array of subjects and to insist even more strenuously on our hermeneutic competence, directing our formation as viewing subjects. The reader of this novel is drawn more deeply into the "productive triangulation" ekphrasis can construct, directed to make a series of aesthetic judgments with modernist cultural and social implications. Here, Cather goes beyond the expanded ekphrasis that accommodated newly valorized objects like the cliff dwellers' water jars, to an elided ekphrasis that challenges the aesthetic value of the commercial object—that questions, in effect, whether the object should enjoy the privilege of ekphrasis. This inquiry is characteristic of Cather's post-1922 writing but also fundamental to the modernist cultural critique, with its distaste for commodity and conspicuous consumption (Stout 3).

Tom Outland, who discovers the cliff dwellings while riding the range near the Blue Mesa, is at first only curious about them, but then he comes to admire the ingenuity of the cliff dwellers as he observes more closely the evidence of their artifacts and their architecture. Soon, however, he begins to aestheticize the remnants of the cliff-dweller civilization. He describes the compound of cliff dwellings as "still as sculpture—and something like that" (200) and again, "more like sculpture than anything else" (201). He says they "seemed to have a kind of composition" (201) and that the people who built them had "a feeling for design" (204). Father Duchêne agrees that "there is unquestionably a distinct feeling for design in what you call Cliff City" (219) and asserts that the decorated pottery is similar, if not identical, to early Cretan pottery (220). His conflation of the cliff dwellers with the classical world, echoed in Tom's reading of the *Aeneid* and Lucretius during his exploration of the mesa, is very like the understanding that flashes upon Thea in Panther Canyon: in both passages, the less familiar art of the ancient Native American world achieves canonical status when characters articulate its essential sameness with more conventionally valorized art. In their display of art, both sites are heterotopian; like Foucault's museum, they are "outside of time," Cliff City suggesting "immortal repose" and "the calmness of eternity" (201), Panther Canyon, "the drama that had been played out . . . centuries ago. . . . a continuity of life that reached back into the old time" (304). The atmosphere of Panther Canyon is "ritualistic" (304); Cliff City is "a sacred spot" that inspires "reverence" (221)—and yet both are, above all, domestic environments. As Tom, like Thea, increasingly observes the evidence of the everyday lives of the cliff dwellers—the tool making, the water carrying, and the baby tending—his appreciation for the artistry of the ancient people increases. Like Cézanne as imagined by Rilke, Tom makes a "saint" out of an ordinary object when he names a mummified body "Mother Eve," and this moment is emblematic of the development in Tom's perception that leads him to value the "aboriginal relation to the land" so important to Cather (204).

As an extended ekphrasis, "Tom Outland's Story" records Tom's shifting perception of the importance of the cliff dwellings and their artifacts, demanding our judgment to shift as well to accommodate the notion that domestic objects, the detritus of a vanished people, might constitute art, and that building a house or shaping a vessel to hold water might be an artistic act. If we look to the ekphrastic descriptions of Tom's discovery of the cliff dwellings to inform our reading of the novel—to interpret the novel's allegory or program—we come to understand that *The Professor's House* is about people forming new understandings of domestic life and its objects (including houses) and of history and time. The social factors that contextualize Tom's ekphrastic encounter—the eradication of the Native population from the Southwest and the cultural imperialism that extends to Roddy Blake an offer he cannot refuse for their remains—likewise contextualize the novel as a whole.

Outside of "Tom Outland's Story," there are no objects of art, conventionally understood, in the novel—no paintings, no sculpture—but we cannot help but notice that *The Professor's House* is filled with color, form, texture, and light. In Godfrey St. Peter's story, which frames Tom's, clothes and bodies are aestheticized to a remarkable degree. Professor St. Peter's physical appearance is described in minute detail and, moreover, specifically as if he were an art object. Not only is his swimmer's body and Spanish coloring described—his "silky, very black hair" and his "tawny skin with gold lights in it"—but his eyes are described in terms of light and color—"brown and gold and green"—and his beard is a "Van Dyke" (13). His daughter Kathleen, a talented painter, appreciates the "modeling of his head between the top of his ear and his crown," a description echoed by the narrator, who describes it as "more like a statue's head than a man's" (13). The physical appearance of the Professor's wife and daughters is also recorded in this aestheticized detail. "Mrs. St. Peter was very fair, pink and gold," and "one did not realize, on first meeting her, how very definitely and decidedly her features were cut" (36). Kathleen "was pale, with light hazel eyes, and her hair was hazel-coloured with distinctly green glints in it" (37). This sort of physical description is very different from the descriptions of Thea's facial features in *The Song of the Lark*, for example, which almost always denote qualities of character—"fierce," "tender," "bleak" (10, 289)—rather than visual detail. Rosamond's "silk suit of a vivid shade of lilac" is "admirably suited to her complexion and show[s] that in the colour of her cheeks there was actually a tone of warm lavender. . . . [S]he seemed very tall indeed, a little out of drawing" (58). Seeing Rosamond in a "coat of soft, purple-grey fur," the Professor remarks, "these things with a kind of lurking purple and lavender in them are splendid for you. They make your colour prettier than ever" (82–83). The painterly and sculptural details of these descriptions identify the members of the St. Peter family themselves as art objects, and our introduction to them is an ekphrastic encounter in itself. Indeed, Doody expands her definition of ekphrasis in the modern novel to include the costumed human body as it is represented in masquerades, charades, and tableaux vivants (401). Modern ekphrasis might then be expanded to meet Valentine Cunningham's broader definition: a "pausing . . . for some words about more or less artistic works . . . not made out of words" (57). Kathleen, whose furs are a poor second to Rosamond's stunning (and stunningly expensive) moleskin, draws her father's—and our—attention to the social space occupied by the beautifully colored Rosamond-object when she tells the Professor that "Rosie comes [to the Guild to sew for the Mission fund] in a handmade French frock that cost more than all our dresses put together" (86). In other words, she corrects her father's aesthetic interpretation to include the circumstances of display; she insists on acknowledging criteria other than aesthetic in appraising a young woman he wants to see only as pretty. Her insistence forces St. Peter to recognize that Rosamond's "emotional penumbra," as Cather called it in "The Novel Démeublé"—the emotional life of the character with which the object is "perfectly synthesized" (48)—is selfish, oblivious of others, materialistic. Kathleen's perception of the social context for this ekphrasis, and her insistence on separating beauty from moral qualities, is consistent with the program of the novel, which interrogates aesthetic judgment and cultural value. It is no surprise that Kathleen was encouraged to go to Chicago to take art classes, while Rosamond goes there to shop.

In *The Professor's House*, Chicago serves as the location for a comparison between the art object and the commercial object. In addition to the reference to the Art Institute, where Kathleen was encouraged to study (65), the Professor is invited to lecture at the University of Chicago (76), and, while he is in the city for the occasion with his wife, Rosamond, and Louie, they attend the opera *Mignon*. The city is thus presented as a showcase for high culture—opera, academic history, art. It is also a showcase for commercial display: Rosamond's emeralds are set by a Chicago jeweler (76), and Louie's choice of hotel, the elegant Blackstone on Michigan Avenue, is compared to the "grimy place on the South side" (92) to which the Professor's budget would have directed him; there are references to restaurant meals and trains. Chicago is the setting for another kind of display as well, Rosamond's "birthday dinner in the public dining-room of the hotel" (95), at which she "was presented with her emeralds" (96). The celebration included some of the Professor's colleagues, who, Mrs. St. Peter tells her husband, "went away from the Blackstone that night respecting Godfrey St. Peter more than they had ever done before" (96). Lillian is "doubtless right" (96)—and the Professor and the reader are both foils for the irony—that the academics are more impressed by their viewing of Rosamond's emerald necklace fashioned by a Chicago jeweler than by their attendance at St. Peters's lectures.

It is the house Louie names "Outland," and the objects associated with it, that the novel's ekphrasis most strongly challenges. The Norwegian manor house, unlike Thea's remembered Norwegian folktale, is not connected to either Rosamond's or Louie's ethnic history; it represents no fusion of people and place. Unlike Panther Canyon or Cliff City or the landscape of Breton's painting, it is neither indigenous nor vernacular; it is quite literally, as Scott's joke has it, "outlandish" (43), a kind of perverse heterotopia. It is a "curated house,"³ a domestic and ethnic simulacrum. Outland is a museum that will display a reconstruction of Tom Outland's laboratory; it is a kind of museum, too, in its display of aestheticized objects. The fact that both the American cultural moment and Rosamond and Louie's taste dictate that the objects on display will be consumer goods rather than art objects reflects Cather's post-1922 concern with market value's replacement of aesthetic value. Although the Professor thinks the painted Spanish bedroom furniture, the object of Rosamond's "orgy of acquisition" (154) in Chicago, is very pretty, when he views it in its social context he understands it is plunder. The historian of conquest and imperialism tells his wife that Rosamond "was like Napoleon looting the Italian palaces" (154). Rosamond's rapacious consumption of goods is as destructive and offensive as Napoleon's acquisition of territory. The Norwegian house, the French dresses, the Spanish furniture—as we "pause" in a kind of ekphrasis before these objects, their commodified ethnicity directs us to interpret the displacement of "aboriginal" culture by an economy of conspicuous consumption in the novel as regrettable. In comparison with the aboriginal culture of the cliff dwellers and with the domestic culture of St. Peters's old home with its French garden, the brave new life of financial prosperity holds little hope for art.

The objects in *The Professor's House* are primarily purchased rather than crafted. They are made, of course, but the act of their making is not central to their value. Their most important relation is to the purchaser, not the maker, and the circumstances of their acquisition and the degree to which they aggrandize the owner bespeak their value. On this point, the reader is certainly called into duBois's "productive triangulation" when Louie directs Kathleen's attention to Rosamond's new emerald necklace and explains, "She doesn't like anything showy, you know, and she doesn't care about intrinsic values. It must be beautiful, first of all" (107). The irony of the necklace having no "intrinsic values"—and intrinsic values being unimportant to Rosamond and Louie—is that it defines the necklace per se as one of those things inferior to the art object. In her essay "On the Art of Fiction," written some five years earlier, Cather says that art "is always a search for something for which there is no market demand . . . where the values are intrinsic and have nothing to do with standardized values" (103; Hilgart 379). Lillian St. Peter had earlier commented that an emerald necklace was "a little out of scale" for Rosamond (76). Lillian's taste in these matters is reliable; we know the necklace most certainly is "showy," and we know Kathleen the artist knows it.

Benjamin argues that in the modern age, the "exhibition value" of art, to which artistry is only incidental, has replaced its cult or magical or religious value (225). Cather's use of ekphrasis in *The Song of the Lark* and *The Professor's House* reflects a similar belief that no object, however beautiful, can be considered art when it is disconnected from its ceremonial origins, as the "standardized" object almost necessarily is. Both Thea Kronborg and Tom Outland see art in terms of history and ritual; for them, the remnants of the cliff dwellers retain their ceremonial value. The "ritualistic" atmosphere of Panther Canyon leads Thea to realize that the ancient pottery is art; Father Duché ne tells Tom that Cliff City must have been the site of "religious ceremonies" (218, 220), and the remnants of domestic artifacts as well as the body of Mother Eve create in Tom what he calls "filial piety," the *pietas* of the ancient Romans (251). Religious ritual is lost to Professor St. Peter—the son of a lapsed Catholic, he must ask the seamstress Augusta to clarify the difference between the Magnificat and the litany of Loreto (99–100)—but domestic ritual remains. Domestic ritual is typically a high order of human endeavor in Cather's fiction, but the Professor seems unable to transfer his cooking, his gardening, and his daily work habits to the new house. He is unsettled by the shift between commercial and aesthetic values in his world and is "adrift," as

222

DIANE PRENATTDIANE PRENATT

David Stouck describes him, "between the Dynamo and the Virgin" (205). In the absence of art and ceremony, in a world governed by commerce, only a kind of degraded ekphrasis is available to St. Peter: of dressmaker's forms that remind him of real women, and a tableau vivant of his sons-in-law that allows him a "little joke" (74).

Cather's description of objects throughout her fiction reflects her own aesthetic sensibility and her sensual apprehension of the material world. In *The Song of the Lark* and *The Professor's House*, Cather finds in the terms of ekphrasis itself the occasion for the kind of painterly description and the modernist interrogation of value that is fundamental to her writing. In *The Song of the Lark*, Cather's use of ekphrasis valorizes noncanonical art; in *The Professor's House*, it challenges the market valorization of the commercial object. In both novels, the relationship between authentic art and vernacular culture is immensely consequential, its representation constituting a critique of twentieth-century consumer culture and the criteria of aesthetic judgment. For Cather, beauty and truth reside in what comes from the "aboriginal" landscape and often appears unrefined—not Rosamond's emerald necklace, but the stones Tom Outland gives to Rosamond and Kathleen, "turquoises, just as they come out of the mine, before the jewelers have tampered with them" (120).

NOTES

1. DuBois acknowledges that at least one scholar of antiquity, Ruth Webb, finds this definition of ekphrasis "reductive," but states that she herself is "still unrepentantly interested" in ekphrasis so defined (45). Versions of this definition of ekphrasis (e.g., "the representation in words of a visual representation" [Bartsch and Elsner i]) recur consistently and unapologetically in the scholarship on ekphrasis. I am indebted throughout this article to the special issue of *Classical Philology* on ekphrasis, edited by Bartsch and Elsner, and particularly to the discussion of historical and theoretical issues provided in their introduction and in the articles by Cunningham, duBois, and Goldhill.

Romy Kozak argues that Cather used "musical ekphrasis" in her fiction. In my view—which seems to be consistent with the available scholarship on ekphrasis—to qualify ekphrasis as "musical" is to create a unique definition that defies the fundamental ekphrastic relationship between the verbal and the visual.

2. My thanks to Kari Ronning for her identification of the Manet painting as *The Street Singer*.

3. "Curated," in the sense of "arranged and maintained with informed aesthetic judgment," is being newly used—it seems to me—in relation to consumer goods and experiences; see, for example, references to "the carefully curated mood of the high-ceilinged rooms" of a newly-decorated apartment (*New York Times* 6 May 2009); "everything you need for the perfectly curated household" (*New York Times Magazine* 17 May 2009); "a good example of the curatorial shopping experience that fashion-conscious women like" (*New York Times* 12 February 2009); "their snug, well-curated apartment in Harlem" (*The New Yorker* 1 March 2010).

WORKS CITED

Bartsch, Shadi, and Jaś Elsner. "Introduction: Eight Ways of Looking at an Ekphrasis." *Classical Philology* 102 (2007): i–vi.

Benjamin, Walter. "The Work of Art in the Age of Mechanical Reproduction." 1842. *Illuminations*. Trans. Harry Zohn. 1955. New York: Schocken, 1968.

Browning, Robert. "My Last Duchess." 1842. *The Poetical Works of Robert Browning*. Cambridge Edition. Boston: Houghton Mifflin, 1974. 252.

Cather, Willa. "The Novel Démeublé." 1922. *Not Under Forty*. New York: Knopf, 1936. 43–51.

———. "On the Art of Fiction." 1920. *Willa Cather on Writing: Critical Studies on Writing as an Art*. Lincoln: U Nebraska P, 1988. 101–4.

———. *The Professor's House*. New York: Knopf, 1925.

———. "Restlessness Such as Ours Does Not Make for Beauty." Interview with Rose C. Feld. *New York Times Book Review* 21 Dec. 1924: 11.

———. *The Song of the Lark*. Boston: Houghton Mifflin, 1915.

Cunningham, Valentine. "Why Ekphrasis?" *Classical Philology* 102 (2007): 57–71.

Doody, Margaret Anne. *The True Story of the Novel*. New Brunswick NJ: Rutgers UP, 1996.

duBois, Page. "Reading and Writing on the Wall." *Classical Philology* 102 (2007): 45–56.

Foucault, Michel. "Of Other Spaces (1967), Heterotopias." Trans. Jay Miskowiecz. *Michel Foucault, info.* 12 Oct. 2009. http://foucault.info/documents/heteroTopia/foucault.heteroTopia.en.html. Trans. of "Des espaces autres." *Architecture/Mouvement/Continuité* 5 (Oct. 1984).

Giorcelli, Christina. "William Carlos Williams' Painterly Poems: Two Pictures from a Bruegel." *Word and Image* 4 (1988): 200–208.

Goldhill, Simon. "What Is Ekphrasis For?" *Classical Philology* 102 (2007): 1–19.

Hilgart, John. "Death Comes for the Aesthete: Commodity Culture and the Artifact in Cather's *The Professor's House*." *Studies in the Novel* 30 (1998): 378–404.

Kozak, Romy. "Sounding Out: Musical Ekphrasis, Sexuality, and the Works of Willa Cather." Diss. Stanford U, 2004.

Hollander, John. "The Poetics of *Ekphrasis*." *Word and Image* 4 (1988): 209–17.

Rilke, Rainer Maria. "Archaic Torso of Apollo." 1907. *Ahead of All Parting: The Selected Poetry and Prose of Rainer Maria Rilke*. Trans. Stephen Mitchell. New York: Modern Library, 1995. 67.

———. *Letters on Cézanne*. Trans. Joel Agee. New York: Fromm, 1985. Trans. of *Briefe über Cézanne*. 1952.

Stouck, David. "*The Professor's House* and the Issues of History." *Willa Cather: Family, Community, and History*. Ed. John J. Murphy, Linda Hunter Adams, and Paul Rawlins. Provo UT: Brigham Young U Humanities Publication Center, 1990. 201–11.

Stout, Janis. "For Use, for Pleasure, for Status: The Object World of Willa Cather." *Willa Cather and Material Culture: Real-World Writing, Writing the Real World*. Ed. Janis Stout. Tuscaloosa: U Alabama P, 2005. 1–14.

Trout, Steven. "Antithetical Icons? Willa Cather, Ernest Hemingway, and the First World War." *Cather Studies 7: Willa Cather as Cultural Icon*. Ed. Guy Reynolds. Lincoln: U Nebraska P, 2007. 269–87.

11 "The Nude Had Descended the Staircase"

Katherine Anne Porter Looks at Willa Cather Looking at Modern Art

JANIS P. STOUT

The phrase quoted in my title, "the nude had descended the staircase," comes from Katherine Anne Porter's essay "Reflections on Willa Cather." Its allusion is of course to the painting *Nude Descending a Staircase, No.* 2 (1912) by Marcel Duchamp, first exhibited in the United States at the 1913 Armory Show in New York. In making her passing reference, Porter assumed that readers would recognize the allusion and understand its significance. And it was a good assumption. Duchamp's cubist nude has long served as an icon of modernism's break with traditional concepts and praxis in art.

I have argued elsewhere that "Reflections on Willa Cather" is an essentially duplicitous essay in which the ever insecure Porter, herself an icon of literary modernism but fearful that her halting production would erode her future place in literary history, sought to strengthen her position in that prospective history by weakening that of her slightly older contemporary. Invoking the nude on the staircase as a touchstone, she sought to position Cather outside the project of modernism altogether where, she strongly implied, Cather persevered in a stodgy and backward-looking aesthetic (Stout, "Porter's 'Reflections'").

225

Porter's essay on Cather was first written as a book review of the posthumous collection of essays and aesthetic statements *Willa Cather on Writing*. Published in the *New York Times* in 1949, it was titled "The Calm, Pure Art of Willa Cather." When it reappeared in greatly expanded and revised form three years later in *Mademoiselle*, it bore the title "Reflections on Willa Cather"—a title that well describes both the loosely associative form of the essay and its shift in emphasis from appreciation to assessment. It appears under this latter title in Porter's *Collected Essays and Occasional Writings* (1970).

The passage in which the nude makes her appearance asserts Cather's indifference to modernism in music and literature as well as visual art:

> Stravinsky had happened; but she went on being dead in love with Wagner, Beethoven, Schubert, Gluck, especially *Orpheus*, and almost any opera. She was music-mad, and even Ravel's *La Valse* enchanted her; perhaps also even certain later music, but she has not mentioned it [in the essays collected in *On Writing*].
>
> The Nude had Descended the Staircase with an epoch-shaking tread but she remained faithful to Puvis de Chavannes, whose wall paintings . . . inspired the form and tone of *Death Comes for the Archbishop*. . . . She loved Courbet, Rembrandt, Millet and the sixteenth-century Dutch and Flemish painters, with their "warmly furnished interiors" but always with a square window open to the wide gray sea. . . .
>
> Joyce had happened: or perhaps we should say, *Ulysses* . . . [but] that subterranean upheaval of language caused not even the barest tremor in Miss Cather's firm, lucid sentences. (37–38)

There can be little question that Porter genuinely admired the "firm, lucid sentences" that characterized Cather's style and paid tribute to her as a stylist and a formalist in her review-turned-essay. At the same time, she reinforces her own position of prominence as a "writers' writer" admired within a circle of other literary modernists—Glenway Wescott, Robert Penn Warren, Allen Tate, Cleanth Brooks, Eudora Welty—while removing Cather to a different category altogether. As a result of such mixed purposes, her "reflections" are skewed, partly right but often very wrong.

Much of the evidence that it is wrong is provided by Cather's letters, which were of course unavailable to Porter. Since the time of her writing, however, hundreds of Cather's personal letters have become available at university libraries. Today's scholars are privileged to read Cather's own expressions of her likes and dislikes, experiences and goals. In contesting Porter's construal of Cather as a writer whose "plain" face was turned squarely toward the past ("Reflections" 30), I will draw freely on these materials and on Cather's nonfiction. Moreover, the enormous theoretical and historical literature on modernism of recent decades has enriched the definitional basis for revisiting the issue of Cather's relationship to modernism in the arts. Three works in particular seem to me both exceptionally cogent and directly pertinent to my discussion here, in that they form linkages among the arts. They are Martha Banta's "The Excluded Seven: Practice of Omission, Aesthetics of Refusal" (1995), Joyce Medina's *Cézanne and Modernism* (1995), and Marc Manganaro's *Culture, 1922* (2002).

My purpose is only secondarily, however, to dispute Porter's contention that Cather was no modernist. She has long since lost that argument as scholars such as Richard Millington, Phyllis Rose, Jo Ann Middleton, and myself, among others, have demonstrated Cather's place within modernism.[1] More important, Porter's argument relating to Cather and modernism provides a useful point of reference for sharpening our own definitions and perspectives. In any event, the comments of one writer on another are almost always of interest, especially since both were women writers at a time when it was still a real struggle to achieve parity of attention with males. Neither Porter nor Cather was eager to make claims based on gender, but both left passages in their letters indicating their awareness that literary publication was very much a man's business. Porter experienced gender exclusivity as a writer primarily as a matter of genre (the short story or sketch versus the more "masculine" novel), while Cather experienced it most directly with respect to admissible or inadmissible subject matter, in reviews of her war novel *One of Ours*. For all these reasons, I find it both interesting and beneficial to place the two in conversation *as modernists* by way of Porter's truly intriguing essay and to use her essay as a springboard for exploring what we can know of Cather's interest in modern art, especially visual art.[2]

A BLURRED REFLECTION

At the time she wrote "Reflections on Willa Cather," Porter was well established as a master of the short story and a stylist whose elegantly crafted sentences and rich symbolism placed her among an elite of contemporary writers. Her stories had appeared in, for example, *Century*, *Transition*, *Hound & Horn*, the *Virginia Quarterly Review*, and the *Southern Review*. But she had yet to achieve a wide popular following; it would be another decade before the publication of *Ship of Fools* (1962) brought her that. She used her essay, then, to reinforce her position as a high-art modernist writer by invoking the names of celebrated modernists in literature, music, and visual art and linking them anecdotally with her own life and artistic maturation. It is a rhetorical strategy implying that the aesthetic represented by this litany of names is to be taken as a measure of artistic status. And by this standard she finds Cather wanting—a kind of mirror reversal of herself. Indeed, we might read the word "reflections" in the title as having dual meanings, referring both to Porter's process of reflecting on (thinking about) Cather and to the likeness or unlikeness between the two of them. The primary unlikeness suggested in the essay, other than an *ad feminam* sniff that Cather was not glamorous (Porter most assuredly was), is that she was not truly modern.

Porter was not alone in thinking of Cather in that way. By 1940, largely through the efforts of Marxist critics such as Granville Hicks, she had been relegated to a kind of pleasant literary backwater. Yet one would think that Porter might have recognized in Cather's work some of the principles and techniques that characterized her own and which, in various combinations, have come to be seen as defining attributes of "high" modernism. These would include gaps and fragmented surfaces, minimalist sculpting, resistance to conventions of form or manner, and a conception of art as a reality of its own counterpoised against an outer world drained of meaning. Readers both then and now would be likely to associate such characteristics with the names Porter invokes in her "Reflections": Henry James, W. B. Yeats, Joseph Conrad, Gertrude Stein, James Joyce; in the visual arts, Klee, Gris, Modigliani; in music, Bartók, Poulenc, Stravinsky. Keeping the focus as much on herself as on Cather, she reminisces about her own first encounter with Stein's *Tender Buttons* and the "great day" (33) on which she picked up a copy of Joyce's *Dubliners*, and recalls her years in Paris during the 1930s as the time when she encountered the work of painters such as Modigliani and became mad for "music hot from the composer's brain."[3]

She associates a very different set of names with Cather. It is true, as she states, that Cather turned to Shakespeare and Beethoven as exemplars of the highest achievement in art. She did so in several of the essays in *On Writing*, the volume Porter was initially reviewing, and had been since her earliest days of newspaper writing. But when Porter goes on to mention Cather's "lov[ing]" Shelley, Wordsworth, and Walter Pater, the accuracy of her assessment becomes problematic. Cather's references to Shelley in *On Writing* are not precisely expressions of adulation. At one point she takes "Citizen Shelley" to task for his mistaken involvement in politics (20), and at another simply mentions his name along with Wordsworth's in making the point that writers can treat traditional subjects without imitating traditional styles such as theirs (27). Cather makes a similar point in praising Sarah Orne Jewett, a writer Porter might well have cited, but did not, as evidence of a premodernist aesthetic taste. Cather praises Jewett, though, not for being traditional but for being independent. Young writers and visual artists alike, she says, should be faithful to their own vision, as Jewett was, not model their work on what has already been done, however fine (51). None of these passages indicates a retrograde devotion to past masters.

Turning next to music, Porter reports that Cather was "dead in love with Wagner, . . . Schubert, Gluck . . . and almost any opera" (37). This is essentially correct; she loved opera. In an undated 1913 letter to Elizabeth Shepley Sergeant she stated (with possible hyperbole) that she was attending operas more often than weekly. To be sure, she was beginning a novel about an operatic singer at the time, and her statement to Sergeant may have been meant as an indication of how devotedly she was preparing for the book. As to Wagner and Schubert, she refers to them with a frequency that does indicate particular preference. But where Porter got the idea, as she goes on to assert, that Cather was "enchanted" with Maurice Ravel's *La Valse*—by which I believe she meant to suggest deplorable taste—I am unable to determine. I have found no reference to Ravel either in *On Writing* or in any of the letters, and Ravel's name is not indexed in either *The World and the Parish* or *The Kingdom of Art*, which reprint much of Cather's newspaper commentary on the arts. As for Porter's musing that Cather may even have liked "certain later music" than Ravel but if so "has not mentioned it in these papers" (37), that too is true, strictly speaking. But with increased availability of her letters we know that in 1934 she attended and enjoyed the New York premiere of *Four Saints in Three Acts*, with text by Gertrude Stein and music by Virgil Thomson (Cather to Luhan).

In the visual arts, my primary emphasis here, Porter was entirely correct in recognizing Cather's great affinity for the work of Pierre Puvis de Chavannes. She clearly indicates that affinity in "On *Death Comes for the Archbishop*," one of the most frequently cited of the pieces in *On Writing* (9). Porter does not seem to have recognized, however—as I believe Cather did—that Puvis, with his stylized flattening of figures, was a significant precursor of modernism. In *The Louvre: French and Other European Paintings*, Michel Laclotte and Jean-Pierre Cuzin write that Puvis's *The Poor Fisherman* (1881, purchased by the Louvre in 1887) "shows how great an innovator" he was. They see in "the subtle arrangement of the simplified and rather stilted forms and the limited range of low-keyed, soft colours" an anticipation of "the young Picasso a few years later" (126). Porter may also have been correct in stating that Cather "loved Courbet" (38), but the only reference to Courbet in the pages of *On Writing* comes in a paragraph deploring the notion that an artist should be so committed to a political cause as Courbet was (20)—one of Cather's most firmly held ideas and one that she in fact shared with Porter, at least so far as politically oriented fiction was concerned. I find no reference to Courbet in any of Cather's letters, nor in either *The Kingdom of Art* or *The World and the Parish*, as indexed.

When singling out Jean-François Millet as an indicator of Cather's aesthetic, Porter is on firmer ground. Cather had in fact expressed an admiration for Millet as well as Jules Breton long before she wrote "On the Art of Fiction," one of the essays Porter was reviewing in her first version of "Reflections." Cather particularly admired the representation of ordinary life in the works of these painters, and as early as January 1898, in a column in the *Lincoln Courier*, she praised their "technical mastery" and "elemental power" (*World and Parish* 2: 574–75). She singled out Breton's *The Song of the Lark* in a column of 10 August 1901 for its affective power and its appeal to ordinary museumgoers who saw it at the Art Institute of Chicago (*World and*

Parish 2: 843). She was still thinking of the broad humanity of Millet's work the following year, 1902, when she made her first trip to Europe. In one of the travel pieces she sent back to the *Nebraska State Journal* she observed that women working in the fields near Barbizon appeared tired toward evening and "grew to look more and more as Millet painted them, warped and bowed and heavy" (*Willa Cather in Europe* 123).

It is surprising that the travel reports Cather sent back to the *State Journal* did not mention going to art museums. Yet we have to believe she did. Indeed, James Woodress points out that her claim in "On *Death Comes for the Archbishop*" to have seen Puvis's "frescoes of the life of Saint Geneviève in my student days" actually refers to her 1902 trip (399). We know from numerous letters that she was a frequenter of museums and galleries throughout her adult life, and her trip in 1902 was her first opportunity to enjoy a European museum. In addition to visits to the Art Institute of Chicago, to be examined more closely below, her letters record museum visits in Pittsburgh (Cather to Ellen Gere); in London, where she more than once stayed across the street from the British Museum (Cather to Hueffer); in Paris, where she stayed near the Louvre (letters in 1923 and 1930, cited below); and in New York, where she was particularly fond of the Frick Collection (Cather to Menuhin).

Cather would obviously have singled out the Louvre as a destination in Paris. We can only wish we knew how many times she went there, how long she stayed, and what pictures stopped her in her tracks, to stand and look. But we do have two letters that give clues. In 1923 she wrote to Edith Lewis that she had stayed for an entire morning and mentioned two seventeenth-century paintings as favorites, a Murillo *Virgin* and a Ribera *Nativity*. She might well have singled out different ones on another day, and indeed she made that point herself in a 1940 letter, saying that we all know our responses to art vary continually from one time to another (Cather to Keppel). In 1930, in the other letter referred to above as having a bearing on her preferences at the

Louvre, she felt familiar enough with its vast collection to give Carrie Miner Sherwood some advice on how to see it. Don't try to do it all, she advised, but stay mainly in the Grande Galerie to see the best of the collection. Which of the many paintings exhibited in the Grande Galerie she numbered among the very best we cannot know. Historical records indicate, however, that there would almost certainly not have been any from the nineteenth or twentieth century. A guide to the Louvre published in 1927 gives detailed indication of what was to be found in the various bays of the Grande Galerie and shows that the few impression-' ist works owned by the Louvre, along with paintings of the Barbizon school so loved by Cather, were hung on the third floor (Heywood xv–xvi, 333–54; see also Laclotte and Cuzin 103).[4]

CATHER AND THE ART INSTITUTE

The interest in Millet and Breton that Cather expressed in newspaper columns around the turn of the century and in her musings while in Europe in 1902 would have begun at the Art Institute of Chicago in either 1895 or 1896. The Institute had opened in its present site at Michigan Avenue and Adams Street in 1893. With a bequest from Mrs. Henry Field in 1894, consisting of a collection of French paintings, primarily mid-nineteenth-century landscapes and genre paintings, it quickly gained the foundation of a developing strength in French art. This early bequest, designated the Henry Field Memorial Collection, included Breton's *The Song of the Lark* as well as two paintings by Millet and one by Corot (*Wounded Eurydice*). The Breton painting would have a major impact on Cather's career when she borrowed its title for her third published novel and used its image on the cover. She would later regret having done so, but her choice reflected a genuine liking for the painting and more generally a belief in the importance of hearing the voice of beauty and inspiration ("the song of the lark") whatever one's circumstances. It is one of the great themes of her work.

Cather made her first trip to Chicago in April 1895, at the age of twenty-one. It is reasonable to suppose that the young Nebraskan, intent on absorbing as much high culture as possible, would have made time in her schedule to see the new museum, which had opened to considerable fanfare sixteen months earlier, but I have found no record that she did. There *is* definite record, though, that only a little over a year later, in 1896, she visited the Art Institute when she passed through Chicago on her way to Pittsburgh to begin her job at *Home Monthly*. Writing to her college friend Mariel Gere in July of that year, she says that she saw a Gustave Doré exhibit. She dismissed it as a splashy extravaganza on the order of billboards for *The Last Days of Pompeii*.[5] Even at that date, to have admired Doré, a French romantic artist of the nineteenth century, would not have indicated avant-garde taste. But her letter did not indicate admiration.

Fortunately, as we have seen, the Institute had much to offer in 1896 besides splashy romantic canvases like Doré's. It also had available for viewing the more realistic and restrained paintings of Millet, Breton, and others of the Barbizon school that would remain favorites of Cather's over the years. In columns published in the same turn-of-the-century years when she was praising Millet and Breton, she also called her readers' attention to Jean-Baptiste-Camille Corot, 1796–1875, generally regarded as a transitional figure, an anticipator of impressionism, and Alfred Sisley, 1839–1899, who belongs solidly among the impressionists (*World and Parish* 2: 761, 808). For her to have noticed and praised the play of light in Corot's and especially Sisley's paintings by 1900 and 1901 (the dates of columns she published in short-lived Pittsburgh periodicals, reprinted in *The World and the Parish*) was by no means to turn her back on what was new in visual art.

Writing almost half a century afterward, Porter may not have recalled that the works of truly innovative and demanding painters like Cézanne had not even been shown in the United States at century's end. In any event, she took Cather's fondness for

Breton and Millet as an indicator of a conservative taste. But Cather's comments on Millet in *On Writing* do not so much emphasize either his realism or his accessibility as his simplification of the field of vision by eliminating extraneous reportage—a characteristic of decided pertinence both to her own work and to modernism itself. Porter either missed or chose to ignore this when writing her review and essay.

It is easy to understand that the representational canvases of Breton and Courbet, Corot and Millet would have been more readily accessible to an early-twentieth-century viewer such as Cather, while the more obviously challenging and nontraditional works of the postimpressionists, futurists, and abstract painters would have been less readily appreciated. Even the late-nineteenth-century impressionists were more challenging for early-twentieth-century museumgoers than the narrative realists who came only slightly earlier. They demanded a real readjustment of appreciative vision. Clearly, though, Cather's liking for the Barbizon painters was not exclusive; she did not refuse to make that adjustment or to appreciate other styles. When she bought prints for her brother Roscoe and his wife, Meta, in 1908, for their house in Wyoming, her selections were fairly eclectic. We know this from a letter to Roscoe in which she dutifully lists her purchases and what she paid. They included prints of Breton's *The Song of the Lark*, two by N. C. Wyeth (then only five years past his first commission), one by Remington, two eighteenth-century Dutch paintings, and an illustration by Maxfield Parrish, *The Dinkey Bird Is Singing in the Amfalula Tree*—all narrative works, none of them very innovative, but her selection was, after all, designed for a domestic space, and not her own.

The familiarity with the Art Institute of Chicago that Cather initiated in 1895 or 1896 was almost certainly maintained in subsequent years. She had reason to travel between New York and Nebraska or destinations farther west with some frequency, and Chicago was a major rail center. Letters show that *after* 1896 she either visited or passed through Chicago a minimum of ten times (in 1897, 1921, twice in 1924, in 1926, 1927, 1931, twice in 1932, and in 1935). Many of these visits were motivated by the need to make train connections, but she sometimes stopped off for a day or more to visit friends, and these stays would have provided opportunities to drop in and see what was being featured at the Art Institute or to revisit her favorites.

By the late 1920s, as a result of deliberate decisions about collection development, the Art Institute of Chicago was a major center of modern art. In 1913 it had been the only American museum to host an exhibition of a large subset of the Armory Show paintings. Indeed, its hosting of this controversial show had produced an outpouring of newspaper commentary, much of it negative.[6] Nevertheless, the Institute not only exhibited the show but purchased several of the works. Additional investments in modern art followed, as well as such major bequests as fifty-two paintings given by Bertha Honoré Palmer in 1924 and the Helen Birch Bartlett Memorial Collection in 1925–27. We do not know to what extent Cather was aware either of the Institute's exhibit of the Armory Show or the arrival of these later major bequests. Given her habit of voracious newspaper reading and the presence of friends in Chicago, it is hard to imagine she did not see the reports, but that is of course conjectural. In any event, we do know that she continued to visit Chicago and that during the years she did, the Institute came to house a permanent collection strong in impressionists and other moderns. Which of these she particularly liked or disliked we do not know.

We do, however, have one very strong indication—a letter stating her wish to see a particular show there that she was unfortunately missing. Her express wish to see this specific exhibit suggests, then, the direction in which her interest was turning in her later life—a direction that included the moderns. On 16 May 1941 she wrote to her longtime friends Irene Miner Weisz and Carrie Miner Sherwood, jointly, lamenting that she had not been able to join them in seeing a major exhibit of French paintings about to close at the Institute. That same exhibition had earlier visited New York, she said, but due to illness and matters of business she had not been able to see it there either.

The show she was referring to was "Masterpieces of French Art Lent by the Museums and Collectors of France," exhibited by the Art Institute from 10 April to 20 May 1941.[7] By consulting the catalog of this exhibit, still available from rare-book dealers or at the Institute itself, we learn what it was that Cather so wished she could have seen. It was indeed a feast of modern art: 170 paintings plus 100 drawings and watercolors that collectively constituted, according to Daniel Catton Rich's introduction to the catalog, "an unforgettable picture of the background and development of modern art." Among the artists represented were Braque, Cézanne, Corot, Courbet, Degas, André Derain (then still living and active), Gauguin, Van Gogh, Matisse, Millet (Cather's old favorite), Monet, Picasso, Pissarro, Puvis de Chavannes (whose presence in such company testifies to his status in relation to modernism), Renoir, Seurat, Sisley, Toulouse-Lautrec, and Vuillard. Obviously, we have no way of knowing which of the paintings in this challenging modern mix Cather would especially have liked, since she never got to see it. But the very fact that she expressed a wish to see this "great" (as she called it) exhibit, almost the whole of it given to recent art, indicates that her interests were not at all so focused on the past as Katherine Anne Porter believed when she wrote "Reflections on Willa Cather."

COMPETITIVE LITERARY SISTERHOOD

Again, one writer's comments on another are almost always of interest. Certainly that is true of Porter's essay on Cather. Contemporaries at a time when women writers were struggling for recognition on a par with men, both were serious artists determined to be recognized as such. Both had emerged from social situations that might not have seemed conducive to literary eminence. Such commonalities might well have positioned them for mutual understanding and appraisal—indeed, for fruitful discussions of technique or of how the fact of gender had affected their experience of the literary profession. Yet so far as I have found, Cather never commented on Porter at all, the two never exchanged letters, and as we have seen, Porter's "reflections" on her sister writer's aesthetic affinities are marred by misunderstandings, perhaps even willful ones. If she had not been so eager to think of Cather as a rival for a position of future eminence, Porter might well have discerned, out of her own practice as a literary modernist, the aspects of Cather's work that share an affinity with that same movement in the arts.

What we see in the varied and complicated record provided by Cather's journalism, literary essays, and letters is not a regressive taste but an eclectic one. At various times Cather expressed a liking for religious art of the Renaissance, realism, and impressionist innovations, and at least an interest in postimpressionism. True, she once expressed to Elizabeth Shepley Sergeant the idea that cubist painting was not comfortable to look at (26 May [1914]), and conveyed to Dorothy Canfield Fisher, in a letter of 1922, a negative reaction to the futurists. On the other hand, she used the word "modern" with no trace of pejorative implication in a letter to Irene Miner Weisz explaining her choice of León Bakst as her portraitist. And as David Porter has demonstrated, she admired the stylized, fully modern paintings of Edith Lewis's friends Earl Brewster and Achsah Barlow Brewster, whose work has been described as having "eliminat[ed] . . . 19th century 'realistic, romantic, sentimental, literary, and scientific' accretions" in favor of "austere, formal, understated" images (149–50). If not an outspoken advocate of the nude who descended the staircase, she was in any event responsive to modern art and recognizably modernist in her own work.

In 1896, when, twenty-three years old and a year out of college, Cather went to Pittsburgh to accept her first job, stopping on the way at the Art Institute of Chicago, she was feeling bedeviled by a label that would not occur to us: her friends were calling her a bohemian. And with good reason. She had exhibited "bohemian" irregularities in her personal life (she smoked, drank cocktails, and sometimes dressed oddly), and her columns in the *Nebraska State Journal* had expressed enthusiasm for the expatriate American painter James McNeill Whistler as well as British aestheticism. To us, the kind of friendly name-calling she experienced as a result may not seem like a very dire problem, but it is clear from her letters that she did not want to be labeled in that way—or indeed, in any way. She is still resistant to labeling. It is useful to identify the traces of particular aesthetic systems in Cather's (or any other writer's) work, as I have sought to do here, but we err when, in the effort to define a Catherian aesthetic, we try to place her in one and only one category, for whatever reason.

Katherine Anne Porter, in her "Reflections on Willa Cather," did not seek to place her in a category but to exclude her from one. She did so by construing the evidence of Cather's artistic vision selectively, choosing to mention some expressions of her taste but to omit contrary evidence even within the few pages of the book she was initially reviewing, *On Writing*. I think, for instance, of Cather's tribute to Katherine Mansfield's "virtuosity" (107), her discernment that certain aspects of Stephen Crane's work made him "one of the first post-impressionists" (69), and most of all, her insistence that, even while revering the Beethovens and the Wordsworths of our heritage, art should not perpetuate "conventional poses" (51). Porter noted none of these in her review. Nor did she recognize in print any of the abundant evidence of Cather's engagement with the very modernist project of reconceiving the nature of the novel, even though that engagement is evident in her experiments with form throughout her career. It was evident too in the *On Writing* essays Porter was reviewing, in her repeated questioning of the definition of the novel as a genre.

Even with the resources we have available today which Porter did not—some three thousand letters and the collected, albeit fragmented, journalism—it is not possible to know precisely

240

JANIS P. STOUT

what Cather thought of the nude's descending of the staircase. She apparently did not go on record about that "epoch-shaking" event. Yet we have other good reasons to believe that she listened attentively to the nude's tread on the stairs and did not find it unwelcome. Katherine Anne Porter's construal of her as a kind of premodern, not so much hostile as immune to the new in the arts, may well have been influenced by the fact that Porter did conceive of herself in modernist terms. Granted that the space among the serious moderns open to occupation by women was limited (though unless they became *too* successful in the marketplace they were welcome to take as much space as they wanted among the middlebrow writers), and granted that Porter fully meant to reserve space there for herself, she had every motivation, conscious or not, to position Cather elsewhere. A zero-sum game enforces competition, and Porter was a fairly devious competitor. She had no intention of giving up her seat.

NOTES

1. Among other fine studies that bear on this subject, I would particularly call attention to Goldberg's, which is perhaps only glancingly pertinent but in important ways.

2. With regard to Cather's taste in art, Bernice Slote's groundbreaking essay "First Principles: The Kingdom of Art" in *The Kingdom of Art* (31–112) remains of general interest here, even though it has very little to say about visual art. Of somewhat more pertinence is my own *Picturing a Different West.* See also Keeler, Al-Ghalith, and D. Porter.

3. In fact, Porter's interest in music also embraced French songs from the twelfth through eighteenth centuries. She spent a considerable portion of her time during 1932 and 1933 translating songs of this period for *Katherine Anne Porter's French Song Book*, published in 1934 by Harrison of Paris.

4. Since these latter were shifted sometime in 1930, it is not entirely clear where they were hung on the day or days Carrie was there. The 1930 shifting of paintings was one of very few changes made in the hangings in the Grande Galerie between the Second Republic (1848) and the Second World War (Loire).

5. Cather may be referring here to *The Last Day of Pompeii* by Russian painter Karl Briullov (1799–1852), which Edward Bulwer-Lytton said had inspired his novel of almost the same title but in the plural, as Cather uses it: *The Last Days of Pompeii.*
6. See Martinez; also the web site of the Art Institute of Chicago, http://www.artic.edu/aic/collections/index.php.
7. I am grateful to Susan Augustine for confirming this.

WORKS CITED

Al-Ghalith, Asad. "Cather's Use of Light: An Impressionistic Tone." *Cather Studies 3.* Ed. Susan J. Rosowski. Lincoln: U of Nebraska P, 1996. 267–84.
Augustine, Susan (Head of Reader Services at the Art Institute of Chicago). E-mail to the author, Nov. 2008.
Banta, Martha. "The Excluded Seven: Practice of Omission, Aesthetics of Refusal." *Henry James's New York Edition: The Construction of Authorship.* Ed. David McWhirter. Stanford: Stanford UP, 1995. 249–60.
Cather, Willa. Letter to Roscoe and Meta Cather. 2 Mar. [1908]. Roscoe and Meta Cather Collection, Archives and Special Collections, U of Nebraska–Lincoln.
———. Letter to Dorothy Canfield Fisher. [17 June 1922]. Bailey Library, U of Vermont, Burlington.
———. Letter to Ellen Gere. 27 July 1896. Willa Cather Foundation, Red Cloud NE.
———. Letter to Mariel Gere. July 1896. Willa Cather Foundation, Red Cloud NE.
———. Letter to Elsie Martindale Hueffer. 20 May 1909. Division of Rare and Manuscript Collections, Cornell U Library, Ithaca NY.
———. Letter to Paul Keppel. 6 Feb. 1940. Butler Library, Columbia U, New York NY.
———. Letter to Edith Lewis. [Summer 1923]. Susan J. and James R. Rosowski Collection, Archives and Special Collections, U of Nebraska–Lincoln.
———. Letter to Mabel Dodge Luhan, 1 May 1934. Beinecke Library, Yale U, New Haven CT.
———. Letter to Yaltah Menuhin, 11 Jan. 1938. Firestone Library, Princeton U, Princeton NJ.

————. Letters to Elizabeth Shepley Sergeant. Morgan Library, New York NY.

————. Letter to Carrie Miner Sherwood. 17 July 1930. Willa Cather Foundation, Red Cloud NE.

————. Letter to Irene Miner Weisz. 11 Aug. 1923. Newberry Library, Chicago.

————. Letter to Irene Miner Weisz and Carrie Miner Sherwood. 16 May 1941. Willa Cather Foundation, Red Cloud NE.

————. Willa Cather in Europe: Her Own Story of the First Journey. Ed. George N. Kates. Lincoln: U of Nebraska P, 1988.

————. Willa Cather on Writing: Critical Studies on Writing as an Art. 1949. Lincoln: U of Nebraska P, 1988.

————. The World and the Parish: Willa Cather's Articles and Reviews, 1893–1902. Ed. William M. Curtin. 2 vols. Lincoln: U of Nebraska P, 1970.

Goldberg, Jonathan. Willa Cather and Others. Durham NC: Duke UP, 2001.

Heywood, Florence. The Important Pictures of the Louvre. 3rd ed. London: Methuen, 1927.

Hicks, Granville. "The Case against Willa Cather." English Journal Nov. 1933. Willa Cather and Her Critics, ed. James Schroeter. Ithaca: Cornell UP, 1967. 139–47.

Keeler, Clinton. "Narrative without Accent: Willa Cather and Puvis de Chavannes." American Quarterly 17 (1965): 119–26.

Laclotte, Michel, and Jean-Pierre Cuzin. The Louvre: French and Other European Paintings. Trans. Diana de Froment and Frances Roxburgh. Paris: Scala; London: Philip Wilson, 1982.

Loire, Stéphane (Conservator in Chief of the Department of Paintings and Chief of Research Service and Documentation, Musée de Louvre). E-mail to author, 12 Feb. 2009.

Manganaro, Marc. Culture, 1922: The Emergence of a Concept. Princeton: Princeton UP, 2002.

Martinez, Andrew. "'A Mixed Reception for Modernism': The 1913 Armory Show at the Art Institute." Art Institute of Chicago Museum Studies 19.1. One Hundred Years at the Art Institute: A Centennial Celebration. Chicago: Art Institute of Chicago, 1993. 30–57, 102–5.

Medina, Joyce. Cézanne and Modernism: The Poetics of Painting. Albany: State U of New York P, 1995.

Middleton, Jo Ann. *Willa Cather's Modernism: A Study of Style and Technique.* Madison NJ: Fairleigh Dickinson UP, 1990.

Millington, Richard H. "Willa Cather's American Modernism." *The Cambridge Companion to Willa Cather.* Ed. Marilee Lindemann. Cambridge: Cambridge UP, 2005. 51–65.

Porter, David. "'Life is very simple—all we have to do is our best!': Willa Cather and the Brewsters." *Willa Cather: New Facts, New Glimpses, Revisions.* Ed. John J. Murphy and Merrill Maguire Skaggs. Madison NJ: Fairleigh Dickinson UP, 2008. 141–57.

Porter, Katherine Anne. "Reflections on Willa Cather." *Collected Essays and Occasional Writings.* Boston: Houghton Mifflin, 1970. 29–39.

Rose, Phyllis. "Modernism: The Case of Willa Cather." *Modernism Reconsidered.* Ed. Robert Kiely. Cambridge: Harvard UP, 1983. 123–45.

Slote, Bernice, ed. *The Kingdom of Art: Willa Cather's First Principles and Critical Statements, 1893–1896.* Lincoln: U of Nebraska P, 1966.

Stout, Janis P. *Katherine Anne Porter: A Sense of the Times.* Charlottesville: UP of Virginia, 1995.

———. "Katherine Anne Porter's 'Reflections on Willa Cather': A Duplicitous Homage." *American Literature* 66 (1994): 719–35.

———. *Picturing a Different West: Vision, Illustration, and the Tradition of Cather and Austin.* Lubbock: Texas Tech UP, 2007.

———. *Willa Cather: The Writer and Her World.* Charlottesville: UP of Virginia, 2000.

Woodress, James. *Willa Cather: A Literary Life.* Lincoln: U of Nebraska P, 1987.

12 "The Cruelty of Physical Things"
Picture Writing and Violence in
Willa Cather's "The Profile"

JOYCE KESSLER

Whatever is felt upon the page without being specifically named there—that, one might say, is created. It is the inexplicable presence of the thing not named, of the overtone divined by the ear but not heard by it, the verbal mood, the emotional aura of the fact or the thing or the deed, that gives high quality to the novel or the drama, as well as to poetry itself.
—*Cather, "The Novel Démeublé"*

As one of her earliest works of fiction, Willa Cather's "The Profile" reveals a great deal about what later became the consistent use of visual imagery and visual art reference in her work. This essay examines the visual semiotics in "The Profile," assessing Cather's knowledge of modern art discourses in relation to her participation in modernist cultural production. "The Profile" can be seen as a product of her interest in and understanding of the modernist experiment in relation to the neoclassic, romantic, and realist art movements. This particular change narrative of art values in conflict was one with which Cather, during her college years of writing art reviews, had become quite familiar, and she exploited it as a suggestive cultural setting for her disturbing tale of the brief marriage between a sensitive portrait painter and his visibly scarred wife. Even this early in her development as a writer, Cather deftly employed visual images and the critical discussion surrounding them in her narrative of the social inequities suffered by women of America and western Europe in the transition from the nineteenth century to the twentieth.

In portraying the struggle between Aaron Dunlap and Virginia Gilbert over the significance of the latter's facial scar, "The Profile" displays the principal visual strategy that Cather notably and consistently employed throughout her writing career. Borrowing her phrase from *My Ántonia*, I identify this strategy as her "picture writing" (p. 237). Included in picture writing, as I am using the term, is her skillful use of the cultural narratives attached to well-known art images, such as the critical furor occasioned by Manet's *Olympia*, mentioned briefly but with intention in this early short work of fiction. The scope of Cather's picture writing, however, takes in her image making generally, and is dependent not just on her knowledge of art movements and their ideals but also on her understanding and use of visual semiosis—of the ways in which objects and materials, colors, marks, and forms all are used in the production of meaning. It was this profound understanding of the visual that she possessed and confidently drew upon, even in the early years of her career.

Since the mid-1990s, Cather's use of the visual in her fiction has become a focus of interest among students of her work. Polly Duryea's exhaustive "Catalogue Raisonné" traces Cather's exposure to the world of images during her college years of extensive critical engagement with exhibits including the French and American impressionists and documents Cather's experience with artists, such as Manet, who departed radically from the romantic and realist traditions (Duryea 6). In "The Observant Eye, the Art of Illustration, and Willa Cather's *My Ántonia*," Janis P. Stout points out Cather's frequent creation of an additional visual layer for the pursuit of truth that escapes the written word. For Stout, Cather's close involvement in the choice of illustrator for earlier editions of *My Ántonia* and her increasing reliance on "visual experience itself" are evidence of a highly developed visual acuity. In her introduction to *Willa Cather and Material Culture*, Stout argues that Cather's embrace of the material culture of her narrative subjects locates her work firmly within the modernist scope (10–11). Catherine Morley also notes the developing importance of the symbol throughout Cather's career in "Voice of the Prairies? Willa Cather and the International Modernist Scene" (9). These similarities of insight assume a paradigm of relationships among images, symbols, and words in a literary text that this essay seeks to revise. The general accord indicates, however, the trend of the ongoing discussion about Cather's visuality, its relationship to her creations of language, and its "fit" within the scheme of modernist cultural production.

Cather's use of visual elements in "The Profile" connects her story to the radical modernity of Manet's *Olympia*, first exhibited in 1865. The story demonstrates her deep understanding of how layers of period and place are linked to art, and of the new forms of visual representation that had emerged in the late nineteenth century. Her commentaries on the public sculpture and painting she viewed during her first trip to Europe in 1902 are clearly founded on her knowledge about studio art practice and an understanding of developments in modern art. They reveal her easy recognition of expertise in the creation of line and composition, in the effective use of color, and in the "truth of tone," a standard that she identified in the portraits of Edward Burne-Jones when she visited his studio (*Willa Cather in Europe* 73–74). As she toured the Barbizon countryside, she noted that the tiring women gleaners appeared "to look more and more as Millet painted them, warped and bowed and heavy" (122–23). Cather consistently blends the visual and the historical for the *Nebraska State Journal* readers for whom she sketched her first experiences of Europe, enlivening her comments on Burne-

Jones's Venus panels or Millet's darker perspectives on peasant labor with their accompanying cultural narratives. In much-noted disclosures on her own art, too, Cather applied her understanding of visual art to elaborate her theories of novelistic technique. She praised the practice of younger novelists whose minimalist ways of writing were parallel to the "suggestive" techniques of modern painters ("Novel Démeublé" 40). Her ability to extrapolate this painterly quality in the works of a coming generation of writers speaks of her ease with both modern visual arts practice and its wider aesthetic influence. In developing this into picture writing, she was able to create narratives that draw a significant portion of their meaning from the quality of her images. Her particular use of visual elements in "The Profile" places Cather firmly within the scope of the modern as revealed in Manet's *Olympia*.

In investigating Cather's modernism, Duryea and others have seen Cather's stylistic development as increasingly informed by the art of the symbolist writers ("Catalogue Raisonné" 16–17). Considering the images in *My Ántonia*, Stout points to Cather's "powerful symbolizing pictures like the plow against the setting sun" as evidence of symbolist influence, in which the simple, unadorned presentation of the object "makes the idea real" ("Observant Eye" 2). In *Willa Cather's Modernism*, Jo Ann Middleton also sees that backlit plow as a symbol mediating Cather's meaning with poetic technique, bringing our associations "of all that it took to tame the prairie" into the field of meaning that this image must suggest (60). Cynthia Griffin Wolff reads Virginia Gilbert's scar as a symbol of general human vulnerability, something physical or material in the narrative that can represent a common understanding or experience for readers (13). These characterizations of Cather's symbolism, or of Cather's imagery as symbolist, are helpful initial approaches to her creative methods, but do not fully account for their specific effects. While the symbolists may have had their influence on her, Cather evolved original methods for communicating meaning visually within her narratives. The disturbing effect of her picture writing in "The Profile" derives not so much from its power to symbolize human suffering generally as from the more potent and specific signifying process by which she has infused her character's physical scar with the particular meaning of the beauty standard's inherent injustice to women.

In "The Novel Démeublé," Cather discusses Tolstoy's masterful infusion of meaning, by realist techniques, into a fictional object. She admired his creation of a numinous narrative in which the physical thing and its emotional significance are entirely integrated as a single, signifying entity. The clear result in Cather is a power of signification that is influenced as much by realist art and literature, such as Tolstoy's, as it is by the symbolist movement. The effect of realist influences on Cather's picture writing may escape us if we place her imagery in "The Profile" within a category of the symbol that is too broadly drawn.

A close consideration of Cather's signifying method in "The Profile" should inquire first into the life experience that set it into motion. On the relationship between Cather and Dorothy Canfield Fisher, Mark Madigan's article "Willa Cather and Dorothy Canfield Fisher: Rift, Reconciliation, and *One of Ours*" has related the meeting, through Fisher, of Cather and Evelyn Osborne, "a young woman with a prominent facial scar and a taste for extravagant clothes" (1). This history reveals the profound hold of the subject on the young writer, despite its resulting negative effects on her relationship with Fisher. Cather's inquiry leads, in fact, to the more descriptive term for the type of sign she has placed on her character's face. Virginia Gilbert's scar does not have the requisite characteristics of a symbol: as a sign, it is better described as a type of index because it indicates or makes reference to the event that produced it. In the semiotic theory of Charles Sanders Peirce, it is "a sign which demonstrates the influence of its object."[1] Cather deploys the scar as a signifier in a variety of ways in her narrative, but in early scenes involving Dunlap's first painful reaction to seeing the affected side of Virginia's face, it reminds him of "the cruelty of physical things" that haunted his childhood (187). It appears to him and to readers also as an indexical sign of an unspecified event of violence to her body, resulting in the theft of her beauty. Thus, Cather positions the criteria for beauty in relation to the idea of justice, moving her readers toward a new conception of their uneasy coexistence.

The documented struggle between Cather and Fisher over the ethics of publishing a story centering on a character whose misfortune had been so obviously drawn from Osborne's own is in itself illuminating. In supporting Cather's vigorous resistance to Fisher's claims, Isabelle McClung wrote the latter tellingly, "it is Willa's scar now" (Madigan 3). McClung expressed a most penetrating insight into the creative process by which Osborne's scar was born into Cather's created narrative. When first meeting Evelyn Osborne, Cather herself may have struggled to construct the meaning of her scar in much the same way that Dunlap, and even the story's readers, struggle with Virginia's disfigurement. From unproductive reasoning backward about the unstated physical and temporal causes of Osborne's scar, Cather might easily have been moved to explore in fictional form the psychological and social effects of disfigurement on an otherwise young, privileged, and attractive woman. Through her character's facial scar, Cather develops an image of complex meaning. Virginia's scar can intensify for the reader Dunlap's sympathy and Virginia's shame, but at the same time it may signify the horror and anger underlying their marital bond, thereby complicating the readers' constructions of Cather's intentions in this text. The semiosis of things visual and material in her story's world enabled Cather to embed within "The Profile" a counternarrative that allows readers to better understand its violent climax.

Her creative process suggests the formation of a conceptual representation of the scar in Cather's mind, one that would have captured for her as a complete visual sign Osborne's inability to meet one of the primary criteria of female beauty during the time period: the smooth pallor of a flawless complexion.[2] As a young writer negotiating her own complex relationship to female beauty, Cather used the image of the scar as a sign of the unjust burdens of the beauty standard that must be carried by young womanhood. Thus, Cather reproduces in her character Dunlap her own movement from understanding a facial scar as an index to claiming it as a specific signifier for larger, if very different, representational purposes. In accounting for Cather's conception and use of the scar as a particular created signifier, we must acknowledge the difficulties of specifying the relationship between thought, language, image, and word.[3] These are the very difficulties that Cather's picture writing, as an independent semiotic dynamic, allows her readers to surmount. Because the visible scars of both Evelyn Osborne and Virginia Gilbert are saliently "unspeakable," Cather melds them into a sign that can speak for itself.

Linguistic production of meaning is a paradigm for Cather's picture writing. On one level, it is analogous to the word in both form and meaning: it is a sign, made up of material signifiers and a corresponding realm of signification. The word, however, is a symbolic convention: its semantic field is established and continuously renegotiated among its speakers. In her picture writing, Cather does not rely solely on this inventory of verbal signifiers and related significations that facilitates human communication. Instead, she invents her sign: the signifier as an image created of words, and its field of signified meanings as visually communicated, seemingly independent of those words. This perspective on her image making allows us to appreciate its originality and to see the difference between symbolism and picture writing. Symbolism makes various uses of the existing, socially assumed meanings of iconic or otherwise symbolic signifiers (in the way that language itself functions), while picture writing deploys images—a plow, a scar, a woman exercising naked, a handful of turquoises, a footprint—that Cather has ordained as signs, for which there are no signifying forms or assumed significations besides what she has invented. It is this distinction between the general operations of the symbolic and the process of specific visual semiosis resulting in Cather's picture writing that leads me to propose the latter as a critical aspect of any approach to the presence of the visual in her art.

"The Profile" gives readers an early and compelling taste of Cather's picture writing. The scar on Virginia Gilbert's face does not function in the manner of a symbol: it functions as a picture writing on her countenance, claiming the significance of which is the central contest between the story's two main characters. The scar is a visual/physical presence within the story, created by Cather out of language, in order to expand her text's inventory of signs, and thus to enhance its semiotic reach, so that her readers' understanding of her text may encompass "the thing not named" ("Novel Démeublé" 41). On the level of transformation from index to picture writing, the metamorphosis of meaning in Virginia's scar constitutes Cather's narrative. This image appears to her readers first as a physical fact of mysterious origin on her character's body, and as the story progresses, the visible mark ultimately becomes a visual sign gradually disclosing its part in the story's meaning. The scar does not invite readers to see or to see more of the nature of its structural referent; it is, rather, a visual signifier that merges with its referent for the reader, one that took total shape in Cather's mind, and exists as a totality in the narrative, through which meaning has been "perfectly synthesized . . . in the emotional penumbra of the characters themselves," one in which "literalness ceases to be literalness" ("Novel Démeublé" 40).

In a number of her other works, such as *My Ántonia*, "Coming, Aphrodite!," *The Professor's House*, and *Lucy Gayheart*, Cather's use of picture writing, which includes her related manipulations of pictorial or other historical referents, creates an additional—and sometimes oppositional—layer of meaning for her narratives, one that is communicated to the reader by the primacy of the visual in the text. This presence of the visual supports our exploration of the complex, the contradictory, and the unnamed within her narrative, and thus offers us the possibility of closing a gap within it. Cather makes us see that the scar on Virginia's face signifies the pathology of women's common struggles with the beauty standard at the turn of the twentieth century.

The central conflict Cather puts before us in "The Profile" is located equally within the art salon and the domestic life of two expatriate Americans who have met and married in Paris. It arises both from the standards of painting practice and from the standards by which women were then judged to be beautiful. Dunlap's immediate horror at the disfigurement of Virginia's otherwise perfect face is a reaction not just to her flesh but to the injustice of her beauty having been despoiled in this manner: "His heart ached at the injustice of it; that her very beauty . . . should, through an inch or two of seared flesh, seem tainted and false" (184). The standard definition of female beauty, as it is recognized among the wealthy classes and the artists of Cather's imagined Paris, has been utterly betrayed for the painter by the sight of the disfigured half of Virginia's face. That the other half of this face meets the standard of beauty Cather makes clear: "a girlish profile, unusually firm for a thing so softly colored; oval, flower-tinted, and shadowed by soft, blonde hair that wound about her head and curled and clung about her brow and neck and ears" (184). That *Olympia*'s harsh charcoal outlines violated this criterion of female beauty Manet's furious critics also made clear. Her embedded mention of *Olympia* in "The Profile" is a subtle signifier: Cather appropriated Manet's challenge to both the beauty and the painting standards of post-Napoleonic Paris in order, similarly, to ask pointed questions about their impact on the women who lived there.

How was the phenomenon of beauty recognized in the Paris of this fateful portrait sitting? In *Face Value: The Politics of Beauty*, Robin Lakoff and Raquel Scherr trace the debate among philosophers as to whether beauty is dependent on overall harmony of physical features (as Aristotle proposed) or on a specific set of properties identifiable as the delicate, soft, and small (as argued by Edmund Burke), and conclude that the idea of beauty is culturally constructed, and therefore varies with time and place (54–55). Cather's turn-of-the-century France, it should be noted, shared many basic cultural assumptions about female beauty with those of Americans of the time period. Cather seems to have caught her female protagonist in a snare of three types of feminine beauty identified by Lois Banner in *American Beauty*, each embodying to the world American national values and international standing as it entered the twentieth century. Virginia's pallor, smallness, and softness are characteristic of the "steel-engraving lady" of the pre–Civil War era, a female type whose physical delicacy and corseted dress were understood as signs of moral rectitude (45). Banner notes that American fashion of the time took its style guidelines from those of the French, and indeed, Cather seems to have modeled the more flamboyant, sensuous style of dress that Virginia was known for in Paris on a slightly later nineteenth-century type that Banner calls "the voluptuous woman," whose fuller figure was the female model preferred by French academic artists commonly exhibiting in America (5). Virginia is typical of American women in having embraced the bolder and more body-conscious fashion of this type, a style that ran to frank emphases of the bosom and buttocks. A third type described by Banner is the well-known Gibson girl of the 1890s, the time period closest to that of the setting of "The Profile." Her tall, slender athleticism and patrician good health, widely popularized in easily reproduced graphic arts, were understood on both sides of the Atlantic to exemplify the "New Woman," who ushered in the new century as the predominant female symbol of American pride and strength (5).

Virginia's scar is a sign of morbidity effectively canceling her young body's health. We are acutely aware of her inability to embody the ideals of the older antebellum or the fresh, new Gibson paradigms of femininity. Despite being a privileged American, she is notorious for following the clothing style of the

voluptuous woman precisely because its seductive message creates a grotesque contrast: "Look at my body and desire; look
at my face and pity." Within Cather's narrative, modeled on a
world awash in images of perfect female beauty, the pain of this
frustration must be very difficult for Virginia to bear. Virginia's disfigurement prevents her from fully meeting the standard
prescribed by any of these images of woman used by Cather as
cultural references to inform her narrative.

Lakoff and Scherr follow the ideal of female beauty through
ages of its varied representation by artists, noting the volup-
tuousness of the standard photographer's or painter's model
in 1895, women with "corseted hour-glass figures" who were
"round, plump, [and] rosy cheeked." They point out the "static,
immobile, frozen, remote faces" of these models, suggesting that
an ideal of both physical and emotional restraint was an additional aspect of late-nineteenth-century conventions in portraiture (70). As a conventional aspect of pose, the depicted cool affect of these models must have produced, for viewers of the time,
a tension contrasting with their seductive, "voluptuous" style of
dress. In Cather's story, this tension is also present, produced by
Virginia's emotional distance in contrast with the beckoning effect of her "toilet."

The pair of illustrations by Walter Taylor on the first and last
pages of the story's original publication in *McClure's Magazine*
extends these tensions within the narrative. Taylor's images create an additional irony between what we see as viewers of his
images and what we know as readers of Cather's story.

At her first sitting, Virginia turns the flawless side of her face
to Dunlap's view and hides from his painter's eyes the grotesque
other side, arranging herself for him in the conventional late
nineteenth century profile pose (fig. 1). Taylor's first image, however, marks the moment in the narrative when she has failed to
hide her scar from Dunlap, who, on the pretext of adjusting the
room's light, has examined it. It is, instead, the readers who view
Virginia's unmarked profile in Taylor's image, and who "read"

Fig. 1. Taylor's first illustration for "The Profile" in *McClure's Magazine* June 1907: 135.

it in narrative terms as providing high contrast to the scar which Dunlap scrutinizes.

The last image visualizes the volcanic anger between the two characters. It replicates their positions in the first illustration, again focusing the reader's eye on Virginia's perfect profile and luxurious décolletage, contrasted with Dunlap's horrified gaze at the scar, which heightens the effect of her "defiant" new gown (141) (fig. 2). In emphasizing the story's ironies of the invisible and unspoken, Taylor's visual effects are similar to Cather's picture writing. A principal irony that Taylor brings to light hints at Virginia's tragic psychological strategy: she perhaps sees herself as a profile portrait of a beautiful woman, an eternal type such as Sargent's *Madame X.*

If the beautiful, high-class woman of fin de siècle Paris had to meet strict codes for her appearance, then her painted likeness was similarly accountable. As Martha Banta has observed in *Imaging American Women: Idea and Ideals in Cultural History,* the Platonism of many artists created standards for representational practice (xxxi). She notes that the resulting images of women, whether on view in print, paint, sculpture, or graphic arts, proliferated among viewers who increasingly took the meanings of these forms to have broader social and cultural significance (xxviii). One symbolic type Banta discusses—"the

Fig. 2. Taylor's last illustration for "The Profile" in *McClure's Magazine* June 1907: 141.

American Girl"—is a model of femininity widely recognized to be physically attractive and pure of heart, but also independent, willful, impulsive, and spoiled (48). Apart from the facial flaw, Virginia Gilbert might have embodied this model. Banta notes that many artists worked from an ideal of a female form they sought to discover in the physical characteristics and poses of their models (178). Cather imprints obliterating complications onto the easily recognized type of the American girl. She creates a character who assuages her psychic pain by seeing herself in her mind's eye and presenting herself in society as the ideal painter's model. This produces a contradictory array of physical and material female signs that amount to an insistent denial of "[t]he comfort offered by Eternal Types in a world of uncertain equilibrium" (411).

A constellation of signs insistently disrupting the comfort of viewers is, according to T. J. Clark, what Manet's public reacted to on their initial experience with his *Olympia*. In *The Painting of Modern Life*, Clark explains that the painted representation of the female body was bound by rules regarding the pose of the figure, the composition of other pictured objects, and, equally important, the production of the brushstrokes that finally negotiate the total image: "all the normal ways in which pigment, texture, and tone declare a likeness" (100). These rules of practice make up the visual grammar within which the meaning of the female image is signified. "The painter's task was to construct . . . a relation between the body as particular and excessive fact . . . and the body as a sign, formal and generalized, meant for a token of composure and fulfillment" (126). Be she society matron dressed to receive or undressed Venus, the image of the female was understood broadly among the bourgeoisie of Second Empire Paris as a sign. Clark's observation, parallel to those of Banner and Banta, is that these icons of womanhood were deeply if not consciously understood by their viewers as icons of the metropolis. Speaking specifically of Manet's painterly discoveries of the emergence of modern Paris, Clark argues

258

JOYCE KESSLER

that the effect of his paintings on the world they sought to investigate "may [have laid] hold of the grammar of appearance in the culture at large, . . . as *specific forms of visualization*" (xxiv). Granting Clark's point, the female image may be understood as a specific signifier of a city in the process of redefining itself, such as Paris was in the mid-nineteenth century.

Clark explains that the common Parisian reaction to the 1865 exhibition of Manet's *Olympia* was outrage at the perception that the nude's flesh had been disgraced and disfigured (134). He quotes a reviewer whose response is typical of the general outcry: "The naked body is the abstract being, and thus it must preoccupy and tempt the artist above all; but . . . to give the facial features all those expressions which are not spoken of, that is to dishonour the nude and to do something disreputable" (128) (fig. 3). Yet Émile Zola defended Manet's technique by asking, "When other artists correct nature by painting Venus, they lie. Manet asked himself why he should lie. Why not tell the truth?" (qtd. in Williams 2).

But the risks in telling the truth are manifold in both Manet's and Cather's Paris. The agon of "The Profile" is located in the two central characters' differing ideas of the truthful representation—either in the form of the image or of the word—of the face of Virginia Gilbert. It dramatizes the ongoing battle between Dunlap and his wife over representative rights to the scar, in word and image. Although neither refers to or names Virginia's disfigurement until late in the story, and Dunlap does not ever give form to it in his portrait, these two modes of representation lie at the polar ends of the increasing line of tension between them, caused by the scar's unnamable presence. The spoken word and the visual image as possible modes of signification for it are equally forbidden. Their ultimate confrontation over the scar results in each invading the other's customary expressive ground—he speaks the word and she makes the mark—in a terminal clash that perpetuates, rather than resolves, their battle over opposing notions of social and personal justice.

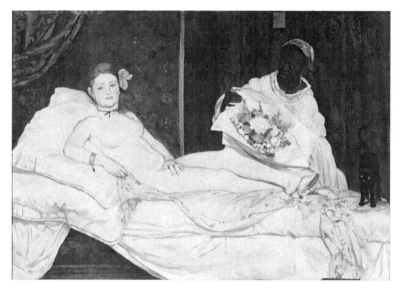

Fig. 3. Manet's *Olympia*, 1865. Musée d'Orsay, Paris. © RMN (Musée d'Orsay)/Hervé Lewandowski.

In the opening scene of "The Profile," the Second Empire painter's commentary on *Circe's Swine* speaks directly to the power of the human image to affront the general sensibilities of the viewer: "They are all errors, these freakish excesses!" (180). As Clark has observed, the art community of the Second Empire placed the ultimate value of the human form in its broader iconic value: any abridgment of this purpose by the disruption of its formal purity was considered a violation not only of the form but of all it represented. Assumed in the old painter's critical values is a link between the realist formal representation of natural form and an idea of the justice that such form must corroborate. His observation that a painter straying from these standards might offend against the "law" that gives primacy to it raises the question of a moral balance between what is right ("The body, as Nature has evolved it") and wrong ("lop away so much as a finger, and you have wounded the creature beyond reparation" [180]).[4] Cather's old painter discusses the whole human figure within the framework of justice values, and the damaged or abridged form as a signifier of justice's failure. His commentary is focused on the distorted male figures, although the pure female form had for centuries been the preferred subject of painters. In reversing the subject of the painted form from female to male, Cather hints at a reversal of justice parallel to the myth's, in which Circe metes out the gods' justice to Odysseus's men. Thus the story's first painting connects purity of the human form and justice, while setting men and women in opposition to one another on the subject of justice.

Presentation of the second painting entailed in this story is embedded as a detail within the early chance meetings of Dunlap and the American millionaire Mr. Gilbert, who is found "standing in a state of abject bewilderment" before Manet's notorious image of a bold-faced, reclining nude. The phrase indicates confusion at the least, or worse, a quality of debasement. Cather is clearly aware of and exploiting public knowledge about the angry rejection of Manet's depiction of his longtime model, Victorine Meurent. Despite the passage of more than three decades, her characters apparently continue to feel the revulsion typical of *Olympia*'s initial critical reception.

The two paintings that appear, however briefly, in "The Profile" are, I would argue, deliberately juxtaposed by Cather to her story's central theme in order to provide it with subtle support. Within this story, she evokes two paintings, both trailing associated cultural narratives. *Circe's Swine* makes visual reference to the narrative of Homer's witch, as she distorts the forms of Odysseus's men in retribution for their flagrant disobedience to the gods in earlier scenes of the *Odyssey*. Manet's nude brings with it the narrative of the scandal that it caused on first showing. Jo Ann Middleton would encourage us to identify the subterranean "stories" attending these two works of art as gaps, or "vacuoles." My perspective on them is slightly different: I see Cather as having brought to light and then exploited an indexical relationship existing between these two icons and their respective "histories," whereby each is used as a sign of that particular associated narrative, casting her paired subjects of beauty and justice in an alternate frame. Cather uses the first image as an index of retributive justice meted out against men by a woman; she deploys the second as an index of the attack of truth on a false ideal of feminine beauty.

To these documented cultural contexts Cather opens a door into her narrative, admitting nineteenth-century rules of representation in art, in their relation to the stable, fiercely defended categories of sexuality and of the gender identities of that time period. In Clark's view, *Olympia* suggested that its reclining subject could be either a courtesan or the idealized female figure, presenting its viewers with mutually irreconcilable signs that "altered . . . identities the culture wished to keep still, pre-eminently those of the nude and the prostitute" (100). Clark's ultimate insight into the effect of *Olympia* on Paris is that the image of an aberrant female form had been posed in relation to the widespread sense of social unease and disrupted certainties suffered by a society engaged in redefining itself on a capitalist model (87–88). Clark thus characterizes the negativity of Manet's critics as stemming from a displaced preoccupation with a "specific form of visualization" (118). In her inquiry into the relationship between beauty and justice, Cather has created a female character whose tragic facial disfigurement is similarly read by her society as a specific visualization of disrupted social values.

Cather sets her story in a Parisian critical establishment still nervous about modern painting. That establishment shares the general public repulsion at the image of despoiled female flesh. In a culture that casts privileged women as emblems of social stability, Virginia's scar makes her vulnerable to reactions of horror and self-loathing on the part of men, in an effect similar to that of Manet's *Olympia*. Her scar is a sign of morbidity, contradicting the significance of her youth and beautiful features, and as with *Olympia*, it can provide a displaced focus for the unconscious fears among those who encounter her.

"The Profile" terminates with striking violence. Dunlap is ultimately driven to violate his wife's silence with words that wound as if with the brutality of his grandfather's strap. In response, Virginia arranges an explosion of the alcohol lamp to mark her niece's face with a disfigurement similar to her own. He succumbs to his revulsion; she to her rage and the only act that will allow her to signify the truth about the cruelty of the ideal of female beauty. Among the story's elements of character and art historical setting, Virginia's scarring of Eleanor is parallel to Manet's manner of depiction in *Olympia*: it corrects the injustice of an ideal of beauty that is not aligned with the truth of human experience.

Dunlap finally sounds one passionate, critical comment, the verbal sign of despoilment that Virginia had so long been able to protect herself from hearing. To match her husband's violence, she transforms herself from a model in a romantic portrait to a painter with a savagely truthful modernist vision. Virginia has marked the youthful purity of Eleanor's face with a sign of the ongoing injustice to women that cannot be modified or erased by the portrait artist's created image of beauty. Dunlap's violence toward her is justified in his mind by his marital expectation of intimacy with his wife; her violence toward him (through Eleanor) is socially unjustified, yet also motivated by the same unjust standard for women that he unknowingly—and on some level, unwillingly—perpetuates. Virginia's redress for the injustice that she has suffered returns us to a gender-reversed version of Circe's harsh punishment of Odysseus's men. Through its development in the story as a focal point for various issues of social and cultural justice (in marriage and in artistic representation), Cather's ultimate semiotic of the scar on a female face comes, at last, to signify injustice to women, broadly defined. This replicated sign on Eleanor's face is a constant reminder to Dunlap of his own part in "the necessity and destiny to suffer, . . . so essential in a woman" (187).

The narrative's ending violence makes readers aware that, as a sign, the scar is Cather's writing about injustice to women, too. Cather proposes through this sign a counternarrative to established justice formulations, along with an alternate standard of justice for those betrayed by such formulations. Her covert argument is silently advanced by the meaning that Virginia's scar gradually accrues as the narrative progresses. Finally, the story will not allow escape from the scar's form as Cather's meaning, no matter how much Virginia seeks to suppress language, or Dunlap avoids his canvas.

Cather's picture writing operates with profound effect, giving readers fascinating images that snag their minds directly and that bear within them subtle arguments. An examination of the picture writing in "The Profile" reveals to us that Cather's distinctive image making was the result of a process of visual semiosis that resulted from her having worked outward toward her final created narrative from an indexical sign of great resonance to her. Like Manet's crudely dark outlines of *Olympia*'s form, Cather's picture writing in "The Profile" results in a visual image that starkly reframes dominant social assumptions by proposing an alternate truth in the matter of women's value. Her invention of this technique and the expressive purposes she sought with it seem to have been significantly parallel to those of Manet. Cather's visual acuity is evident in her deep engagement with the visual arts and with visual form, but it was in her discovery and use of picture writing that she created a modern way to exploit her own process of visual semiosis for the intensification of her narrative art.

NOTES

1. The category of "sign," according to Peirce, holds within it three basic subcategories: the symbol, the icon, and the index (Atkin).

2. In *American Beauty*, Lois Banner describes the pale tone and unblemished skin surface that were two paramount attributes of beauty as defined at the turn of the twentieth century.

3. W. J. T. Mitchell has called this visual totality a "verbal icon," connecting it to notions of "pure form" as they were conceived by the imagist poets. Mitchell proposes an intermediate visual form for the thought that precedes its formal manifestation, whether in word or image. Opposing Mitchell's notion of the preverbal image, Derrida's idea of "writing" admits of no formless thought or verbal icon to which created language or image gives form. Within the scope of his claim that there is no thought without language, both conceptual and manifest forms are a species of linguistic phenomenon.

4. Duryea speculates that Cather's source for her fictional painting, *Circe's Swine*, may have been a work by the French symbolist painter Gustav Moreau (119).

WORKS CITED

Atkin, Albert. "Peirce's Theory of Signs." *Stanford Encyclopedia of Philosophy.* Spring 2009 ed. Ed. Edward N. Zalta. 12 July 2008. http://plato.stanford.edu.

Banner, Lois W. *American Beauty.* New York: Knopf, 1983.

Banta, Martha. *Imaging American Women: Idea and Ideals in Cultural History.* New York: Columbia UP, 1987.

Cather, Willa. *My Ántonia.* Willa Cather Scholarly Edition. Ed. Charles W. Mignon with Kari A. Ronning. Lincoln: U of Nebraska P, 1994.

———. "The Novel Démeublé." *Willa Cather on Writing: Critical Studies on Writing as an Art.* Ed. Stephen Tennant. Lincoln: U of Nebraska P, 1976. 35–43.

———. *Willa Cather in Europe: Her Own Story of the First Journey.* Ed. George N. Kates. Lincoln: U of Nebraska P, 1976.

———. "The Profile." *McClure's Magazine* June 1907. *Willa Cather Archive.* Ed. Andrew Jewell. U of Nebraska–Lincoln. 2 Apr. 2008. http://cather.unl.edu.

Clark, T. J. "Olympia's Choice." *The Painting of Modern Life Paris in the Art of Manet and His Followers.* Rev. ed. Princeton: Princeton UP, 1984. 79–146.

Derrida, Jacques. *Of Grammatology.* Trans. Gayatri Chakravorty Spivak. Baltimore: Johns Hopkins UP, 1976.

Duryea, Polly. "Paintings and Drawings in Willa Cather's Prose: A Catalogue Raisonné." Diss. U of Nebraska–Lincoln, 1993. *Willa*

Cather Archive. Ed. Andrew Jewell. U of Nebraska–Lincoln. 17 May 2008. http://cather.unl.edu.

Lakoff, Robin Tolmach, and Raquel L. Scherr. *Face Value: The Politics of Beauty.* Boston: Routledge and Kegan Paul, 1984.

Madigan, Mark. "Willa Cather and Dorothy Canfield Fisher: Rift, Reconciliation, and *One of Ours.*" *Cather Studies 1.* Ed. Susan J. Rosowski. *Willa Cather Archive.* Ed. Andrew Jewell. U of Nebraska–Lincoln. 20 May 2008. http://cather.unl.edu.

Manet, Édouard. *Olympia.* 1865. Musée d'Orsay, Paris. Réunion des musées nationaux, Agence Photographique (27 May 2010).

Middleton, Jo Ann. *Willa Cather's Modernism: A Study of Style and Technique.* Teaneck NJ: Fairleigh Dickinson UP, 1990.

Mitchell, W. J. T. "What Is an Image?" *New Literary History: A Journal of Theory and Interpretation* 15.3 (1984): 503–37.

Morley, Catherine. "Voice of the Prairies? Willa Cather and the International Modernist Scene." *Willa Cather Newsletter and Review* 51.1 (2007): 7–10.

Stout, Janis P. Introduction. *Willa Cather and Material Culture.* Ed. Janis P. Stout. Tuscaloosa: U of Alabama P, 2005. 1–14.

———. "The Observant Eye, the Art of Illustration, and Willa Cather's *My Ántonia.*" *Cather Studies 5: Willa Cather's Ecological Imagination.* Ed. Susan J. Rosowski. *Willa Cather Archive.* Ed. Andrew Jewell. U of Nebraska–Lincoln. 2 Mar. 2007. http://cather .unl.edu.

Taylor, F. Walter. Illustrations for "The Profile." *McClure's Magazine* June 1907. *Willa Cather Archive.* Ed. Andrew Jewell. U of Nebraska–Lincoln. http://cather.unl.edu.

Williams, Mary Elizabeth. "Manet's *Olympia.*" *Salon.com.* 13 May 2002. http://dir.salon.com.

Wolff, Cynthia Griffin. "The Artist's Palette: Early Cather." *Willa Cather Pioneer Memorial Newsletter* 40.1 (1996): 1–14.

13 "Before Its Romanzas
Have Become Street Music"

Cather and Verdi's *Falstaff*, Chicago, 1895

JOHN H. FLANNIGAN

In March 1895, as Willa Cather was about to graduate from the University of Nebraska, she traveled with a university librarian friend, Mary Jones, to Chicago to hear five opera
performances featuring Metropolitan Opera stars making their
annual visit to the Auditorium Theatre.[1] The trip was a momentous one for Cather. She had not been outside of Nebraska since
arriving there at the age of nine, and she would hear some of the
finest singers then active in Europe and the United States in roles
that made them famous.[2] The Metropolitan's offerings were a
veritable feast for music lovers, yet Cather, who for some time
had been actively writing music and theater criticism for the *Nebraska State Journal*, published a single column for the *Journal*
mentioning only two events from that memorable week. Cather devoted a brief paragraph to the American soprano Emma
Eames, who sang the role of Desdemona in the Saturday, 16
March, performance of Verdi's *Otello*; the rest of her review is
given over to the Thursday, 14 March, performance of Verdi's
final opera, *Falstaff*.[3] Her column, an extraordinarily perceptive
piece of work for a twenty-one-year-old college student, represented Cather's debut as a critic of musical events beyond Lincoln, Nebraska, and makes interesting reading today now that

Falstaff, after more than a century of lukewarm critical responses, has found a more or less secure place in the operatic canon. The review is all the more interesting given Cather's almost
complete lack of musical training. A reluctant piano student and
raised on a diet of light opera and mediocre performances by
touring groups, Cather nonetheless proved herself a sharper and
more perceptive critic of Verdi's unabashedly modern opera than
others with far stronger credentials and wider experience.

The resistance *Falstaff* met as it made its way into opera companies' repertoires has its roots in both musical and cultural
shifts in the late nineteenth century. On the musical front, the
explosion of interest in Wagner's complex musical dramas had
caused a general backlash against Italian opera. For many early
audiences and critics, however, Verdi had unfortunately ended
up on the "right" side of the Wagnerian controversy: the music
of *Falstaff* was too Germanic, too Wagnerian, and not sufficient-
ly Italian to satisfy audiences used to Verdi's traditional musical
vocabulary (Hepokoski 138–41).

Broader cultural shifts had also affected public tastes in theater and symphonic music as well as in opera. According to historian Lawrence W. Levine, the cultural hierarchies that privilege
"serious" entertainments over "popular" ones began hardening
into ironclad divisions as early as the mid-nineteenth century
(33). For Levine, this "sacralization of culture" began with nineteenth-century America's turning away from popular parodies of
Shakespeare's plays and ended with a "society in which Shakespeare is firmly entrenched in the pantheon of high culture" (4).
This shift in taste was repeated in the public's increasing disdain
for popular opera and orchestral music and the gradual adop-
tion of rigorous "categories of culture"—"high" and "low"—
that are "fixed and immutable" (8). Because of the fossiliza-
tion of such hierarchies, Verdi's *Falstaff*, with its rollicking story
and genuinely funny music deriving from perhaps Shakespeare's
most broadly humorous comedy, seemed destined to fall on the
wrong side of these cultural developments.

Upon her arrival in Chicago, Cather had already joined this struggle between high and low cultures, and in her *Falstaff* review she clearly states her sympathies: "To be present at the fourth American presentation of Verdi's 'Falstaff' was more than a pleasure: it was a privilege and a great opportunity. There is something especially wonderful and sacred about any great masterpiece in its first youth, before its romanzas have become street music, before the concocters of comic opera have stolen the choruses, while it is played by the first cast, and the ink of the score is scarcely dry" ("As You Like It"). The constellation of images in these opening sentences—"sacred," "street music," "concocters of comic opera," "stolen" choruses—implies a tension between the real and the fraudulent, the legitimate and the counterfeit, and the sacred art object and its profane imitation. These tensions are worth exploring, as they not only appear again and again in Cather's fiction and nonfiction but also have to a great extent explained modern American tastes and attitudes toward "culture" (Levine 9).

Interestingly, however, Cather struggled for much of her personal and professional life with her own attitudes toward these cultural hierarchies. In her review of *Falstaff* she addresses these hierarchies in curious if conflicted ways and furnishes a helpful benchmark for measuring how, throughout her life, she alternately participated in and resisted this process of "sacralization." At the age of twenty-one, she seems to suggest that great art such as *Falstaff* can be corrupted by prolonged association with its inferiors, a conception of culture that, for Levine, signifies the loss of "a rich shared public culture that once characterized the United States" (9). Yet Cather also revels in the "great opportunity" afforded by her encounter with Verdi's opera, for she can become a participant in an artistic event instead of being a mere spectator. In Levine's analysis, American audiences had once taken this kind of freedom for granted, but by the end of the nineteenth century they were less comfortable with it (9). Cather relishes the possibility of playing a collaborative role with Verdi: "On such an occasion one feels dimly what it must be to create" ("As You Like It"). Moreover, when she remarks that it was a "privilege" to hear *Falstaff* "before its romanzas have become street music," she was not so much expressing her opposition to such vulgarization as conceding that it was an inevitable, perhaps even a constructive, process.

Later in her writing career, especially after she began to know very well "what it must be to create," Cather withdrew from the elevation she occupied during the *Falstaff* performance and sometimes sought relief in lower artistic and musical altitudes. Or perhaps it is more accurate to say that she would always be comfortable inhabiting both the Apollonian and Dionysian artistic worlds, the temple as well as the street. Her youthful enthusiasm for *Falstaff* is certainly strong evidence that, even at the beginning of her writing career, she understood and relished engaging in the artistic struggle between the new and the traditional, the fresh and the timeless, the fleeting and the permanent, and perhaps came to realize that, despite attempts to insulate "high art" from the masses, "the perimeters of our cultural divisions have been permeable and shifting rather than fixed and immutable" (Levine 8). As she grew older, she continued to discover artistic fulfillment in personal encounters with music and artists of all stripes, encounters that her more sophisticated friends perhaps disdained or for which they were too embarrassed to admit their fondness. In her later years she may have had in mind how her own youthful exuberance and naïveté had once crossed paths with the mellowness of Verdi in his sunset years when she wrote in the prose fragment "Light on Adobe Walls" that "Art is too terribly human to be very 'great'" (125).

In his late seventies, Giuseppe Verdi (1813–1901) unexpectedly returned to writing comedy, an operatic genre he had abandoned more than a half-century earlier after the disastrous premiere of his comedy *Un giorno di regno* (*A Day's Reign*) in September 1840. (His intervening twenty-five operas were decidedly not comedies, although more than a few had comic moments.) He combined this sudden turn toward comedy with a lifelong love for Shakespeare and in 1888 began collaborating with composer/librettist Arrigo Boito (1842–1918) on an adaptation of the character Sir John Falstaff from Shakespeare's *Henry IV, Parts 1 and 2* and, more significantly, *The Merry Wives of Windsor*. In the resulting collaboration, some of the most graceful and elegant music to be found in opera effectively illustrates Falstaff's gluttony, lechery, and shameless egotism.

But by selecting *The Merry Wives of Windsor* as a major source for their opera's plot, Verdi and Boito were going to the bottom of the barrel for a Shakespearean subject. As Gary Schmidgall has observed, "There are many more or less sacred cows in the Shakespearean canon. *The Merry Wives of Windsor* is not one of them" (321). Schmidgall notes the unusual ratio of prose to poetry in the play—88 percent of the lines are in prose—and argues it is one of Shakespeare's "least inspired efforts" (134). American audiences were dismissive of the play at the same time their reverence for "serious" Shakespeare was increasing. As Levine argues, by the end of the nineteenth century, "Shakespeare had been converted from a popular playwright whose dramas were the property of those who flocked to see them, into a sacred author who had to be protected from ignorant audiences and overbearing actors threatening the integrity of his creations" (72). When it came to productions of *The Merry Wives of Windsor*, however, American critics felt that Shakespeare had to be protected even from himself. One Chicago critic, reviewing a November 1886 performance, concluded that it was "almost impossible . . . to enter into the spirit of the blunt and gross humor of those buxom days." The same critic offered backhanded praise of William H. Crane's performance of the leading role: "[I]f it is not the Falstaff of Shakespeare, the actor may reply and truly that the Falstaff of Shakespeare is not in the 'Merry Wives of Windsor'" ("Falstaff of Farce"). The "blunt and gross humor" of *The Merry Wives of Windsor* had begun to appear "un-Shakespearean" to American audiences of this era, and an operatic comedy based on it—especially one composed by the revered Verdi—would probably be even more difficult to swallow. The action of Verdi's opera revolves around Sir John Falstaff's attempts to seduce Mistress Alice Ford and Mistress Meg Page. A subplot involves the love affair between Nanetta, the daughter of Mistress Ford and her husband, and Fenton. Ford forbids Nanetta to marry Fenton, and the two lovers have only fleeting moments together throughout most of the opera. In act 1, Mistresses Ford and Page learn that Falstaff has sent both of them identical love letters, and they vow revenge. When Alice Ford invites Falstaff to her home for a tryst, Falstaff falls for the bait. In act 2, she hides him from her husband by burying him in a laundry basket and instructs her servants to throw it out the window into the Thames. In act 3, Falstaff, often depicted in productions as emerging dripping wet from his dunking, is still convinced he is loved by both women and accepts the ladies' invitation to come to Herne's Oak in Windsor Forest at midnight. There, Alice, Meg, and Dame Quickly stage an elaborate masque with Nanetta Ford as the Queen of Fairies. Falstaff is frightened out of his wits by the faux-supernatural encounter and, when the joke is exposed, takes a beating from the ladies. Unbeknownst to her husband, Alice has also disguised Nanetta and Fenton and arranges for them to be married by the unsuspecting Ford. The opera concludes with a vocal fugue sung to the words "But he laughs well who laughs / the last laugh" (Hepokoski 1–18).

Verdi had had a brilliant success in 1887 with *Otello*, and the premiere of *Falstaff* (La Scala, Milan, 9 February 1893) was eagerly awaited by opera lovers around the world. Both *Otello* and *Falstaff* had concise, beautifully constructed libretti by Boito; both featured the great French baritone Victor Maurel in leading roles; and both productions were marvels of scenic design, costuming, and careful preparation. But whereas *Otello* had made a deep impression on audiences as it toured the world's opera houses, *Falstaff* stumbled early in its international travels. A review of the first Rome performances of *Falstaff*, in April 1893, is typical and pinpoints a problem:

> There was considerable astonishment—perhaps even disappointment—among many of the innumerable admirers of Verdi's immortal genius. . . . "Is this our Verdi?", they asked themselves. "But where is the *motive*; where are the broad melodies that decorated his earlier operas; where are the usual *ensembles*; the *finales*? Alas, all of this is buried in the past. At the age of eighty, then, does he acknowledge having changed course? Are *Rigolettos*, *Traviatas*, and *Aidas* no longer beautiful and fresh?" (Montefiore 129)

Whether Verdi appreciated it or not, audiences had sacralized him for his earlier successes and resisted having to rewrite their standards for sacralization.

Outside Italy, audiences were likewise confused by *Falstaff*'s strangeness. Within only two years of its first performance, *Falstaff* had traveled to nearly all the corners of the Western musical world—from Milan to Naples, Rio de Janeiro, Mexico City, St. Petersburg, Berlin, Madrid, Paris, London, and elsewhere—but failed to gain a foothold anywhere (Hepokoski 130). Even when critics wrote favorably of the work, audiences stayed away (Hepokoski 129). It fared somewhat better in New York in February 1895, one month before Cather encountered the work, but even there critics were nagged by doubts. According to the *New York Times*, "it may be that the remarkable ingenuity of the score passes into a subtlety which will escape the hearer at first, and it is certain that no one will ever fairly appreciate this opera who cannot follow the text line by line" ("Verdi's Great 'Falstaff'").

Major difficulties for critics have included "reconciling [*Falstaff*] with the rest of Verdi's career" and deciding the question, "is the subtlety of *Falstaff* an advance or a retreat?" (Hepokoski 138). No critic has claimed that Verdi or Boito was careless in his work—quite the opposite. In fact, the enormous sophistication of Boito's poetry and Verdi's musical ingenuity—the tonal relationships and juxtapositions between scenes, the amazingly vivid orchestration, the composer's uncanny ability to match musical sounds with words and images in the text—is clear to a listener who follows a performance or a recording with an orchestral score. But therein lies a huge stumbling block for most audiences, only a small minority of whom wish to "enjoy" a performance by following along with a score. *Falstaff* is too subtle for most audiences to appreciate after a single encounter, and the opera's lack of approachability discourages opera companies from staging it as often as other, more "approachable" works, thereby in turn preventing audiences from becoming more familiar with its novelties.[4]

The controversy surrounding *Falstaff* as it made its way around the world no doubt increased audience excitement in Chicago, and its premiere there—Cather saw the first of two performances—was the subject of intense anticipation in the press. Even Martin T. Dooley, the fictional Irish bartender and raconteur beloved by Chicago newspaper readers, reported that he attended the premier and enjoyed a spirited political debate while the singers on the stage "was whalin' away in Eyetallian" (Dunne). But the mood of Chicago's more sober operagoers was rather sour. The newly founded (1891) and already greatly respected Chicago Symphony Orchestra, organized by Theodore Thomas, was on its own tour and would not accompany the Auditorium performances as it had in previous seasons (Marsh 61). And worse, the Metropolitan's managers, Abbey, Schoeffel and Grau, had raised ticket prices by fifty cents over the previous year's tour: prices for the March 1895 performances ranged from $1.50 to $3.50, with boxes going for $30.00 ("Grand Opera"). (To put these prices in perspective, Cather likely was paid $1.00 per column for her *Nebraska State Journal* work [Lewis xxxi].)

In a provocative article titled "The Operatic Revolt" that appeared in the *Tribune* four days before the *Falstaff* premiere, an anonymous critic complained about the sloppy preparation, capricious cancellations, and, in particular, the ever-rising ticket prices that marked the Metropolitan tours:

> Taking everything together, it is no wonder that the oppressed peoples have risen in revolt. To all this the managers will reply that Italian opera is a luxury and that luxuries are always costly, and that the salaries of operatic artists are so high that they cannot afford to charge reasonable rates. To this it may be answered that there is a limit even to the cost of luxuries, and that the price of luxuries even should be reduced to a reasonable rate when the managers are making large profits, as they are in this case. ("Operatic Revolt")

Opera, like performances of Shakespeare and symphonic music, was indeed becoming a "luxury" and unaffordable for less-wealthy audience members. By contrast, on the evening of the same day that Cather had attended a matinee performance of *Otello* at the Auditorium, the American local-color author George Washington Cable was performing "Creole-African Songs and Stories, with Illustrative Examples" at Chicago's Central Music Hall, a first-class concert venue, with reserved seats priced at fifty cents, seventy-five cents, and a dollar (Central Music Hall).

No doubt due in part to the higher ticket prices, the *Falstaff* audience of 14 March, though "good," was "not remarkably large" ("First Week"). The Chicago critics, moreover, were deeply divided about the performance. Reviews in the *Inter Ocean* ("'Falstaff' Is Heard"), the *Record* ("Maurel Won Laurels"), and the *Evening Post* ("Verdi's 'Falstaff'") were generally positive, and Cather may have drawn on these notices when writing her own review.[5] The notices in the city's most powerful papers, the *Tribune* and the *Daily News*, however, were mostly negative. Witnessing the same performance attended by Cather, the *Tribune*'s critic found the music "threadbare" and noted "the first act impresses one as the work of an old man" ("Much Humor"). The same critic lamented a "fatal lapse of memory" by the American soprano Zélie de Lussan in the role of Nanetta Ford that threw the performance into disarray and elsewhere in the review mostly summarized the plot without commenting directly on Verdi's music. In its Sunday edition following the premiere, the *Tribune* ran a general review of the Metropolitan's performances to date in which the critic again lamented the "unfortunate break" in act 3 of *Falstaff* triggering an "unprecedented disaster" that was "painful to the audience as well as to those engaged on the stage" ("First Week").

The critic covering the performance for the *Daily News* was the extremely colorful and caustic Amy Leslie, a legendary actress-turned-journalist who, a generation older than Cather, was the doyenne of Chicago music and theater circles for half a century. Her scathing review proves that Cather was not the only "meatax" critic terrorizing singers and actors in their forays around the Midwest. For Leslie, "the first act of Verdi's 'Falstaff' is null and empty as a drunkard's flagon. There is neither art nor luxury, no rhythm, no robust phrasing, no comedy, no music. . . . Even the richness of Maurel's classic performance of Falstaff could not emphatically illumine Verdi's soulless, stupid and vapid attempt at light harmony for a heavy clown." She enjoyed the second act somewhat better, but the pleasure did not last. "[T]ouched by a gleam of music in Anne's [Nanetta's] solo and cheapened by a slovenly and lifeless ballet movement, the third act is tasteful only because of the presence of so masterful an interpreter of Sir John as Maurel proved to be." The memory lapse noted by the *Tribune*'s critic also did not escape Leslie, although she blamed not de Lussan but soprano Emma Eames in the role of Mistress Ford, "who looked very beautiful without trying and sung very wretchedly also without trying." Leslie's overall impression of the work has been echoed by other critics down to our own day: "'Falstaff' is the spectacled accomplishment of genius in dotage and is neither a laurel for the adored name of Verdi nor a truce to his tone-posing antagonists of the noisier, nobler school."

JOHN H. FLANNIGAN

The Chicago *Falstaff* reviews illustrate the generally shifting tastes of American opera audiences in the late nineteenth century. Verdi's earlier operas such as *Rigoletto*, *Il trovatore*, and *La traviata* had been wildly popular in the United States, and Verdian "romanzas"—arias detached from their operatic sources and with texts translated into the American vernacular—had supplied a huge number of popular songs that entertained Americans in the parlor and concert hall.[6] This was the world that Cather herself had known in Nebraska and that informed her own musical tastes. Well before Cather's Chicago visit, however, Wagner's revolutionary musical dramas had begun to eclipse the works of Rossini, Donizetti, and Verdi himself. Indeed, "Italian opera, which had been dominant in the first half of the century, came under attack in the second" (Levine 220). In Cather's "A Wagner Matinée" (1904), for example, Clark gently chides his Aunt Georgiana, "Well, we have come to better things than the old Trovatore at any rate" (328). By the time *Falstaff* appeared on the American scene, Verdi's works in general were slipping in popularity and Verdi himself was being labeled, in Amy Leslie's phrase, a "genius in dotage."

Additionally, *Falstaff*, with its combination of physical comedy (the title character's enormous size and grossness) with elegant wordplay and music of extreme delicacy and ethereal beauty, still represents an unusual mixture in the operatic canon. The jarring juxtaposition of "high" and "low" art in Verdi's final opera likely discomfited American audiences who were already used to canonizing Shakespeare's plays as "high art" and for some time had been turning their backs on the parodies and interpolations that had characterized Shakespearean performances in the nineteenth century (Levine 21–23). On several levels, Verdi's *Falstaff* probably struck Chicago audiences as a curious anachronism.

Against the backdrop of the *Tribune* and *Daily News* reviews, Cather's article in the *Nebraska State Journal* makes a powerful contrast. Even the Shakespearean title "As You Like It," which

Cather had earlier adopted for some of her critical articles in the *Journal* and under which the *Falstaff* review appeared, seems a strategic and not merely coincidental choice for the review, for it underscores the whimsy and introspection that infuse Cather's writing. There is no carping about high ticket prices or sloppy production values. Instead, more than one quarter of Cather's review treats the subject of the general excitement triggered by the appearance of any new work of art, an event so remarkable and significant that even a performer's memory lapses contribute their own magic: "Something of the very personality of the composer seems to cling to it. Its bloom, its freshness, the wonderful charm of its novelty, even the slight uncertainty with which some of the principals carry their parts, all emphasize that one is witnessing an absolutely new creation, a new work that did not exist yesterday, that has been called up out of nothingness and that henceforth will be a part of the art of the world" ("As You Like It").

In the above passage, Cather luxuriates in the moment when Chicago audiences have passed from living in a "pre-*Falstaff*" to a "post-*Falstaff*" world and focuses her attention on the audience's reception, not the performers' labors or mistakes. (Interestingly, the "unprecedented disaster" of the act 3 memory lapse noted by the *Tribune* critic—it is conceivable that the conductor stopped and restarted the performance—was for Cather merely a "slight uncertainty.") Cather's identification with her fellow audience members strongly evokes the mood of Levine's elegiac description of early-nineteenth-century American audiences of Shakespeare: "they are participants who can enter into the action on the field, who feel a sense of immediacy and at times even of control, who articulate their opinions and feelings vocally and unmistakably" (26). For Cather, the Auditorium audience that Thursday night had not yet surrendered the freedom whose passing, Levine notes, was already well under way in the 1890s.

Like other critics of early *Falstaff* productions, Cather detects something new and radically different in Verdi's musical lan-

guage, but she is much more accepting of it than were most critics: "it seems almost as wonderful that [*Falstaff*] should come
from Verdi as it is impossible that it should have come from any
other man living." She praises the "titanic comprehensiveness"
of the work while also appreciating "the decided flavor of the
opera comique that separates it from Verdi's earlier work"—a
mingling of genres noticed by few other critics. Moreover, she
appreciates the demands Verdi makes on an audience used to
a "different" Verdi and grants him the right to make such demands: "The whole composition is as difficult as it is beautiful and is less in the florid Italian style than any other of Verdi's
works. Instead of largely consisting of the lengthy solos so pro-
nounced in 'Il Trovatore' and even in 'Aida' and 'Otello,' the
dialogue is short and choppy; made up of one line recitations
and caught up rapidly by the singers." In fact, the almost total
absence in *Falstaff* of "set" musical pieces—Cather uses the term
romanza for such "detachable," discrete segments of music—
separates *Falstaff* not only from Verdi's earlier works but also
from those of almost all of Verdi's contemporaries.

Cather may have heard *Falstaff* with more open ears than did
other audience members, but her attitude toward the work is
nonetheless conflicted. At the same time Cather exults in Verdi's creative spirit, she expresses an ambiguous attitude toward
the cultural hierarchies that were hardening into impenetrabil-
ity in the 1890s. She expresses no disappointment in Verdi for
having attempted something new in this groundbreaking work,
but she nonetheless tries to construct an insurmountable barrier
around *Falstaff* to prevent its slide into mere popular entertain-
ment. "'Falstaff' has none of the rich arias and beautiful romanzas which abound in 'Il Trovatore,' 'Aida,' and 'La Traviata,'"
she writes. "With perhaps the exception of Oberon's song [sung
by the character Nanetta in disguise] in the scene in Windsor
Forest there are no airs in the opera that will ever be garnered
into 'Treasuries of Song' and other popular collections." After
savoring the thrill of encountering *Falstaff* before contamination

by the street will change forever how audiences hear its music, Cather ultimately expresses her belief that Verdi's opera will remain apart from audiences who no longer thrill to its newness—as if Verdi has somehow inoculated his work against contamination from inferior listeners.

Early in her career, Cather is beginning to formulate a personal aesthetic credo that would shape her later fiction and criticism and help define her relationship with readers and critics in our own time as well. The uncompromising integrity, even aloofness, that Verdi proclaimed in writing *Falstaff* appealed strongly to Cather even while she was a college student: "On such an occasion one feels dimly what it must be to create, to dream and to send out of one's dreams golden song that shall be immortal." Conspicuous by its absence from Cather's review is any mention of the importance of an artwork's immediate popular appeal in determining its immortality. Cather seems to believe that, even if other critics panned it and audiences sat on their hands, *Falstaff* was here to stay. Her growing confidence as a critic is clear in this review, and Bernice Slote was right to recognize how, in the columns Cather wrote after her Chicago trip, "one may sense a new kind of vitality, often freer, more ecstatic language. She knew that the best was real, and her own independence and authority in the arts could be based on that knowledge" (20). At twenty-one, Cather already seems to understand and even to envy a great artist's independence—the ability to do fresh and groundbreaking things without merely indulging an audience's taste for something "new." Verdi's unwillingness to compromise his art and give his audiences a new version of the same formula they had come to expect from him—the same strength she later identified in such influences as Flaubert—commanded Cather's deepest respect even at a young age and perhaps helped supply a model for her own career path as a writer.

Given her theater experience in Red Cloud and Lincoln, Cather understandably has much to say in her review about baritone Victor Maurel's acting ability in the title role, devoting almost half its space to ecstatic praise of his stage movements, costumes, gestures, and so on. (Strangely, however, in her column's brief reference to the *Otello* performance of Saturday, 16 March, which featured Maurel as Iago, she makes no mention at all of the great singer's legendary portrayal of the role he had created only eight years earlier.) Her comments on Verdi's orchestrations, however, a subject about which Cather knew almost nothing from experience or study, are perhaps most interesting for modern opera fans and set her review apart from almost every other contemporary assessment:

> In Verdi's youth he was accused of light and superficial orchestration, but certainly his last opera, a crowning glory in more senses than one, once and forever refutes that charge. It is a wonder, a marvel, a miracle of clever orchestration. . . . [T]here are a hundred little things, like the prodigious sigh of satisfaction among the wind instruments every time Falstaff lifts his cup of sack to his lips, the lively crescendo when fat Sir John is dumped into the moat, the monotonous mezzo forte of the orchestra as Falstaff runs over the items of his bill at Garter Inn and then, when he reaches the total, suddenly forte!

Cather's familiarity with *Henry IV* and *The Merry Wives of Windsor* would have prepared her for the situations portrayed in Verdi's opera, but it is unclear how she understood so quickly and confidently the musical evocations of these situations.

Cather probably had read at least some of the Chicago newspapers' extensive coverage of *Falstaff* in the days leading up to and following its premiere, but even these accounts—some of them consisting of several columns devoted to careful musical analysis, thematic quotations, and plot synopsis—do not approach Cather's strikingly precise discussion of Verdi's handling of the orchestra. (For example, the critic for the *Evening Post* praises Verdi's orchestration but fails to mention particular instruments ["Verdi's 'Falstaff'"]). In fact, few other critics, Eu-

ropean or American, of this era whose reviews I have read seem
to match Cather's grasp of two of the most powerful aspects of
Verdi's score: its eroticism and its purely *musical* humor:

> The second part of the third act opens with some of the
> most beautiful lyric music Verdi ever wrote, music breath-
> ing all the witchery of a summer night of moonbeams and
> uncertain shadows, of fairy festivals and of elfin trumpet-
> ers. And then those rare mellow strains of which the opera
> is full, now racy, snappy and piquant as one of Sir John's
> jests which were best not told before ladies. Now blood-
> stirring, amorous to grotesqueness, with a sort of yearning
> sensuousness like the naughty dreams which flitted through
> the fat knight's tipsy slumber. Tantalizing strains of reel-
> ing, sweeping sweetness that were rudely broken off before
> they were half begun, that pleased and excited and irritated
> and went to one's head like champagne, and over and over
> again came that royal laughter of the king of jolly good fel-
> lows; now crashing out of the whole orchestra, now picked
> lightly upon the strings amid the chatter of women, now
> sighing from the wind instruments in the summer breezes of
> Windsor Forest, now chuckling in the bellies of the big bas-
> soons, repeated in every kind and degree of mirth, the rib-
> ald laughter of Sir Jack Falstaff.

Cather's gnarled, jagged sentences and obvious fun in joining
words to images and impressions seem to aspire to Verdian
heights, as if her writing has been infused with the very spirit
of *Falstaff*. The sheer pleasure she seems to take in writing also
supplies a strong but not entirely dissonant counter-melody to
the otherwise exalted tone of her review. Early in her career as a
writer, Cather is actually confirming the observation made many
years later by Edith Lewis on Cather's writing: that "her style,
her beauty of cadence and rhythm, were the result of a sort of
transposed musical feeling" (48).

Cather easily reconciles Shakespeare's gross, lecherous glutton with the sometimes brassy, sometimes gossamer, and sometimes breathtakingly beautiful music with which Verdi surrounds him. And yet the humor in Verdi's music—its lightning-fast alternation between broad comedy and charming sentiment, the delicacy and wit of its orchestration, its mock-serious themes—was a long time gaining acceptance by audiences (Hepokoski 138–44). In Cather's day and well into the twentieth century, most audiences seemed not to grasp at all what was going on musically in *Falstaff*. Cather's confident, almost effortless ability to explain how orchestral color itself can make a story amusing gives her review an uncanny, exhilarating quality.

More than two weeks separated Cather's attendance at *Falstaff* on 14 March from the date of her review's publication in the *Nebraska State Journal* on 31 March. During that period, Cather contracted a serious illness ("typhoid-pneumonia") that was attributed to the killing pace of her trip to Chicago (Bennett 156). While she recovered in Lincoln, she may have had time to relive and reflect on her whirlwind trip to Chicago and to "replay" the *Falstaff* experience. Although her written recollections of the *Falstaff* performance have much of the spontaneity and warmth found in other columns that she wrote to meet tight deadlines, the new "ecstatic" tone identified by Slote in Cather's post-*Falstaff* criticism seems to have its roots in a period of thoughtful reflection during which her personal relationships to art and artists, to her home and family in Nebraska, and to the larger world represented by Chicago and points beyond probably underwent a reexamination.

Almost a year after the *Falstaff* performance, Cather wrote her stern manifesto on the rigors of being an artist, a column that seems to temper her youthful hubris with a mature understanding of the risks undertaken by any artist: "In the kingdom of art there is no God, but one God, and his service is so exacting that there are few men born of woman who are strong enough to take the vows" ("Mighty Craft" 417). Seen through the prism of Cather's later, more austere judgment, the March 1895 encounter with *Falstaff* appears to have triggered a recognition that her own critical voice was perhaps as lonely and irrelevant to the masses as Verdi's opera had seemed to many audiences and even to distinguished critics with impeccable credentials. Instead of weakening Cather's confidence in her own taste and standards, however, this recognition may have bolstered her resolve to resist conforming to the conventional viewpoint and to trust her own artistic tastes and instincts.

Clearly, Cather's high artistic standards—already taking shape while she was a college student—are confirmed by her later rejection of solicitations to popularize her fiction through filmed adaptations and paperback editions and by her efforts to prevent republication of her earliest writings. Her gentle mocking, for example, of Lucy Gayheart's starry-eyed intoxication at a performance of *Lohengrin* at the Auditorium can be read as a parody, albeit a fond one, of her own youthful tendency to go weak-kneed in the presence of art, great or not so great. I think it is just as likely, however, that when it came to music, Cather simply knew what she liked and never tried to fool anyone—least of all herself—into taking her ideas about it too seriously. As Richard Giannone points out, Cather "was devoted to music but as a member of the laity. She listened to music to add to her dreams" (4).

But music also had practical importance for Cather's criticism and fiction. The *Falstaff* review may be an early attempt by Cather to preserve and relive a deeply memorable event by describing the particular sounds that have anchored various sensory images in her memory. These images can be conjured up by Cather by "playing" the sounds in her memory and matching them to words. Music thus supplied a language that helped Cather translate memories such as the *Falstaff* performance into words to be shared as images among her readers. This "musical language," although essentially private, has a strong narrative component and enables Cather to write with unusual clarity and color about stories in which plot and characters already have been clothed in musical dress by a composer. As early as March

1895, writing, for Cather, furnished a "transposing" tool that enabled her to render remembered sounds into "definite effects with words" (Lewis 48).

Given the sophistication of this transposing skill, it is understandable that Cather occasionally sent mixed signals about her general musical expertise. In November 1931, for example, H. L. Mencken shared a Carnegie Hall box with Cather while attending a concert by the Boston Symphony Orchestra under its director, Serge Koussevitzky, and was very surprised to learn that Cather, whose taste Mencken had long respected, had preferred a suite from Ravel's ballet *Daphnis and Chloe*, a "very cheap piece of trash" in Mencken's opinion, to the evening's major work, Mahler's Symphony no. 9, receiving its New York premiere. In his diary, Mencken recalled, "I had always thought of Cather as a musician, but she told me she really knew very little about music, and thus preferred Ravel's obvious banalities to Mahler's very fine writing" (41).

The Carnegie Hall episode shines light on Cather's honesty and her reluctance to make "high" and "low" distinctions when explaining her attraction to particular music or composers. As far back as the 1895 performance of *Falstaff*, she had been able to respond almost intuitively to a work that, to many audiences and professional critics, lacked the seriousness and weight that Wagner's operas possessed. Although in the years after 1895 Cather became an ardent Wagnerite, her musical tastes apparently remained catholic without becoming indiscriminate. Even though she prized the chance in Chicago to hear music that had not yet been played to death, she did not disdain *romanzas* merely because they *had* become "street music." Mildred Bennett relates an incident involving Cather and her childhood friend Carrie Miner Sherwood, who were riding the Hoboken ferry during one of Sherwood's visits to New York. Sherwood recalled that "on the boat was an old Italian playing many familiar operas on his accordion. When the ferry docked, Willa said, 'Do you mind if we stay on for another trip? I do enjoy that music'" (155).

No doubt the Italian accordionist was playing early Verdi,

not the quirky, fleeting melodic fragments that steal through the score of *Falstaff*, but Cather appreciated art wherever and whenever she could. Throughout her life she seems to have retained a strong populist streak in her musical tastes that enabled her to enjoy, without embarrassment or irony, art, be it great or modest, in artistic temples as well as in streets—and even on ferryboats. It is this side of Cather—the artist who finds room in *My Mortal Enemy* for Myra Henshawe's tipping of the boy with no overcoat playing "The Irish Washerwoman" on a pennywhistle, in *Lucy Gayheart* for Lucy's enthusiastic embrace of Michael Balfe's hackneyed opera *The Bohemian Girl*, in "Old Mrs. Harris" for Hillary and Victoria Templeton's attending Robert Planquette's once wildly popular but now entirely forgotten operetta *The Chimes of Normandy*, and so on—that seldom receives much critical attention.

Yet these fictionalized encounters with "low" art illustrate Cather's own respect for art that could not be rendered "inauthentic" merely because of where it was encountered or what kind of people made up its audience. Certainly, Cather's remarkably eclectic taste, her unembarrassed embrace of musical belly laughs in Verdi's *Falstaff* and Ravel's opulent, wonderfully sensual ballet score *Daphnis and Chloe*, never deadened her taste for more cerebral works, such as Beethoven's last string quartets. Her enthusiasm for high and not-so-high art—for both Wagner and opéra comique—helps to explain and to reconcile the apparent contradiction between the youthful seriousness of her 1896 manifesto—"In the kingdom of art there is no God, but one God"—and the mature wistfulness of "Art is too terribly human to be very 'great.'" The cultural chasm between these two artistic credos seemed to shrink rather than grow during Cather's life, if indeed there ever was a chasm at all.

NOTES

1. Early in its history, the Metropolitan Opera (founded 1883), under the direction of various impresarios, began assembling touring com-

panies to present operas outside New York. The Metropolitan made its first tour to Chicago in January 1884, and by the time of Cather's visit in 1895 it had settled into a more or less regular pattern of annual visits. The March 1895 performances were under the management of the Abbey, Schoeffel and Grau Italian Grand Opera Company (Marsh 256–59). Cather used the Auditorium Theatre, designed by Dankmar Adler and Louis Sullivan and opened in 1889, as the venue for the performance of Ambroise Thomas's *Mignon* attended by Godfrey and Lillian St. Peter in *The Professor's House* (1925) and for the opera performances that Lucy and Harry attend in *Lucy Gayheart* (1935).

2. Cather saw five operas during her visit: Verdi's *Falstaff*, *Otello*, and *Aida*; Meyerbeer's *Les Huguenots*; and Gounod's *Roméo et Juliette* (Woodress 102). The cast lists for these performances read like a who's who of the 1890s opera world. They include Victor Maurel, Emma Eames, Sofia Scalchi, and Zélie de Lussan (*Falstaff*); Francesco Tamagno, Eames, and Maurel (*Otello*); Tamagno and Pol Plançon (*Aida*); Nellie Melba, Lillian Nordica, and Jean and Édouard de Rezske (*Les Huguenots*); and Melba and the de Rezskes (*Roméo et Juliette*) ("First Week"). Cather saw Tamagno (Otello) and Maurel (Iago and Falstaff) in roles they had recently created under Verdi's supervision.

3. Cather's column appeared under the title "As You Like It" (one of her regular column titles for theater reviews) in the *Nebraska State Journal*. Andrew Jewell, editor of the *Willa Cather Archive*, provided me with a page image and transcription before the column's publication as part of the digital edition of Cather's journalism. Items in the *Chicago Tribune* were accessed via Proquest Historical Newspapers, while other Chicago newspapers were accessed on microfilm.

4. Chicago audiences did not hear the work again until the 1908–9 season, when a single performance was given by the Metropolitan Opera's touring company (Marsh 261). When the work was revived by the Chicago Opera Company in December 1916—again for only one performance—the critic for the *Chicago Tribune*, Frederick Donaghey, called *Falstaff* a "fiscal flivver," the equivalent of modern-day "box-office poison."

5. The critic for the *Evening Post*, for example, wrote of the performance of 14 March, in words that anticipate Cather's review of two weeks later, that *Falstaff* "is not tuneful—that is, not full of detachable airs that can be sung on the concert platform or whistled in the street" ("Verdi's 'Falstaff'").

6. Levine notes that, as early as the 1790s, the American popular song "Away with Melancholy" was derived from an aria from Mozart's *The Magic Flute* (1791) and that Verdi's operas of the 1850s furnished material for many American popular songs, sheet music of which "sold side by side with the music of such perennial [indigenously American] favorites as Henry Russell, the Hutchinsons' and Stephen Foster" (96). The song remembered by the character Clark in Cather's "A Wagner Matinée" ("Home to our mountains, oh, let us return!"), an adaptation of the Azucena-Manrico duet from act 4 of *Il trovatore*, is an example of such American borrowing from Italian originals.

WORKS CITED

Bennett, Mildred. *The World of Willa Cather.* 1951. Lincoln: U of Nebraska P, 1961.

Cather, Willa. "As You Like It." *Nebraska State Journal* 31 Mar. 1895: 13.

———. "Light on Adobe Walls." *Willa Cather on Writing.* Lincoln: U of Nebraska P, 1988. 123–26.

———. "A Mighty Craft." *Nebraska State Journal* 1 Mar. 1896: 9. Slote, *Kingdom of Art* 415–17.

———. "A Wagner Matinée." *Everybody's Magazine* Mar. 1904: 325–28. *Willa Cather Archive.* Ed. Andrew Jewell. Oct. 2007. U of Nebraska–Lincoln. 5 June 2010. http://cather.unl.edu.

Central Music Hall. Advertisement. *Chicago Tribune* 16 Mar. 1895: 6.

Donaghey, Frederick. "Campanini Effects Lively, Well-Cast Revival of Verdi's Great Comic Opera." Review of Verdi's *Falstaff*, Chicago Opera Company, Auditorium Theatre, 18 Dec. 1916. *Chicago Tribune* 19 Dec. 1916: 13.

Dunne, Finley Peter. "Dooley at the Opera." *Chicago Evening Post* 16 Mar. 1895.

"'Falstaff' Is Heard." Review of Verdi's *Falstaff*, Auditorium Theatre, Chicago, 14 Mar. 1895. *Chicago Inter Ocean* 15 Mar. 1895: 1+.

"The Falstaff of Farce." Review of Shakespeare's *The Merry Wives of Windsor*, Chicago Opera House, Stuart Robinson and William H. Crane, 22 Nov. 1886. *Chicago Tribune* 23 Nov. 1886: 5.

"First Week of Opera." *Chicago Tribune* 17 Mar. 1895: 37.

Giannone, Richard. *Music in Willa Cather's Fiction.* Lincoln: U of Nebraska P, 1968.

"Grand Opera." Advertisement. *Chicago Tribune* 12 Mar. 1895: 8.

Hepokoski, James A. *Giuseppe Verdi: "Falstaff."* Cambridge Opera
Handbooks. Cambridge: Cambridge UP, 1983.

Leslie, Amy [Lillie West]. "The Falstaff of Maurel." Review of Verdi's
Falstaff, Metropolitan Opera, Auditorium Theatre, Chicago, 14
Mar 1895. *Chicago Daily News* 15 Mar. 1895: 4.

Levine, Lawrence W. *Highbrow/Lowbrow: The Emergence of Cultural
Hierarchy in America*. Cambridge: Harvard UP, 1988.

Lewis, Edith. *Willa Cather Living: A Personal Record*. Lincoln: U of
Nebraska P, 2000.

Marsh, Robert C. *150 Years of Opera in Chicago*. Completed and ed.
by Norman Pellegrini. DeKalb: Northern Illinois UP, 2006.

"Maurel Won Laurels." Review of Verdi's *Falstaff*, Auditorium
Theatre, Chicago, 14 Mar. 1895. *Chicago Record* 15 Mar. 1895: 1+.

Mencken, Henry Louis. *The Diary of H. L. Mencken*. Ed. Charles A.
Fecher. New York: Knopf, 1989.

Montefiore, T. Review of Verdi's *Falstaff. La tribuna* (Rome), 19 Apr.
1893. Hepokoski 129.

"Much Humor in the Opera's Music." Review of Verdi's *Falstaff*,
Metropolitan Opera, Auditorium Theatre, Chicago, 14 Mar. 1895.
Chicago Tribune 15 Mar. 1895: 1.

"The Operatic Revolt." *Chicago Tribune* 10 Mar. 1895: 28.

Schmidgall, Gary. *Shakespeare and Opera*. New York: Oxford UP,
1990.

Slote, Bernice, ed. *The Kingdom of Art: Willa Cather's First Principles
and Critical Statements 1893–1896*. Lincoln: U of Nebraska P,
1966.

"Verdi's 'Falstaff' and Maurel." Review of Verdi's *Falstaff*,
Metropolitan Opera, Auditorium Theatre, Chicago, 14 Mar. 1895.
Chicago Evening Post 15 Mar. 1895: 4.

"Verdi's Great 'Falstaff.'" Review of Verdi's *Falstaff*, Metropolitan
Opera, New York City, 4 Feb. 1895. *New York Times* 5 Feb. 1895:
5.

Woodress, James. *Willa Cather: A Literary Life*. Lincoln: U of
Nebraska P, 1987.

Sarah Clere is a graduate student at the University of North Carolina at Chapel Hill, where she is completing a dissertation on Willa Cather. Her work has appeared in *Mississippi Quarterly.*

Mark A. R. Facknitz is a professor of English at James Madison University, where he has taught since 1983. His essay on Willa Cather's frontier gardens appeared in *Cather Studies 5.* From the Shenandoah, he reports that his nostalgia for trains and prairies is as fierce as an amputee's longing for a missing limb.

John H. Flannigan is a professor of English at Prairie State College, Chicago Heights, Illinois. His essays on Cather have appeared in *Cather Studies 2, Studies in Short Fiction, Modern Fiction Studies,* and elsewhere.

Richard C. Harris is the John J. McMullen Professor of Humanities and assistant dean at Webb Institute on Long Island. He has published on Willa Cather in a number of journals, including *Cather Studies, Studies in American Fiction,* the *Journal of Narrative Theory,* the *Midwest Review,* and the *Willa Cather Newsletter and Review.* He was the volume editor for the Scholarly Edition of Cather's Pulitzer Prize–winning novel *One of Ours* (Nebraska, 2006).

Amber Harris Leichner is a doctoral candidate in English with a Women's and Gender Studies specialization at the University of Nebraska–Lincoln. Her scholarly and creative work has appeared in *Teaching the Harlem Renaissance*, the *Dos Passos Review*, *Relief*, and elsewhere. She teaches courses in writing, literature, and women's and gender studies at UNL.

Melissa J. Homestead is Susan J. Rosowski Associate Professor of English and program faculty in women's and gender studies at the University of Nebraska–Lincoln. She is the author of *American Women Authors and Literary Property, 1822–1869* (2005) and many essays on American women authors, such as Susanna Rowson, Catharine Sedgwick, Harriet Beecher Stowe, Sarah Orne Jewett, and Willa Cather. She is at work on a digital edition of *Every Week Magazine* (1915–18), of which Edith Lewis, Cather's domestic partner, was managing editor.

Joyce Kessler is chair of the Liberal Arts Environment and associate professor of English at the Cleveland Institute of Art. In addition to this article on Willa Cather, Dr. Kessler has published on subjects ranging from eighteenth-century gendered written language to the contemporary poetry of Derek Walcott. She is currently engaged in a study of the uses of visual culture in Willa Cather's fiction.

Matthew Lavin is a doctoral candidate in English at the University of Iowa. He earned a master's degree in American studies at Utah State University in 2006 and a bachelor's degree from St. Lawrence University in 2002.

Michelle E. Moore is a professor of English at the College of DuPage, in Glen Ellyn, Illinois, where she teaches courses on American and European modern literature and film. She has published articles on William Faulkner, Don Delillo, Henry James, and Todd Solondz's films.

Julie Olin-Ammentorp is a professor of English and of gender and women's studies at Le Moyne College in Syracuse, New York. She has published essays on Henry James and Edith Wharton and is the author of *Edith Wharton's Writings from the Great War* (2004). She has also published on the works of Willa Cather in *Cather Studies 8* and the *Willa Cather Newsletter and Review*. She is currently working on a monograph tentatively titled "Edith Wharton and Willa Cather: Complementary Stories."

Diane Prenatt is a professor of English at Marian University in Indianapolis, where she teaches courses in American and European literature as well as the literature of Catholicism. She is especially interested in the construction of ethnic identity and the depiction of domestic acts in Cather's fiction. She is currently working on a biography of Elizabeth Shepley Sergeant.

Guy J. Reynolds is a professor in the Department of English at the University of Nebraska–Lincoln, where he also directs the Cather Project and serves as the general editor of the Cather Scholarly Edition. He is the author of *Willa Cather in Context: Progress, Race, Empire* (1996), *Twentieth-Century American Women's Fiction* (1999), and *Apostles of Modernity: American Writers in the Age of Development* (2008).

Kelsey Squire is an instructor and PhD candidate at Marquette University. Her dissertation investigates the manifestation of regional consciousness in American literature between 1860 and 1930. In addition to Cather and Fitzgerald, her dissertation addresses works by Mark Twain, Sarah Orne Jewett, John Muir, and various contributors to the *Atlantic Monthly* during the turn of the century.

Janis P. Stout, professor emerita of Texas A&M University, has been a prolific Cather scholar for many years. She is the author or editor of *Willa Cather: The Writer and Her World*

(2000), *A Calendar of the Letters of Willa Cather* (2002), *Willa Cather and Material Culture* (2005), and *Picturing a Different West: Vision and Illustration in the Tradition of Cather and Austin* (2007). Her latest book is *This Last House: A Retirement Memoir* (2010).

John N. Swift teaches English and American literature at Occidental College in Los Angeles. He is the author of many essays on Cather and other modern authors, the coeditor of *Willa Cather and the American Southwest* (2002), and a past president of the Willa Cather Pioneer Memorial and Educational Foundation.

INDEX

298

ekphrasis (*cont.*)
interpretive nature of, 206–7;
in *The Professor's House*,
xviii, 205, 215–21, 222; and
social-political context, 211–
12, 217, 218–19; in *The Song
of the Lark*, xviii, 205–15,
222
Eliot, T. S., 209
ethnographers, 21–22, 41n2
European trips, 89, 246

*Face Value: The Politics of
Beauty* (Lakoff and Scherr),
252–53, 254
Facknitz, Mark, xiv–xv, 53, 67–
92, 289
Falstaff (Verdi): action in, 271;
Cather's enthusiasm for, 269,
285; Cather's review of, 266–
69, 276–82, 286n3; Chicago
performances of, 274–75,
286n4; critical reception of,
271–76; and cultural hierar-
chies, 267, 276; and *The
Merry Wives of Windsor*,
270–71
Farrar, Geraldine, 5
Faulkner, William, ix, 56
Fauset, Jessie, 155n6
Feld, Rose C., 45–46, 48, 49–50,
57
feminism, 108, 134, 154
Fetterley, Judith, 47
Field, Mrs. Henry, 233
Fisher, Dorothy Canfield, 125,
163, 166, 238, 248, 249
Fisher-Wirth, Ann W., 102–3
Fitzgerald, F. Scott, ix; and

Cather, 54–55; "Echoes of the
Jazz Age," 54–55; *The Great
Gatsby*, x, 46, 55, 56–57,
60–61, 62, 123; on literary art
in America, 55, 63n6
Flannigan, John H., xix, 266–88,
289
Flaubert, Gustave, 67, 279
Foote, Stephanie, 63–64n7
Ford, John, 1
Forum, 168, 170, 171, 172
Four Saints in Three Acts
(Thompson/Stein), 230
France, 89, 253; art in, 49–50,
161, 236–37, 259
France, Anatole, 114
*From Mesa Verde to "The Profes-
sor's House"* (Harrell), 117
Frost, Robert, 209
Fuisz, Lisbeth S., 41n5
Fuller, Henry Blake, 95–97, 106,
119, 123; about, 115–16; *Bertram Cope's Year*, 115, 125–
27, 128nn1–2; and Cather,
114–15, 116, 117, 120, 125,
127; *The Cliff-Dwellers*, xv,
95–97, 104–5, 115, 118–20,
128n2; "My Early Books,"
119; on homosexuality, 126–
27; *On the Stairs*, 117; "A
Plea for Shorter Novels," 117,
125; *With the Procession*,
115, 119, 123
futurists, 238

Garland, Hamlin, 46, 103, 105–
7, 116
Garvey, Ellen Gruber, 135, 138
gender: and Cather's self-defini-

music, xii, 229, 240n3, 281, 282;
Cather's tastes in, xix, 230,
280, 283, 284–85

Nation, 115
Native Americans, 22, 30, 33, 38;
and antimodernism, 25; appropriation of culture of, 27–
29; in Death Comes for the
Archbishop, 39–41; as interior
and exterior, 26; metaphoric
conceit about, 38, 42n10;
playing Indian, 21, 26, 31, 36;
removal and extermination of,
22; in The Song of the Lark,
1, 25, 26–28, 31, 36–37,
38–39, 214; of the Southwest,
21–22, 41nn1–2
Navajos, 38–39, 41n2
Nealon, Christopher, 64n8
Nebraska State Journal, 239,
246–47, 266, 276–77, 282,
286n3
neurasthenia, 25
New Age, 28–29, 41n6
New Republic, 115
New Woman, 25, 134, 136,
155n6; Cather's depictions of,
137, 140, 150, 154. See also
women
New Yorker, 116
New York Evening Post, 115
New York Times, 115, 226, 272;
interview with Cather, 45–46,
48, 49–50, 57
Nordenskiöld, Gustav, 114
Norris, Frank, 55, 163
nostalgia, xi, 4, 13, 15, 64n8

Nude Descending a Staircase
(Duchamp), 225

O'Brien, Sharon, 37, 107
Odyssey (Homer), 260
O'Farrell, Mary Ann, 124
O'Keefe, Georgia, 56
Olin-Ammentorp, Julie, xvii,
182–203, 291
opera, 266, 267, 268, 274,
286n2. See also Falstaff
Orientalism, 187, 201n3

Page, James Franklin, 34–35
Palmer, Bertha, 107–8, 109,
129n7, 236
Palmer, Scott, 77–78
Parrish, Maxfield, 235
Pater, Walter, 229
Peattie, Elia, 128n4
Peirce, Charles Sanders, 248,
263n1
picture writing, xix, 245, 248,
250–51, 263
Pilkington, John, 119
Pittsburgh Leader, 139
Pittsburgh Press, 133, 143–44
place, xi, xvi, 49, 208; and
community, 52–53; F. Scott
Fitzgerald on, 55, 56, 62;
insiders and outsiders of,
52, 63n4; in The Professor's
House, xiv, 5, 45, 46, 49–54,
58, 61, 62, 63n5, 114; topo-
philia and, 50, 63n3
Planquette, Robert: The Chimes
of Normandy, 285
poetry, 164
Poetry: A Magazine of Verse, 115

CPSIA information can be obtained at www.ICGtesting.com
Printed in the USA

267862BV00002B/3/P

9 780803 237728